CHILDREN AND FAMILIES IN COMMUNITIES

THE NSPCC/WILEY SERIES
in
PROTECTING CHILDREN

The multi-professional approach

Series Editors: Christopher Cloke,
NSPCC, 42 Curtain Road,
London EC2A 3NX

Jan Horwath,
Department of Sociological Studies,
University of Sheffield,
Sheffield S10 2TU

Peter Sidebotham,
Warwick Medical School,
University of Warwick,
Coventry CV4 7AL

This NSPCC/Wiley series explores current issues relating to the prevention of child abuse and the protection of children. The series aims to publish titles that focus on professional practice and policy, and the practical application of research. The books are leading edge and innovative and reflect a multi-disciplinary and inter-agency approach to the prevention of child abuse and the protection of children.

All books have a policy or practice orientation with referenced information from theory and research. The series is essential reading for all professionals and researchers concerned with the prevention of child abuse and the protection of children.

CHILDREN AND FAMILIES IN COMMUNITIES

Theory, Research, Policy and Practice

Jacqueline Barnes, Ilan Katz, Jill E. Korbin and
Margaret O'Brien

John Wiley & Sons, Ltd

Other Wiley Editorial Offices

John Wiley & Sons Inc., 111 River Street, Hoboken, NJ 07030, USA

Jossey-Bass, 989 Market Street, San Francisco, CA 94103-1741, USA

Wiley-VCH Verlag GmbH, Boschstr. 12, D-69469 Weinheim, Germany

John Wiley & Sons Australia Ltd, 42 McDougall Street, Milton, Queensland 4064, Australia

John Wiley & Sons (Asia) Pte Ltd, 2 Clementi Loop #02-01, Jin Xing Distripark, Singapore 129809

John Wiley & Sons Canada Ltd, 22 Worcester Road, Etobicoke, Ontario, Canada M9W 1L1

Wiley also publishes its books in a variety of electronic formats. Some content that appears in print
may not be available in electronic books.

Library of Congress Cataloging in Publication Data

Children and families in communities : theory, research policy and practice / Jacqueline
   Barnes . . . [et al.].
      p.   cm. — (The NSPCC/Wiley series in protecting children)
   Includes bibliographical references and index.
   ISBN-13: 978-0-470-09357-3 (cloth)
   ISBN-10: 0-470-09357-9 (cloth)
   1. Community-based child welfare.   2. Community-based family services.   3. Child
   development.   4. Community psychology.   I. Barnes, Jacqueline.   II. Wiley series in child
   protection and policy.
   HV713.C39573 2006
   362.73—dc22

                                                                                    2006001297

British Library Cataloguing in Publication Data

A catalogue record for this book is available from the British Library

ISBN-13 978-0-470-09357-3
ISBN-10 0-470-09357-9

Typeset in 10/12pt Palatino by Integra Software Services Pvt. Ltd, Pondicherry, India
Printed and bound in Great Britain by Antony Rowe Ltd, Chippenham, Wiltshire, UK
This book is printed on acid-free paper responsibly manufactured from sustainable forestry
in which at least two trees are planted for each one used for paper production.

Dedicated to Professor Urie Bronfenbrenner (1917 to 2005) whose writings have been so influential in bringing the topic of the community to the forefront for all those concerned with the well-being of children and their families. And to our children: Wesley and Max; Daniel, Gideon and Talia; Michael; Patrick and Rosie.

CONTENTS

ABOUT THE AUTHORS

Jacqueline Barnes is Professor of Psychology at Birkbeck, University of London, based at the Institute for the Study of Children, Families and Social Issues. After undergraduate study at University College London and qualifying at the University of Wisconsin to be an educational psychologist she returned to the UK and was awarded her PhD in Psychology from London University in 1983. A member of the newly-formed Fatherhood research group she co-edited a book about the emerging interest in fathers in the UK, *Fathers: Psychological Perspectives*, with Nigel Beail. In the 1980s she also developed the *Early Years Behaviour Checklist* with Naomi Richman, a widely used measure of the behavioural problems of young children in group settings published by the UK's leading test distributor, NFER. Since then she has worked at Harvard in the USA, returning then to London University. Her current research interests are: evaluation of early intervention programmes related to children's health and development and parenting; community characteristics and the environment as they relate to family functioning and children; the impact of parental illness and the use of assisted reproduction on parenting and child behaviour; and the use of child care in the early years, particularly factors associated with mothers returning to work after having a new baby. Professor Barnes is one of the directors of the national evaluation of the UK government's Sure Start local programmes initiative.

Ilan Katz is Professor and Acting Director of the Social Policy Research Centre at the University of New South Wales in Sydney, Australia. He has had many years of policy, practice and research experience in children's services. After training in South Africa he started his career as a social worker and manager in London, working in both the statutory and voluntary sector. He was head of practice development and research at the National Society for the Prevention of Cruelty to Children. He left to become a civil servant and was Team Leader of the Children's Fund policy team in the Children and Young People's Unit, and Head of the Children in Need and Family Support Section of the DfES. He has subsequently returned to research and was Deputy Director of the Policy Research Bureau before emigrating to Australia. He has written extensively on a wide range of topics relating to children and families, including race and ethnicity, parents with mental illness, adoption, youth justice, community and social capital, early intervention, family support and child protection. He is currently the Chief Investigator of both the national evaluation of the Australian Government's Stronger Families and Communities Strategy, and the New South Wales Government Early Intervention Program.

Jill E. Korbin is Professor of Anthropology, Associate Dean in the College of Arts and Sciences, and Co-Director of the Schubert Center for Child Development and the Childhood Studies Program at Case Western Reserve University. She earned her Ph.D. in 1978 from the University of California at Los Angeles. Korbin is a cultural and medical anthropologist. Her awards include the Margaret Mead Award (1986) from the American Anthropological Association and the Society for Applied Anthropology; a Congressional Science Fellowship (1985–86) through the American Association for the Advancement of Science and the Society for Research in Child Development; and the Wittke Award for Excellence in Undergraduate Teaching at Case Western Reserve University. Korbin served on the National Research Council's Panel on Research on Child Abuse and Neglect, and the Institute of Medicine's Panel on Pathophysiology and Prevention of Adolescent and Adult Suicide. She is Co-Director of the Schubert Center for Child Development and of the Childhood Studies Program. Korbin teaches a range of courses from introductory anthropology to upper division and graduate courses in medical anthropology and on child and family issues from an anthropological perspective. Korbin has published numerous articles on culture and child maltreatment, including her edited book, *Child Abuse and Neglect: Cross-Cultural Perspectives* (1981, University of California Press), which was the first volume to examine the relationship of culture and child maltreatment. She has published and conducted research on women incarcerated for fatal child maltreatment, on cross-cultural childrearing and child maltreatment, on health, mental health and child rearing among Ohio's Amish population, and on the impact of neighbourhood factors on child maltreatment and child well-being.

Margaret O'Brien is Professor of Child and Family Studies and Co-Director of the Centre for Research on the Child and Family at the University of East Anglia. She was awarded her Ph.D. in 1984 from the London School of Economics and qualified as a Clinical Psychologist (British Psychological Society) in 1987. She was one of the early figures in fatherhood research in the UK, founding the Fatherhood Research group and co-editing two influential books *The Father Figure* (1982) with Lorna McKee and *Reassessing Fatherhood* (1987) with Charlie Lewis. O'Brien's current research interests are on fathers and family life, children's neighbourhoods and children's services. Recent publications include: *Children in the City: Home, Neighbourhood and City* (with Pia Christensen) (2003, London: Falmer Press) reporting on findings from the *Childhood, Urban Space and Citizenship: Child Sensitive Urban Regeneration, ESRC* funded Child 5–15 Research Programme; *Children's Trusts: Developing Integrated Services for Children in England* (2004 London: DFES); *Working Fathers: Earning and Caring* (2003, London: Equal Opportunities Commission). Professor O'Brien is one of the directors of the national evaluation of the UK Government's Children's Trust intervention to develop integrated children's services.

FOREWORD

COMMUNITY-BUILDING – SO WHAT?

[By natural law,] we are bound together in what the Bible calls 'the bundle of life.' Our humanity is caught up in that of all others.... We are made for community, for togetherness, for family, to exist in a delicate network of interdependence. Truly, 'it is not good for man to be alone,' for no one can be human alone. We are sisters and brothers of one another whether we like it or not and each one of us is a precious individual. (Tutu, 1999, pp. 196–197)

All of us, at some time or other, need help. Whether we're giving or receiving help, each one of us has something valuable to bring to this world. That's one of the things that connects us as neighbors – in our own way, each one of us is a giver and a receiver.... (Rogers, 2003, p. 135)

In the giving of help, a parent experiences one of the best feelings that any of us can have: that life has meaning because we are needed by someone else. Watching a baby grow with our help tells us other things we like to feel about ourselves: that we are competent and loving. (Rogers, 2003, p. 82)

Ubuntu does not say, 'I think, therefore I am.' It says rather: 'I am human because I belong. I participate. I share.' (Tutu, 2004, p. 27)

In *Children, Families, and Communities*, authors Jacqueline Barnes, Ilan Katz, Jill Korbin and Margaret O'Brien have undertaken the ambitious task of description of the relationship between community life and the well-being of children and families. The resulting volume is without peer in its breadth. *Children, Families, and Communities* is remarkable in at least two ways.

First, reflecting the authors' own cosmopolitan backgrounds, the reference points for the volume nearly span the globe. Although Barnes et al. acknowledge that a disproportionate number of relevant studies and programmatic innovations have occurred in the United States, the examples are drawn from the various countries in Europe, North America and Oceania in which the majority of people speak English as their first – and often only – language. Second, *Children and Families in Communities* integrates research findings with lessons from experience in family services. Going beyond relevant evaluation research, the authors also review practice- and policy-relevant basic research about topics in community sociology and environmental psychology. Thus, *Children and Families in Communities* is distinctive in the scope of the cultures studied, the sources of knowledge drawn upon and the settings to which the conclusions are applied.

COMMUNITIES AS VENUES FOR SERVICES

Building on the conceptual underpinnings of the family support movement (see, e.g., http://www.familysupportamerica.org), Barnes et al. endeavour to make their multi-cultural integration relevant in an era in which 'community-based programmes' and, subsequently, 'community initiatives' have dominated efforts to improve the well-being of children and families. Of course, what such projects *do* varies enormously, even if there is some commonality in *where* they work. Further, that these projects reflect the conventional wisdom about 'best practice' – in effect, much of the focus of *Children and Families in Communities* – does not necessarily mean that modal practice is even a close facsimile.

In several respects, the programmatic efforts chronicled in *Children and Families in Communities* have often been largely reactive. First, community-based programmes have often been defined in terms of what they are not. They ordinarily do not require people to leave their homes or relinquish the simple liberties of everyday life. Often, as in school-based services, community-based programmes are located within neighbourhood settings or primary community institutions. Such settings are likely to be 'friendlier' than hospitals (even the outpatient clinics) or correctional facilities – an important but modest accomplishment in the quest to protect the dignity of children and their families.

Second, community-based services often have been developed in response to particular local service gaps. The proliferation of community-based services is apt, almost by definition, to increase the accessibility of professional help. As a practical matter, especially in communities that are remote or that lack public transportation, this increased proximity to clients often results in greater availability of services, not just greater convenience in using them. Such a translation of nearby location into increased availability of services may be especially significant for individuals (indeed, most children) who are usually dependent on caregivers to transport them to service providers.

Although such increases in the help available to families in the most underserved communities are by no means trivial, their significance is often overstated. Rarely do they *transform* the services to make them more respectful and humane, better adapted to the setting, more family- and community-oriented, or better grounded in research. Creation of a school-based human services programme, for example, does not necessarily result in a qualitative change in the services delivered (see Melton, Limber & Teague, 1999; Melton & Lyons, in press; Motes, Melton, Pumariega & Simmons, 1999). *School-based* rarely means *school-oriented*. Instead, school-based mental health services, for example, often are organised in traditional 30- or 50-minute blocks for individual therapy, as if they were delivered at an ordinary community mental health centre. Often such school-based services are even less family- and community-oriented than are clinic-based services, because the hours of operation are limited to the school day, and only the children themselves are 'captive' during that time.

Third, community initiatives have emerged as a reaction to problems of operation of the service system itself. As the example of school-based mental health services illustrates, co-location by itself does little to eliminate the generations-old artificial division of the lives of children and families into overlapping domains (e.g., education; health; justice; welfare) or, worse, into co-extensive problems (e.g., conduct disorder; juvenile delinquency; poverty; special educational needs; school misbehaviour). Common sense leads to the conclusion that the current child and family service system is hopelessly inefficient. Worse, the panoply of agencies that serve (or control) more or less the same populations with more or less the same repertoire of interventions means that reform in one without concomitant change in all of the others typically accomplishes little more than to shift children and families to other service tracks that are the new paths of least resistance (Melton, Spaulding & Lyons, 1998).

Such effects are surely unintended, and almost everyone would agree that they are undesirable. De jure policy goals are frustrated, the lives of children and families are purposelessly invaded, and money is wasted. Nonetheless, elimination of the redundancies in the service system has proven to be a formidable challenge – maybe even an intractable problem. Not only is the need for coincident change in many laws and practices virtually impossible to engineer, but the historic categorisation of services is sustained by large and well-entrenched bureaucracies and professional guilds.

For example, some political jurisdictions have attempted to eliminate the redundancies by merging the traditional panoply of youth service agencies into an omnibus department or ministry of child, youth and family services or even simply 'human' services. As a practical matter, however, the result of the 'radical' reorganisation typically has been the creation of one more layer of bureaucracy laid atop new 'divisions' (not 'departments') of child welfare, juvenile justice, child mental health, etc. Indeed, agreement on an organisational chart that comports with common sense is itself such a difficult task that the creation of services that are closely tailored to families' and communities' needs and resources often seems to be a mere pipedream.

As the colloquial guidance goes, the response typically has been, 'If you can't beat 'em, join 'em'. All US states and, I suspect, most or all of the other jurisdictions discussed in this volume have undertaken major initiatives in the past two decades – typically multiple times – to increase *coordination* and *collaboration* among agencies providing services to children and families.

At root, such projects have had three assumptions. First, re-stating the thesis about the malfunctioning of the service system, virtually all observers both inside and outside agency leadership concede that the rampant fractionation of child and family services impairs their efficiency and effectiveness. Second, noting the unimpressive history of service system restructuring, most would contend that fundamental reform – in effect, starting over – is impractical and, many would argue, undesirable. (In this instance, *undesirability* refers to the widespread belief that the present ineffectiveness of child and family services is the product of inefficient administration, not inherent problems in the service array itself.)

Third, most directly driving the emphasis on service coordination, many contend (naïvely, in my view) that, if only agency administrators were enabled – or forced – to talk more often with each other, the efficiency and effectiveness of services would increase substantially. Reflecting the strength of this belief, such inter-agency initiatives have often begun with great hoopla, they sometimes have included substantial financial incentives from federal or state governments and large private foundations, and the resulting councils, teams and other structures and processes to facilitate coordination of services have typically consumed much time and effort of key staff.

THE NEED FOR A BROADER APPROACH

As Barnes et al. discuss, however, these projects have typically had disappointing, even if unsurprising results. Inter-agency communication – even when inter-agency decision making and case management are added – generally fails to increase the efficiency and effectiveness of services. These results should be unsurprising. Well coordinated and even well financed ill-conceived services are still ill-conceived!

There are two related problems that underlie these conceptual failures. First, traditional services, even if administered in community settings, typically are logically linked neither to clients' needs nor to families' and communities' resources. When a family lacks sufficient income to enable parents to meet their child's basic needs, when the child (actually, usually adolescents) lag several grade-levels in educational achievement behind the mean for their age, when they have well-entrenched patterns of misbehaviour, and when their family has a multitude of other social problems (also often of long standing), then why should one expect a chat with a psychotherapist for 30 or 50 minutes every week or two to make a difference in the well-being of the child or the family? Despite the obvious lapse in common sense, this was the usual prescription when mental health professionals were given a blank cheque in the largest and best evaluated initiative ever undertaken to build a coordinated system of child mental health services (Bickman, 1996, 2000).

Second, the 'players' in the model coordinated services generally have been primarily – or only – the formal service providers. The 'community' involved in many purportedly comprehensive community initiatives has been narrow indeed!

This narrow construction is unfortunate at one level because the 'clinical' approach that relies only on professionals and bureaucrats has long been known not to be cost-effective, at least in the aggregate. Volunteers and paraprofessionals have long been known to be at least as effective as professionals in eliciting change on mental health variables among children (Berman, 1985; Weisz & Berman, 1987).

More generally, the nearly exclusive attention to formal programmes (especially those that are problem-focused rather than developmental; cf. Commission on Positive Youth Development, 2005) inherently diminishes both the reach and the effectiveness of help for children and their families. The incorporation of informal networks and natural helpers into service plans, whether at the family or the community level, enables immediacy and ubiquity of assistance. Such attributes are valuable in themselves. Help that comes sooner rather than later when one is hurting is nearly universally regarded as better. So is help that is available when one needs it most. Help that *prevents* pain altogether is still better, and help that does not simply prevent distress but that actually promotes a better quality of life is surely best of all.

Both common sense and principles of behaviour change also suggest that intervention is apt to be most effective when rehearsal is in vivo and the contingencies used to maintain the change can be made 'natural' in the settings of everyday life. When these conditions can occur without payment of professional fees and the stigma of identification as a patient or a client, such help is both more feasible and more likely to be accepted.

The epidemiology of child and family problems also suggests the need for an approach that gives due weight to the potential contributions of relatives, friends, neighbours and primary care professionals (e.g., family physicians; clergy; schoolteachers; recreation leaders). A panoply of factors push toward enlistment of the community as a whole as helpers and 'friendly' agents of control: the high proportion of children and families with serious problems in meeting the demands of everyday life, the multiplicity of problems that they typically have, and the ubiquity of the settings in which such problems are manifest. To use a US sports metaphor, a 'full-court press' in which *all* of the local players (not just the coach [the agency administrator or consultant] or the team captains [the credentialed professionals]) are engaged in coordinated action to address an issue of common concern sometimes is the only sensible course of action. It also may be the only approach that has a chance to be effective in combatting multifaceted problems of formidable strength. (New Zealand's family group conferences – and, even more so, the community-driven steps to implement the resulting plans – are illustrative.)

Apart from the immediate effectiveness of a system of care that relies in substantial part on the good will of concerned community residents, such a system is likely to have important positive side effects. For example, Reissman and Carroll (1995) brought social scientists' attention to the *helping paradox*, the familiar phenomenon in which helpers receive more benefit than those whom they assist. It is indeed more blessed to give than to receive.

Further, if a community-wide safety net is to be woven for children and families, it must be used often enough and visibly enough that all of those who are needed as weavers perceive the importance and efficacy of their contributions, it must be big enough to blanket the community, and all must perceive the responsibility to lift the net into place where it is needed. As the metaphor suggests, we need a universal norm of mutual assistance. This norm must extend from 'haves' to 'have nots', and it must encompass young people as well as adults.

In that regard, observation of neighbourhood residents having a positive effect on the community may be important for both parents and children in building a sense of collective efficacy and, for parents, of parental efficacy – dimensions that are important elements in improving both objective and subjective quality of life for families. As Barnes et al. discuss, participatory planning may be one mechanism for such action. Regardless of the particular strategy, however, the effects of one's own participation are likely to be multiplied by the effects of observation of neighbours' involvement. Such collective experiences are first steps toward construction of new norms of mutual assistance.

THE IMPORTANCE OF COMMUNITY BUILDING

The Questions of Concern

Barnes et al. conclude this volume with an expression of 'considered optimism'. Their lukewarm enthusiasm for the approaches that they review appears to be based on a lack of definitive evaluation studies using conventional indicators of child outcomes and a suspicion that community change may be too distal from individual well-being to be an effective strategy.

There is a more fundamental problem, however, than the instrumental query of whether a given approach 'works' in affecting individual behaviour. As a matter of social policy and public morality, the experience of *belonging* – of being sheltered by a community, of being treated with respect as a *person* in that community and ultimately of contributing to the well-being of other people in the community, individually and collectively – ought to be a part of every child's life. This is a *bonum in se* (a good in itself) – perhaps even the *summum bonum*. As implicit in the Golden Rule, everyone should expect to be treated as a person of worth who will be noticed and cared for, and, by their own behaviour, all should contribute to such expectations in the community at large.

There is good reason to believe that the experience of belonging and the corollary immersion in a sea of relationships within and across the generations are indeed critical elements of effective strategies for reduction of problems of childhood and family life. These experiences are too important in themselves, however, to relegate them in public discussions to consideration merely as intermediate outcomes.

The Ideas of Mr Rogers and Archbishop Tutu

The significance of this idea is suggested in the quotes of Fred Rogers and Desmond Tutu that opened this foreword. The humanitarian instincts of these two men were, in my judgment, among the most heroic in the 20th century. At first glance, they had little in common. Fred Rogers, known to a generation of American children as 'Mr Rogers', starred in a US public television show for preschoolers, and Archbishop Tutu provided much of the moral and intellectual leadership for the transformation that occurred in South Africa late in the century. One was White, and the other is Black. One was American, and the other is South African. One was a media celebrity, and the other is a spiritual and political leader. Mr Rogers was so legendary for his 'niceness' that he was often the subject of satire, but, as indicated by his Nobel Prize, Archbishop Tutu is a larger-than-life figure who now is virtually beyond criticism and who, even during the apartheid years, was largely invulnerable to the government's disdain. (This observation is not meant to denigrate the courage that undoubtedly was required for a Black man to be a vocal critic of the then-prevailing social and political order.)

In my own mind, however, Mr Rogers and Archbishop Tutu had much in common. Although Mr Rogers' viewers and most of their parents knew little about his background, he was also a Protestant clergyperson (specifically, a Presbyterian minister). The major point of commonality that struck me, however, was not their similar educational and professional background or even their common religious faith. Although these experiences probably contributed to the similarities in their public personas, the feature that united Mr Rogers and Archbishop Tutu in my mind was their gentleness. Whether in the company of young children or heads of state, each compellingly communicated respect for others through a demeanor of grace and humility. Although their words were memorable (whether in Mr Rogers' simple songs about 'the people in your neighbourhood' or Archbishop Tutu's thoughtful homilies integrating Anglican theology and African experience), these two kind men's soft demeanor was the foundation for their power.

The blend of medium and message is overt in Archbishop Tutu's ubuntu theology, which blends East and West (perhaps more precisely, South and North) to show the compatibility of a strong sense of community and respect for human rights (see Battle, 1997, for a detailed exposition of the integration of these ideas with Judeo-Christian theology, specifically the belief that human beings are created in the image of God). *Ubuntu* is a Xhosa word, which apparently does not have a direct English equivalent but which is translated roughly as *humanity*. It subsumes a statement of worldview, a code of ethics, a mode of social relations and a characteristic of personality.

In 1993, Tutu gave an address to an African American audience in 1993, in which he described ubuntu as the embodiment of welcoming, giving, and sharing, just as a neighbourly person acts as a friend to a stranger. As he commonly does, Tutu described the human condition as a 'delicate network of interdependence', so much so that self-discovery arises only within the context of community:

> We say a person is a person through other persons. We don't come fully formed into the world. We learn how to think, how to walk, how to speak, how to behave, indeed how to be human from other human beings . . . We are made for togetherness . . . This is how you have ubuntu [in effect, how you discover your personality] – you care, you are hospitable, you're gentle, you're compassionate and concerned. (Battle, 1997, p. 65, quoting Tutu's 1993 speech at Morehouse Medical School)

To return to the quotes of Mr Rogers, the value that one adds to the world (stated in psychological and philosophical terms, the *meaning* that one's life has) is discovered most directly in acts of generosity. Further, when families and communities are functioning well, this interdependence as giver and receiver is the framework for everyday experience.

It is this experience that is most fundamental to community life and, in particular, to the growth of children as uniquely important persons. As succinctly stated in the seminal global expression of human rights, '[e]veryone has duties to the community in which alone the free and full development of personality is possible' (Universal Declaration of Human Rights, 1948, art. 29, § 1). In recent years, the international community has joined in a pledge to support 'the development of the child's personality, talents and mental and physical abilities to their fullest potential' (Convention on the Rights of the Child, 1989, art. 29, § 1(a)) and in 'the preparation of the child for responsible life in a free society' (art. 29, § 1(d)) – a society grounded in 'the spirit of peace, dignity, tolerance, freedom, equality and solidarity' (preamble).

A Personal Anecdote

To concretise these grand pronouncements, I hope that readers will permit me to indulge in the presentation of a personal story. Several years ago, my older daughter Jennifer and her then-fiancé Tom chose to hold their wedding in the small-town Methodist church in North Carolina where my great-grandfather had been minister and in which his heirs had been active. Although Jennifer had spent little time in that community in which I grew up, she felt connected by the family ties across five generations. These connections were made even more obvious because, by happenstance, the wedding was held on the day of the town's centennial anniversary. Several of the guests noted an exhibit in the festival displays that chronicled my late grandfather's service as mayor.

The wedding was clearly a family affair, but there was a touch of globalisation even in Granite Quarry. One of my brothers (a United Methodist minister) officiated, and the other (an accountant by day but a semi-professional classical singer by night) sang love songs by Grieg. The international flavour came not only from Jennifer's selection of music by Grieg but also her choice of her best friend from the folk school that she attended in Norway as her matron of honour and as the folk-music soloist at the reception.

Although these personal touches in themselves made for a memorable wedding, the most striking aspect for me was the relationships in which Jennifer now joined, perhaps unintentionally. The setting vividly suggested the strength of the community connections that sustained several generations before her when, as the vows go, our family had been richer or poorer, in sickness or in health. Those relationships could be found not just in the church but also in and among the bridge group, the Civitan civic club, the women's club, the Little League baseball team, the Scout troop, the street dance, the town council meeting and the school classroom.

When my siblings and I attended church the next day, we were struck not only by the number of childhood mentors whom we saw but also by the number and specificity of their memories of my family's involvement in the everyday life of the community about 40 years earlier. For example, the minister told the congregation a story that had not entered my own memory in years about one of my brothers' quiet attentiveness to a Little League teammate who lost first a leg and then his life to bone cancer.

I have since visited the church several times and each time become re-acquainted with more now-elderly adults who were important to my parents, one of my siblings, or me. Each time I am reminded about new stories of shared celebration or mourning. The stories are not always ones of pride; most notably, racial segregation was a fact of life throughout my childhood. However, the stories are uniformly grounded in a strong web of *relationships* that gave shape to me as a person. From an early age, I had no reason to doubt that my friends, my relatives, my teachers and youth group leaders, these adults' own friends and relatives and I myself all were important members of the community – Tutu's delicate network of interdependence.

Re-experiencing these connections is always a bittersweet experience, however. My ambivalence comes from the fact that my own daughters and most of their peers have not experienced the same depth and breadth of connections. They are less likely than the generations that came before to have friends who share their burdens of disability and loss and their joys of creation and union. They are less likely to notice and be noticed when there is cause for celebration and sorrow. If current long-standing trends continue, the next generation will be even less likely to experience the personal meaning that comes with community.

CONCLUSION

I am not telling the story of Jennifer's wedding because of a sense of nostalgia or an idyllic view of life in the small-town US South. Rather, I combine it with the observations of Fred Rogers and Desmond Tutu because that weekend and the connections that it re-awakened demonstrate what community means. Such experiences are at the centre of our humanity, and they have particular significance for the personal development of children.

There is no question that the decline in social capital has been adverse for our children (see, e.g., Seligman, 1995, on the trend toward greater depression among young people, and Twenge, 2000, on the analogous trend toward greater anxiety). Nonetheless, my point is that the primary reference point for understanding community initiatives ought not to be in a traditional evaluation of their efficacy as a strategy to replace older means of human service delivery in responding to particular problems of individual children. Although that is a legitimate question, the more important concern rests in their effectiveness in fostering community itself.

In that regard, I suspect that the ultimate contribution that Barnes et al. will have made in this volume lies in their beginning to address the basic question of the nature of children's involvement in communities and of the significance of that involvement for their development. We need a better understanding of the 'glue' that binds communities together – especially communities fully inclusive of children. (I was struck recently by the evidence that the most attractive and 'renewed' cities in the United States – e.g., San Francisco; Seattle; Minneapolis; Boston; Austin – are also the cities with the lowest proportion of children in their population.) The acquisition of personal meaning in a time of community fragility is a profound question indeed and one that will be important for generations to come.

Professor Gary B. Melton
August 2005

REFERENCES

Battle, M. (1997) *Reconciliation: The Ubuntu Theology of Desmond Tutu*. Cleveland: Pilgrim.

Berman, J.S. (1985) Does professional training make a therapist more effective? *Psychological Bulletin* 92, 401–407.

Bickman, L. (1996) A continuum of care: More is not always better. *American Psychologist* 51, 689–701.

Bickman, L. (2000) The Fort Bragg continuum of care for children and adolescents: Mental health outcomes over five years. *Journal of Consulting and Clinical Psychology* 68, 710–716.

Commission on Positive Youth Development (2005) The positive perspective on youth development. In D.L. Evans, E.B. Foa, R.E. Gur, H. Hendin, C.P. O'Brien, M.E.P. Seligman & B.T. Walsh (eds), *Treating and Preventing Adolescent Mental Health Disorders: What We Know and What We Don't Know* (pp. 497–527). New York: Oxford University Press.

Convention on the Rights of the Child, G.A. Res. 44/25, U.N. GAOR Supp. 49 at 165, U.N. Doc. A/44 736 (1989).

Melton, G.B., Limber, S.P. & Teague, T. (1999) Changing schools for changing families. In R.C. Pianta & M.J. Cox (eds), *The Transition to Kindergarten* (pp. 179–213). Baltimore: Paul H. Brookes.

Melton, G.B. & Lyons, P.M., Jr. (in press). *Mental health services for children and families: Building a system that works*. New York: Guilford.

Melton, G.B., Spaulding, W.J & Lyons, P.M., Jr. (1998) *No Place to Go: Civil Commitment of Minors*. Lincoln: University of Nebraska Press.

Motes, P.S., Melton, G.B., Pumariega, A. & Simmons, W.E.W. (1999) Ecologically-oriented school-based mental health services: Implications for service system reform. *Psychology in the Schools* 36, 391–401.

Reissman, F. & Carroll, D. (1995) *Redefining Self-help in the Human Services: Policy and Practice*. San Francisco: Jossey-Bass.

Rogers, F. (2003) *The World according to Mr. Rogers: Important Things to Remember*. New York: Hyperion.

Seligman, M.E.P. (1995) *The Optimistic Child*. New York: Harper.

Tutu, D. (1999). *No Future Without Forgiveness*. New York: Doubleday.

Tutu, D. (2004). *God Has a Dream: A Vision of Hope for Our Time*. New York: Doubleday.

Twenge, J.M. (2000). The age of anxiety? Birth cohort change in anxiety and neuroticism, 1952–1993. *Journal of Personality and Social Psychology* 79, 1007–1021.

Universal Declaration of Human Rights, G.A. Res. 217 A (III) (1948) (available at http://www.un.org/Overview/rights.html).

Weisz, J.R. & Berman, J.S. (1987). Effectiveness of psychotherapy with children and adolescents: A meta-analysis for clinicians. *Journal of Consulting and Clinical Psychology* 55, 542–549.

PREFACE

Sustainable communities meet the diverse needs of existing and future residents, their children and other users, contribute to a high quality of life and provide opportunity and choice. They achieve this in ways that make effective use of natural resources, enhance the environment, promote social cohesion and inclusion and strengthen economic prosperity (*Egan Review. Skills for Sustainable Communities*, ODPM, 2004, p. 7).

In the 1990s there was a resurgence of interest in policy, practice and research relating to communities and their significance for children and families, which has continued into the current century. This has been accompanied by increasing concern about the breakdown of families and communities in post-modern society, and a belief that this breakdown is a contributory cause (and an effect) of social problems. Improvements in data collection and analysis have shown that problems such as child abuse, juvenile crime, substance abuse, school expulsion, mental health problems of children and parents and marital discord are not only concentrated in certain types of families, but also in particular geographic locations. This realisation has resulted in a growing recognition (accompanied at times by almost religious fervour) that the community or neighbourhood environment may be a significant factor in enhancing children's well-being. Community development and regeneration, once relatively neglected disciplines, have recently received a great deal of attention in a number of countries in the Western world. This in turn has led to the recognition that effective programmes to prevent and treat these social problems need to be targeted not only at high-risk individuals or families, but also at neighbourhoods and communities themselves.

In the USA evidence of increasing interest in communities can be seen in the formation of the Roundtable on Comprehensive Community Initiatives for Children and Families (Connell et al., 1995). This has led to a range of catchy book titles – '*From Neurons to Neighbourhoods*', '*It takes a village*', '*Does it take a village?*' – and many other less catchy but equally important volumes. Following the election in the UK of the Labour Government in 1997, a range of initiatives such as Sure Start, New Deal for Communities, On Track and the Children's Fund have been developed and rolled out to target high-risk communities or neighbourhoods. Indeed, there are now over 20 'Area-based initiatives' either wholly or partly focused on children in the UK. In other countries community initiatives are burgeoning – Better Beginnings Better Futures in Canada, Stronger Families and Communities in Australia, CoZi schools in the USA – to name but a few.

The theoretical underpinning for many of these interventions is the 'Ecological Model' originally proposed by Bronfenbrenner in 1979, which provides a framework for understanding how different levels of the ecology interact to affect the lives of children. There is a growing body of empirical and theoretical literature emerging about the effects of the environment on children and families, and this literature is pointing towards a rather complex relationship between communities, families and children. In particular, the relationship between community-level interventions and child outcomes is not at all straightforward.

Another area which has been growing has been the participation of children in communities, prompted in some ways by the greater attention being paid to children's rights following the UN Convention on the Rights of the Child, ratified currently by 192 nations. Only recently has it been acknowledged in both policy and research that children and young people themselves may have a distinctive view of communities and a specific role to play in improving and developing communities (or indeed in degrading and undermining them). Whilst participation by children and young people has now become an important focus of policy and practice, there is a relatively small theoretical and evidence base for this work, and much of the discussion ignores or downplays the role of parents and families. This book considers the research, theorising and some of the policy implications of involving young people in communities. In so doing it draws on the emerging disciplines of childhood sociology, childhood geography and anthropology.

This book brings together some of the latest current thinking on the relationship between children, families and communities, exploring the theoretical, policy, research and practice implications for the emerging knowledge in this area. It adds to a growing literature which is aimed at building up the theoretical and evidence base for intervening in family life to reduce poverty and social exclusion.

The book addresses the theoretical bases of community and childhood, the extent to which it is known (rather than assumed) that communities influence children and parents, what has been done to involve young parents and young people in community strengthening, and the knowledge-base regarding community interventions for infants and preschoolers and their families, for school-age children and for adolescents.

The first three chapters deal with theory and methodology, examining the many and varied definitions of community, the theoretical approaches to understanding the influence of communities on children and parents and the developments in the measurement of communities. The next two chapters summarise research, first examining ways that community features may (or may not) influence child development and parenting behaviour, and second the role of children in communities is examined in detail by looking at how children use communities and move about in them.

The remainder of the book focusses on policy and practice. The concept of a community intervention is clarified in the context of current policy agendas. There follow reviews of a range of interventions grouped according to whether they primarily focus on young children and their parents, older children, schools as communities, or on preventing adolescent problems and in particular juvenile crime.

Finally, we provide some conclusions and thoughts about future directions, particularly on the future of community interventions for children and families.

$$\boxed{1}$$

INTRODUCTION

ECOLOGICAL THEORY AND ITS APPLICATION TO CHILD DEVELOPMENT AND PARENTING

It has always been recognised that a child's circumstances are likely to have an influence on their developmental progress. In the past psychologists in particular have focused predominantly on the behaviour and skills of parents, looking at the extent to which they have gained educational qualifications, attained employment at different levels of the occupational 'ladder', or provided opportunities for their child – to play, to meet other children, to attend schools of good quality and so on. Personal characteristics of the parents such as their personality, attitudes or mental health were also considered to be of importance in understanding both their child's development and their parenting behaviour. In contrast, sociologists paid more attention to community influences.

What has changed in the past few decades is the acknowledgement by a number of disciplines concerned with child and family development, such as psychology, sociology, anthropology, psychiatry and social policy, that parents and children occupy systems beyond the family system, that they need to be understood in context, and that their environment makes a difference to their health, well-being and progress. Now it is recognised that individual, family and wider community factors need to be addressed together rather than being considered separately. For instance, 'broken windows' in a neighbourhood have long been associated with levels of criminal and delinquent behaviour (Wilson & Kelling, 1982). Wilson and Kelling hold that if someone breaks a window in a building and it is not quickly repaired, others will be emboldened to break more windows. Eventually the broken windows create a sense of disorder that attracts criminals, who thrive in conditions of public apathy and neglect. Their argument in relation to interventions to reduce crime and delinquency was that, if you send the message that people care about this neighbourhood (by fixing windows), this also sends the message that if something happens someone may catch you or at the very least notice. The theory would predict that this attention to the structural 'well-being' of the neighbourhood will change people's behaviour, not just about whether they break windows but whether they mug old ladies and whether or not they burgle houses and so forth. More recently structural aspects of a geographical community such as the broken windows indicator, or general community neglect, have been linked with a range of other issues including health problems (Cohen et al., 2000), parenting problems (Garbarino & Eckenrode, 1997), children's educational achievement (Gibbons, 2002) and child behaviour (Boyle & Lipman, 1998).

The environment of a child or a family, including their immediate dwelling and conditions in the home, has been intensively studied by researchers around the world using instruments such as the HOME inventory (Bradley & Caldwell, 1976; Caldwell & Bradley, 1984). However, as much if not more attention is now also being directed towards understanding the importance of neighbourhoods or communities, and towards the relationships that children and parents have within their neighbourhoods with non-family groups or communities of interest. Thus there is both a physical community in which they are placed, and a community of relationships that may influence them.

Although talk about 'ecological influences' and 'community intervention' is becoming commonplace[1] it is important to understand the theoretical underpinnings of this trend as well as the limitations of current knowledge. Much of the literature pertaining to the possible relevance of the community to children and parents has been inspired by, and gives credit to, the theoretical work of Bronfenbrenner (1979). His ideas provided the mainspring for a wealth of research and writing over the following decades. Very simply put, he proposed that a child's development should be examined as an evolving interaction between the person and the environment; that development is defined as the way in which the environment is dealt with. It was his concept of the environment that was original, described as a 'set of nested structures, each inside the next, like a set of Russian dolls' (p. 3). Some of these 'dolls' would be actual settings in which the child moved (microsystems; e.g. the home, the classroom), others would be 'virtual dolls', the interaction between settings that the child occupied (mesosystems; e.g. between home and school), and yet other layers would be settings in which the child did not move, but which were occupied by key figures in their world (exosystems; e.g. their parents' workplaces). Finally the complex inter-relationship between nested levels will be influenced by the prevailing culture or subculture (macrosystems). He stressed that 'what matters for behaviour and development is the environment as it is *perceived* [his italics] rather than as it may exist in "objective" reality' (p. 4). He further suggested that, rather than basing social policy on research evidence 'Basic science needs public policy even more than public policy needs basic science', going on to conclude:

> Knowledge and analysis of social policy are essential for progress in developmental research because they alert the investigator to those aspects of the environment, both immediate and remote, that are most critical for cognitive, emotional, and social development of the person (1979, p. 8).

---

[1] For instance, a Google search using the terms 'ecological, influence, child, development' produced 905,000 hits; 'ecological theory' produced more than three million (3,370,000); using the terms 'community, intervention, child, development' produced 11,100,000 results; and entering the terms 'community, intervention, child abuse) led to 4,560,000. A Psychlit search entering 'ecological' produced 32,407 hits, and the term 'Bronfenbrenner' produced 14,000 results.

Belsky (1980), expanding on Bronfenbrenner's ideas, linked child maltreatment with ecological theory and in turn to neighbourhood influences. He showed that child maltreatment is multiply determined by 'forces at work in the individual, in the family, and in the community and culture in which the individual and the family are embedded' (1980: p. 320), allowing for a broader perspective on vulnerability and on ways to support families. With respect to the 'exosystem' he concluded that two factors played an important role in the aetiology of maltreatment – the world of work and the neighbourhood. The extent of social isolation and absence of local support systems had been seen to typify many parents who were identified as maltreating their children. While Belsky suggested that the absence of local support systems may indicate familial deficits, an inability to establish and maintain friendships, rather than a real neighbourhood feature (the absence of neighbours who are friendly), he also emphasised the relevance of the values of the society towards violence, corporal punishment and to children in general. Although values towards parenting behaviour such as smacking are often reported at a cultural level, or at the individual level, it is important to recall the many subcultures that exist, often associated with particular communities.

A decade later, influenced by a number of subsequent publications (Belsky, 1993; Garbarino, 1985; Gelles, 1992; Melton & Berry, 1994; Pelton, 1981; Schorr, 1988), the United States Panel on Research on Child Abuse and Neglect of the National Research Council was asked to review and assess research on child abuse and neglect so that priorities could be identified for the future. They adopted an 'ecological developmental perspective' to reflect the transactions between the growing child and the social environment or ecology, commenting 'The panel's ecological perspective recognizes that dysfunctional families are often part of a dysfunctional environment' (1993, p. 4). While this approach may now seem the only logical way to proceed, at the time it was a bold step, taking the focus away from individuals and their inter-personal relationships and recognising that support for children and families needs to be conceptualised at levels beyond the individual or the family, in the communities in which they live. Similarly, the working group of the American Psychological Association Coordinating Committee on Child Abuse and Neglect concluded that:

> Research has shown that prevention programs that target single risk factors are not nearly as effective as prevention programs that assume an ecological model and examine risk factors in the context of the individual, the family, community, and society (Willis, 1995, p. 3).

In the UK, somewhat later, the Department of Health revised their guidelines for social workers undertaking comprehensive assessments of families. Areas seen to be crucial in their assessments of potential risk included not only 'the child's developmental needs' and 'parenting capacity', but also 'family and environmental factors' (DoH, 2000, p. 1). While the recommended measures focused on somewhat narrow aspects of the environment, such as home cleanliness or safety, the tri-partite model for assessing families does allow for those involved in working with children in need and their families to incorporate important aspects of the family's community and their integration into community networks.

In addition to work directed at supporting families and children in need, the UK Government has become community-focused in its work to reduce crime and in particular to prevent delinquency. The Home Office established the Active Citizenship Centre which is part of its Civil Renewal effort, designed to increase the extent to which residents become involved in their local communities. Their website states:

> Civil renewal is at the heart of the Home Office's vision of life in our 21st century communities. As a political philosophy it has been around for centuries but it is, increasingly, being taken up by public bodies, people working in the voluntary and community sector, and active citizens in their own communities, as the effective way to bring about sustainable change and improve the quality of people's lives. Civil renewal is the development of strong, active, and empowered communities, in which people are able to do things for themselves, define the problems they face, and tackle them in partnership with public bodies. A key reason for pursuing civil renewal is that local communities are just better at dealing with their own problems. They have the networks, the knowledge, the sense of what is actually possible, and the ability to make solutions stick . . . The ethos of active citizenship is derived from the Athenian tradition which unites the values of democratic self-determination with mutuality and solidarity. It is about reconnecting citizens to their communities and institutions to become more actively involved in addressing their common problems and enhancing the political process (http://www.active-citizen.org.uk, February, 2005).

Involvement in one's community is now being conceptualised more broadly than in the past, including not only the more traditional activities associated with community development such as improving the environment and bringing local groups together, but widening to focus on individuals within the environment, their health and well-being, to integrate micro-, meso- and macro-levels. For example, in Canada throughout the 1970s and 1980s there were calls for community participation in health. New social movements challenged traditional authority, questioning the efficacy of the medical model and supporting disadvantaged groups in the public policy process (Labonte, 1994). In 1980, the Health Promotion Directorate of Health and Welfare Canada launched the Health Promotion Contribution Program (HPCP) to implement the government's community participation strategy (Boyce, 2002). The aim was to provide financial resources to community groups for projects to help them to identify and solve their health problems. This was based to a large extent on the ideas of one government minister (Epp, 1986) who suggested that community participation was a strategy for 'helping people to assert control over factors which affect their health . . . and enhancing people's capacity to cope' (p. 9), citing self-care groups and mutual aid voluntary associations designed to enhance coping skills in disadvantaged persons as prime mechanisms for community participation. This community health approach is perceived to differ from traditional thinking in that it contextualises power inequalities within multiple ecological levels of analysis leading to interventions that are community-driven, involving partnerships between professionals and disadvantaged people (Nelson, Prilleltensky & Peters, 2003).

Thus, the ecological approach to understanding child development and family life has been incorporated not only into much of the more traditional developmental

psychology research, but has also proved the basis for re-thinking ways to intervene to enhance the lives of those living in disadvantaged circumstances. The
rest of this book describes, discusses and evaluates ways it has been used to
understand the development of children and parents, and to make their lives
more rewarding.

DEFINITIONS

Communities and Neighbourhoods

Throughout this book the terms 'community' and 'neighbourhood' will appear
frequently. It is important, therefore, to look into their meanings in order to understand how they are used, why one is used specifically rather than the other, and
why some writers use them interchangeably. Communities and neighbourhoods
provide the places and the contexts for children to develop. There is widespread
agreement that they have an impact and that, in some cases, community change is
desirable and achievable. Nevertheless, the development of relevant and sensitive
indicators and strategies that are directed at enhancing circumstances for children
and families pose numerous conceptual and methodological challenges; in
particular, there is the question of what is meant by the terms (Coulton, 1995).
Issues related to methods of assessing communities are dealt with in detail in
Chapter 3; here the discussion is limited to definitions. It becomes clear, when
reading the literature, that there is little theoretical agreement about the nature of
the concept 'community', or whether it is synonymous with 'neighbourhood'.
Definitions of one sometimes include the other and the distinction between them
is not consistent (Chaskin, 1997).

   Historically, the German sociologist Ferdinand Tönnies (1855–1936) provided a
definition of 'community'. He is best remembered for his distinction between two
basic types of social groups (Tönnies, 1957). He argued that there are two basic forms
of human will: the essential will, which is the underlying, organic, or instinctive
driving force; and arbitrary will, which is deliberative, purposive, and future-(goal-)
oriented. Groups that form around essential will, in which membership is self-
fulfilling, Tönnies called *Gemeinschaft* (which is often translated as 'community'). In
contrast, groups in which membership was sustained by some instrumental goal
or definite end he termed *Gesellschaft* (often translated as 'society'). *Gemeinschaft*
was exemplified by the family or neighbourhood; *Gesellschaft*, by the city or the state.

   Comparing dictionary definitions in a review for the US Advisory Board on
Child Abuse and Neglect, Barry (1991) concluded that the term 'community' is
more general than 'neighbourhood' saying:

> The terms "community" and "neighborhood" are used frequently, and at times
> seemingly interchangeably, to denote a grass roots approach. However there are real
> differences in meanings and they are important...the term "community" is the more
> general of the two. It may refer either to a place, or to a class of people having some-
> thing in common...the idea of a broader sense of community which transcends
> place is a relatively recent theoretical concept, resulting from advances in communi-
> cation and mobility. The term "neighborhood" has not taken such a leap however. All

Webster's definitions still involve the concept of nearness, proximity or "neighborliness", which presumably means geographic proximity. People may belong to a number of communities, depending on their interests, affiliations, and the way community is defined. But most will presumably belong to only one neighborhood, based on the location of their primary residence (1991, pp. 4–5).

However, in their report the US Advisory Board on Child Abuse and Neglect embeds the concept of community within its definition of a neighbourhood saying 'A neighborhood is a small geographic unit consensually identified as a single community' (cited by Garbarino, Kostelny & Barry, 1998, p. 288).

The debate about the meaning of these terms is by no means new, some writers using only the term community but giving it several meanings, others making a distinction between community and neighbourhood. Yet others use the terms interchangeably. A review completed several decades ago (Hillery, 1964) noted 94 different definitions of community, arising from two broad camps: advocates of a territorially-based conception of community (neighbourhood), and advocates of a notion of community based on social network relationships. This dichotomy was noted by others (e.g. Gusfield, 1975) who similarly asserted that the relational type of community is concerned with 'the quality of character of human relationships, without reference to location' (p. xvi). However, the existence of such a large number of competing definitions within each of these general camps indicates that there is much ongoing debate and disagreement (Puddifoot, 1996).

Willmott (1989) enlarged on Hillery's (1964) distinction by proposing subdivisions between the two basic uses of the term: the population of a particular geographical area (the territorial or spatial community), and people who share in common something other than physical proximity (the interest community). He made a second distinction, applicable to either of the basic types, between local and non-local communities. He went further by suggesting a third dimension, the 'community of attachment' that brings together a density of social relationships and sense of identity with a place or group.

Chaskin's review of the concepts of neighbourhood and community (1997) provides further differentiation between the two terms, mirroring to a great extent those identified by Hillery (1964) and Barry (1991). He states:

On the one hand, "community" implies connection: some combination of shared beliefs, circumstances, priorities, relationships, or concerns. The networks that bind individuals of a given group to one another as a community may or may not be rooted in place. Ethnic and religious communities are bound by culture and systems of beliefs; professional communities and other "communities of interest" are connected by common interests, circumstances or priorities...although local communities are place based, they are not seen as simply geographically bounded subdivisions of land ... in both the local community and the community of interest, it is the existence of some form of communal connection among individuals – whether or not such connection is locality based – that provides for the possibility of group identity and collective action. "Neighborhood", on the other hand, is clearly a spatial construction denoting a geographical unit in which residents share proximity and the circumstances that come with it. The neighborhood is a subunit of a larger area and is usually seen as primarily, if not exclusively, residential (1997, pp. 522–523).

While these terms, thus described, appear to be distinct, he goes on to explain that they are not really so clearly separated:

> In the urban context, in fact, the neighborhood is often considered the more primary unit of actual and potential solidarity and social cohesion. Thus there is a conflation of community-like expectations of solidarity and connection within the geographical construction of neighborhood (1997, p. 523).

Chaskin concludes that, despite definitional difficulties, sub-areas of cities are recognised and recognisable, both to residents and to outsiders (such as researchers or those planning interventions). However the delineation of boundaries is a 'negotiated process', combining individual cognitions or mental maps, collective perceptions and organised attempts to codify boundaries.

Overall, Chaskin (1997) suggests that it is best to think about neighbourhoods not just as spaces on a map but as open systems linked to other systems, which may become more or less important to an individual or a family. Indeed he concludes that:

> Individuals may claim and value membership in more than one [local community] at a time. The local community may thus be seen as a set of (imperfectly) nested neighborhoods – a hierarchy of local constructions – and individuals often recognize such localities by name and are comfortable with more than one name to describe local areas differently constructed (1997, p. 540).

Although recognising that relational networks can be dispersed beyond the neighbourhood, Chaskin reinforced the importance of physical neighbourhoods, concluding that instrumental relationships between neighbours remain common and provide important support and identity and may be the basis for collective action, particularly in areas of residential stability. However he also noted that neighbourhoods are experienced and used differently by different populations (e.g. women, married people, those with higher incomes, children, the elderly), and that this must be taken into account in any attempt to describe a neighbourhood or introduce neighbourhood-intervention programmes.

The UK Government, while focusing strongly on community development in many of its policies (see Chapter 6), has concluded that the term 'community' cannot easily be defined, though taking the approach that it is usually taken to mean either an area or a group of people with a common interest. To answer the question 'What is the government's definition of community?' the Home Office-sponsored active citizenship website provides the following information:

> There is no one definitive definition of "community". A community is a specific group of people who all hold something in common. Community has tended to be associated with two key aspects: firstly people who share locality or geographical place; secondly people who are communities of interest. Communities of interest are groups of people who share an identity – for example Afro-Caribbean people; or who share an experience – for example people with a particular disability. (http://www.active-citizen.org.uk. February, 2005).

Space and Meaning

The size of a community or neighbourhood and its boundaries may be defined by administrative demands, political expediency or historical accident, and it can indeed vary widely in scale: from a few streets to an area as large as a nation, or even a nation group (e.g., the European Community, now known as the European Union). The most common scale in the communities discussed in much of the research literature, however, is much more local, a few adjacent streets, a neighbourhood (usually between 3,000 and 10,000 residents), or a small town or district in a city (up to 75,000 residents). Indeed, recent evidence suggests that individual definitions of personal neighbourhoods are fairly small and limited, which can differentiate them from territorial communities. In a study of Chicago communities (Sampson, 1997a) residents were asked if their neighbourhood had a name, and to indicate its boundaries on a map. Almost three-quarters (70%) were able to name their neighbourhood, and the average, mapped size was 30 city blocks, equivalent to a population of approximately 7,500 people. This is significantly smaller than the 77 traditional Chicago communities with populations of 39,000 on average. These smaller areas identified in this study were termed 'neighbourhood clusters' by the researchers. Barry (1991) made a different type of distinction with regard to territorial communities, suggesting that the term 'neighbourhood' may be used more often in an urban context while the term 'community' is used more frequently when describing rural settings. However he also suggested that 'community' may be used to denote an entire town, city or county while a neighbourhood is much smaller.

Whether boundaries are statistical, political or phenomenological, some areas are well-defined, often by barriers such as major roads, rivers or large buildings, while others are amorphous. Some neighbourhoods have names that are widely used and understood by residents and outsiders while others exist only in the eyes of the census or the local political parties. Still others exist according to residents' experiences and the concreteness or reality of a community's boundaries may be related to its impact on residents. If a political ward has no impact on one's life it will be ignored, while a boundary related to local policing may have much more relevance if it means that you do (or do not) benefit from a new initiative such as Community Support Officers (http://www.policecouldyou.co.uk February 2005).

However, a neighbourhood is more than boundaries drawn on a map, the land that is covered or even the perceptions of that area by the people resident within its boundaries. It also encompasses the physical structure and conditions and events taking place within those boundaries (such as crimes). None of the definitions discussed takes the physical attributes of the areas or events occurring within them into account, focusing more on the way in which an area is perceived, or labeled, by residents.

Garbarino, Kostelny and Barry (1998) suggest that, beyond a spatial dimension, most definitions of neighbourhood include some sense of history represented by the evolution of residential patterns and 'psyche', a sense of shared identity among residents, indicated for example by a common usage of the same name for the neighbourhood (p. 288). They propose that, apart from the spatial element of a neighbourhood, there are three other components: social, cognitive and affective. This suggests that one could only say that a neighbourhood exists after conducting some kind of survey of residents to verify that these other components are also present – social interaction as indicated by informal social support and social networks, a shared cognitive understanding of the area and an affective dimension indicating a shared sense of belonging and an attachment to the neighbourhood. Thus in these terms a neighbourhood has to be a community as well, though a community does not have to be a neighbourhood. The affective dimension of neighbourhood, viewed in this manner, is most closely akin to the concept of 'psychological sense of community' (McMillan, 1976), the sense of mutual help, support and attachment to a neighbourhood felt by a parent or child (see Chapter 2).

It could be argued that neighbourhoods of residence have little relevance if individuals have minimal involvement with others locally. It is certainly less likely that they will be influenced positively or negatively if they do not talk to anyone, are not out and about in the streets at times when neighbours are about (possibly going everywhere by car or other means of transport), and do little shopping in the immediate area. With the focus on home-improvement that is so much part of culture in Western societies it is possible to be immersed in a private world within one's home, set within a locality but without any sense of being in a neighbourhood. This can change once there are children in the family. For many, and especially in areas of disadvantage, young children are taken to local health facilities such as doctors' surgeries or child health clinics. Then they may attend local schools where there is a chance to meet other parents, although this recedes as they move on to secondary (junior high and high) school. It is at that time that the community becomes important to the children themselves. Even if they do not attend a school in their local area, they are likely to have to travel through their neighbourhood to reach school and to return home again. In addition, as they are allowed more freedom, they become concerned about the quality of resources for their sporting, shopping and other leisure pursuits.

At all these stages in a family's life cycle, children and parents may be more distanced from their immediate area if they have more financial resources. Favoured doctors may be sought in other areas, children may be sent to fee-paying schools at some distance, and leisure activities may be organised using the family car rather than locally or by public transport. The parents themselves may commute to work in other towns or cities, or in some cases even other countries. Based on this idea, that with affluence comes a separation from the community, Barry and Garbarino (1997) noted that many professionals responsible for decision-making about communities, for whom geographical boundaries no longer have significance, may underestimate the relevance of neighbourhood with respect to its impact on the poor and on child and youth outcomes. Parents, particularly those living in deprived areas, may not occupy the world of work or move large distances from their place of residence, especially if they have few resources, and for them the territorial community could be of greater relevance.

Communities of Interest

Community may of course not refer to a physical space at all. It has been suggested that, in today's urban centres, the notion of a community based on relationships linked by ideology such as shared political affiliations, beliefs or religion, has most relevance (Crump, 1977, cited in Glynn, 1986) and that urbanites have 'portable personal communities' made up of social networks detached from any specific locality. As long ago as the 1960s the likelihood of 'community without propinquity' was discussed, most notably in the seminal work of Webber (1963). In response to current sociological writing suggesting that there was a loss of 'community' in (then) modern-day cities, Webber showed that friendships could be maintained at a distance and community could emerge on the basis of professional groupings and other organisations in addition to those developed on the basis of a common neighbourhood. His ideas have proved prophetic in view of the current usage of the Internet to develop communities, and hence those ideas have been revisited.

The ever-changing developments of the Internet have led to greater attention being paid to communities of interest. Wellman (2001) proposed that, in view of the concept of 'communities without propinquity', people may live closely within a geographical area (their neighbourhood) but they may not feel close socially with their neighbours, instead having strong links outside the area (their community). However, Calhoun (1998) questioned Webber's original conception. When discussing the relevance of the Internet to communities of interest, he had some doubts about the quality of virtual communities. He suggested that community to Webber meant no more than 'clusters of personal relationships characterized by some common identity and perhaps some emotional warmth.' He asserted that there was no clarification of the differences in the patterns of relationships that might vary with degrees of propinquity, and that make 'the community of a remote coalmining town a different thing from the professional bonds and personal friendships of say the more dispersed "community" of social theorists' (p. 374). Calhoun suggests that the excitement over the new technology had led to an overstatement of its relevance to community, pointing out that most members of multi-user domains (MUDS) remain anonymous or shielded by pseudonyms, that commitment levels are low, and that participation is episodic. However he goes on to say that the Internet certainly matters to communities of interest, though mainly as a means of supplementing face-to-face contact, and to gain technical information. This is supported by a number of researchers who have argued that virtual communities can increase involvement within people's face-to-face communities by increasing democratic participation and other community activism (Bakardjieva & Feenberg, 2002; Blanchard & Horan, 1998; Schuler, 1996). This has been substantiated in some empirical research (Wellman et al., 2001).

It has also been demonstrated that members of some virtual communities do have a shared psychological 'sense of community' (discussed in detail in Chapter 2) with clear rules about membership, boundaries, group symbols, exchange of support and emotional connectedness (Baym, 1993; 1995; Greer, 2000; Preece, 1999; Rheingold, 1993), indicating that, far from being virtual, some at least if not all Internet communities can be real communities.

Membership of communities of interest may for children and parents be defined by personal characteristics such as ethnic group, religious affiliation, or some defining feature such as being the parent of twins, having a child with a handicapping condition, being a single parent, or being in a same-sex parent household. These communities are sometimes, but not always, formed as a means of collective empowerment, in the context of being ignored or treated negatively by society (Gilchrist, 2004). Under these circumstances there is less debate about what defines the community since it is clearly defined by its members. The Gingerbread organisation is a good example of this (www.gingerbread.org.uk). Established in 1970, at a time when the needs of lone parents were seen to be ignored by society at large in the UK, it was created by one lone mother who was finding survival in London a struggle following her divorce. It now provides a range of support and advice; local groups have been created so that they can meet each other, and a number of additional features include reasonably priced holidays for single parent families, who generally pay more than two-parent families for package deals, and can feel socially isolated from 'typical' holiday-makers. The organisation also acts as an advocate for its members with politicians and with businesses that appear to discriminate against single parents.

More recently, groups have emerged for non-traditional families, such as Pink-Parents UK (http://www.pinkparents.org.uk/index.shtml) which provides support to reduce the isolation and discrimination that lesbian and gay families face; and the Internet-based IVFworld.com, supporting parents who are attempting or have conceived using in vitro fertilisation techniques, which opens its home page with the statement 'Welcome to the community'.

A community designed to provide more tangible activities and linking ethnic status and identified needs of children, is the African-Caribbean Network for Science and Technology. This educational charity was established in 1995, stating as its mission:

> The singular objective is to advance the educational achievements and career aspirations of Black youth within the fields of Science, Mathematics and Technology, by engendering the ethos that the pursuit of such qualifications and careers can be fun, empowering and achievable (http://www.ishangohouse.com/index.html. Accessed April, 2005).

With evidence since the 1950s of poor achievement by African-Caribbean children in school, it aims to develop links throughout the African-Caribbean community in the UK to increase the number of youth with that background taking up careers in science and technology. Science clubs in schools draw on ethnic pride in past scientific achievements in Africa. For example, the Ishango Science Clubs are named after the Ishango Bone, a carved bone, over 11,000 years old, discovered at Ishango, on the shore of Lake Edward in Zaire (Congo), indicating early evidence of a calendrical/numeration system, in that part of Africa.

What becomes clear from the debate surrounding these two terms, neighbourhood and community, is that almost all people live in neighbourhoods (unless they live in isolated rural housing), but they may not necessarily all be part of the neighbourhood in the sense of taking any active role in its improvement or having any social interactions with neighbours. They may also be members of a number of communities. However, members of a community – be it virtual or one that comes together in real space and time – will in all likelihood have some vested interests and interact socially, though they may never meet in person. Whether or not communities of interest in fact provide any benefits to other community members is a separate issue altogether. Indeed it is easy to think of examples of members of certain communities, defined on the basis of a common interest in, say, taking illegal drugs, who may lead other members of the group into situations that will be deleterious to their health, well-being and freedom. Similarly, some communities defined according to rigidly structured patriarchal societies may provide a great deal of social contact for community members, but it may be designed to control their behaviour in ways that are oppressive rather than providing any benefits.

It is all too easy to think that the labels associated with glossy new initiatives have only a positive interpretation, when the terms have historically been otherwise. While community-building is currently in favour, it is well to remember that communities benefit from diversity in addition to cohesion. A sense of 'them' versus 'us' can lead to conflict and violence, and minority groups, while benefiting to a certain extent from liaising with each other to create communities, may not always prosper through this kind of community involvement.

CONCLUSIONS

The concept of individuals developing within ecological frameworks is now accepted as one of the most useful ways both to understand development and to effect change. While there has been a considerable amount of progress in theory, basic research and community-focused intervention relevant to enhancing parenting and improving children's development in the past two decades, it is important to rethink the links between child outcomes and ecological influences in more detail. In order to plan effective intervention strategies it is necessary to understand specifically what impact the community or neighbourhood may have on family functioning and on the lives of parents and children. It is clear, however, that it may be difficult to understand how to interpret research related to the impact of communities on parents and children, or to develop ways to intervene, while the concept remains so nebulous and open to debate. One might argue that this kind of ambiguity is common to much of social science, take for instance the concept of intelligence. However, there are more tried and tested methods of assessing intelligence. At the moment the science of measuring communities or neighbourhoods is not so well developed. In the remainder of this volume we lay out the theories that have been developed to explore and explain the importance of communities for children and families. Then measurement methods are reviewed, providing more clarity about definitions. Research will then be presented to understand more about what is known regarding the importance of communities, and whether they can be manipulated to enhance developmental outcomes. Finally, we consider what the implications are for future policy, practice and research to further the understanding of the role of communities.

2

THEORIES OF COMMUNITY INFLUENCE

The debate about the effect of neighbourhoods (especially poor neighbourhoods) on the development of children, and in particular on their behaviour, has raged for decades. In the United States attention was directed towards community poverty during the 1960s as products of the federal government's War on Poverty. Subsequently, interest in neighbourhoods and urban policy was revived through President Clinton's introduction of the Empowerment Zone and Enterprise Communities Program in 1993 (Gittell et al., 1998). In Canada, interest in improving neighbourhoods occurred in the 1970s when urban planners came to accept that the social dimensions of neighbourhood life, such as mutual support and participation in neighbourhood events, were as important as the physical structure (Novick, 1979). More recently in the UK, the Labour government elected in 1997 established the Neighbourhood Renewal Unit in 2001 to find solutions to the problems of the most deprived communities in England, so that no one would be disadvantaged by where they lived (Social Exclusion Unit, 2001).

THE UNDERCLASS, SOCIAL EXCLUSION AND THE CULTURE OF POVERTY

In recent years debates about the role that poor neighbourhoods play in the lives of children and families have crystallised around the related notions of the Underclass, Social Exclusion and the Culture of Poverty. Although these are different constructions, having different provenances and research traditions associated with them, they are all features of the basic question '*Are (very) poor people different from "normal" or mainstream people in terms of their behaviours, attitudes and lifestyles*?' Some theorists assume that poor or socially excluded people are inherently different and therefore address the question of *why* they are different. All assume that they will be different and all these approaches also assume (although some more explicitly than others) that 'different' in this context really means 'inferior'. Thus although the object of study might vary – educational outcomes, child abuse, antisocial behaviour, mental health, self-esteem and so on – it is assumed that the 'norm' – which usually means the middle class norm – is the optimal condition for children and families, and that poor families are in some ways deficient, and that they live in communities that are deficient. Inter-generational transmission of beliefs and lifestyles is a key facet of these theories, and therefore they focus explicitly on the behaviour and attitudes of parents and on the ways they socialise their children. The theories assume that at least part of the question which underlies these debates is *'Are poor parents responsible for their poverty and for the poor outcomes for their children?'* Models disagree about the degree to which poor parents are responsible for their children's poor outcomes, but explicitly or implicitly they assume that parents do have some responsibility. Whilst none of these theories directly addresses the issues around neighbourhoods, they all imply a neighbourhood effect. They assume not only that poor families are different and therefore socially separate from the norm, but also that they are geographically separate, and therefore that part of the problem related to the dislocation of poor children from society is the nature of their neighbourhoods.

The Underclass

The term 'underclass' has a long provenance but emerged in the academic and policy arena during the late 1980s and early 1990s. It has subsequently been succeeded in the UK and Europe by 'social exclusion' – a term that has fewer of the powerful negative connotations of 'underclass'. However the fundamental issues relating to social exclusion are presaged and in some ways enhanced by the underclass debates. Interestingly the term is used by writers from both the political left (e.g. Field, 1989; Wilson, 1987) and the right (e.g. Murray, 1990, 1994). There is considerable debate as to whether there is an underclass, and if so why it exists and what should be done about it (Lister, 1996) but the central tenet of the underclass thesis – from both left and right – is that poverty is not a uniform phenomenon, and that different groupings of 'the poor' can be identified. In particular some elements of society have become dislocated from mainstream society not only in terms of income, but also in terms of their lifestyle, beliefs, values and engagement with the labour market. Briefly, members of the underclass are said to have the following characteristics:

● dislocation from the labour market – (don't want to or can't work);
● illegitimacy;
● anti-social behaviour, especially street crime;
● disrespect for authority or for mainstream institutions;
● low aspirations and lack of future orientation;
● poor parenting skills;
● live in self-contained (urban) ghettos;
● (in the USA) are ethnically distinct from mainstream society.

Other important aspects of the underclass are its persistence over time, its reference to groups and transmission from generation to generation. So a single individual who behaves anti-socially and who is materially deprived is not part of the underclass, which refers, rather, to a group of people who collectively withdraw from societal norms and values.

The most significant proponent of the underclass theory from the right is Charles Murray (1990, 1994). In a series of provocative articles he claimed that the underclass is a growing 'cancer', which is threatening to destroy Western society. Citing rising street crime, single parenthood and unemployment statistics in the USA and the UK, Murray claimed that there is now an epidemic sweeping these societies:

> I am not talking here about an unemployment problem that can be solved by more jobs, nor about a poverty problem that can be solved by higher benefits. Britain has a growing population of working-age, healthy people who live in a different world from other Britons, who are raising their children to live in it, and whose values are now contaminating the lives of entire neighborhoods – which is one of the most insidious aspects of the phenomenon, for neighbors who don't share those values cannot isolate themselves (Murray, 1996, p. 26).

Unlike accounts of the underclass provided by left-leaning authors such as Wilson (1987) in the USA and the Member of Parliament, Frank Field (1989), in the UK, Murray's account emphasises the *behaviour* of underclass members rather than structural economic factors as the most important defining feature of the underclass. He does not claim that members of the underclass are the poorest in society. Rather they are distinguished from other poor people by their antagonism towards and/or disengagement from mainstream society. What distinguishes them from other poor people is that, even though they are capable of being engaged in mainstream society (albeit as poverty-stricken), they choose to behave in 'deplorable' ways.

From the left and with a particular focus on ethnic minorities, the American sociologist, William Julius Wilson, after studying Chicago communities, focused more on the influence that the neighbourhood might have on its residents, in conjunction with discrimination and associated lack of opportunity. He focused on the concentration of low-income individuals and households in his investigation of community erosion, typical of Black and Hispanic neighbourhoods in the city (1987). He argued that poor children with *poor neighbours*, living in *run-down neighbourhoods*, would do less well and become the 'underclass' and that this was likely to have inter-generational effects. His conception of the 'underclass' links family deprivation with the collapse of employment opportunities, the lack of good quality public services, the exodus of Black middle-classes to the suburbs, and the counter-attractions of a delinquent subculture in communities with few legitimate opportunities. Wilson puts forward the hypothesis of the 'marriageable pool' to explain the link between single parenthood, long-term unemployment and neighbourhood poverty in black communities.

According to Wilson, Black ghettos were in the past similar to the historical Jewish ghettos in Europe – i.e. they were whole communities with leadership structures, codes of conduct and clear identities. However, after the Second World War, middle-class black families moved out of the ghetto, and the remaining men were not 'marriageable' – i.e. they were not able to support a family because they lacked basic work skills or had mental health, criminal or substance abuse issues.

This left a community without structure and leadership, and largely populated by female-headed single parent families and single men. He notes (1991) that the proportion of poor families in the USA who live in poor 'ghettos' varies by race. While 21% of Black poor and 16% of Hispanic poor live in poor neighbourhoods, only 2% of poor White families live in ghettos. Several commentators have attributed this social and economic phenomenon to racially segregated housing policies and the concentration of Whites in affluent suburbs (Leventhal & Brooks-Gunn, 2000).

Although the social trends identified by both Wilson and Murray are not really disputed, and seem to be common to most industrialised countries, the underclass thesis has been challenged by many theorists. Some of the challenges, especially to Murray, are ideological rather than factual, in particular his use of language and tendency to 'blame the victim' (Walker, 1996). Another set of challenges relate to his focus on illegitimacy as the main cause of moral decline in the underclass, and his differentiation between marriage and cohabitation and his insistence that cohabitation is a form of 'illegitimacy' and therefore, with single parenthood, has a pernicious effect on children. Finally there are challenges to the idea that there is a definable 'underclass' at all – i.e. that there is a specific group of people who are distanced from mainstream society and the labour force, live in single parent families, pay little due to social mores and who pass on these characteristics to their children.

Nevertheless, the underclass theory has important consequences for the issue of neighbourhood and family links, and for the effects of global social and economic trends on communities. It points towards the rather paradoxical conclusion that the more social mobility there is in a society, the more those at the very bottom will become disengaged from the mainstream and will be concentrated in dysfunctional communities. However, the extent to which these phenomena may be unique to the USA, with its particular social and racial mix, is still disputed (Deakin, 1996).

Social Exclusion

The concept of social exclusion has its origins in Europe rather than the USA, but describes a similar phenomenon to the underclass – i.e. a group of people who are not only materially deprived, but who have lost contact with 'mainstream' society. However, the term is much more fluid than the underclass thesis and it describes a much more diffuse occurrence. Individuals and groups can be socially excluded in different ways, to different degrees and for different periods of time. Thus there is not one group, 'the socially excluded', as there is deemed to be one 'underclass'.

Although there is little consensus as to what the term actually means or how to measure it (Atkinson, 1998), the concept of social exclusion has proved useful in widening the policy debate towards a more dynamic and holistic view of poverty and inequality. The UK government's definition is:

> A short hand label for what can happen when individuals or areas suffer from a combination of linked problems such as unemployment, poor skills, low incomes, poor housing, high crime environments, bad health and family breakdown (Department for Social Security, 1999, p. 23).

Levitas's (1998) influential model sets out three different 'discourses' of social exclusion; redistribution discourse (RED), social inclusion discourse (SID) and moral underclass discourse (MUD; see Box 2.1). These are not 'real life' policy positions, rather:

> RED, SID, and MUD are presented as distinct discourses. They are of course ideal types. All of them posit paid work as a major factor in social integration, and all of them have a moral content. But they differ in what the excluded are seen as lacking. To over simplify, in RED they have no money, in SID they have no work and in MUD they have no morals. (Levitas, 1998, p. 27).

Whilst this analysis applies mainly to the labour market, these discourses are relevant to many of the current tensions that are apparent in the development of policy towards parenting. According to Room (1995) social exclusion is the process of being detached from the organisations and communities of which the society is composed and from rights and obligations they embody. In broad terms this is a move from a focus on *distributional* to *relational* issues.

Room (1995) describes five ways in which there have been changes of emphasis from poverty to social exclusion in research:

- the move from the study of financial indicators to multi-dimensional disadvantage;
- the move from a static to a dynamic analysis;
- the move from the individual household to the local neighbourhood;
- the move from a distributional to a relational focus;
- the connotation of separation and permanence, a discontinuity in relationships with the rest of society.

Box 2.1   Levitas's discourses of social exclusion

Redistribution Discourse (RED). According to the RED discourse social exclusion is seen in terms of material deprivation, and the solution is a redistribution of wealth. This is the 'Old Labour' socialist ideology.

Social Inclusion Discourse (SID). The SID discourse portrays exclusion not just as a matter of poverty, but of dislocation from the mainstream of society. It is related to the 'dynamic' view of poverty. The policy objective of SID is to involve socially excluded people in the workforce and in mainstream society (including mainstream services).

Moral Underclass Discourse (MUD). This is the view held by Murray (1989) discussed above – i.e. that socially excluded people are (at least to some extent) responsible for their own marginalisation, and that policy towards these groups should not only involve 'carrots' such as job seekers benefits, but also 'sticks' such as Parenting and Anti-Social Behaviour Orders or withdrawal of benefits for parents who do not participate in welfare to work programmes.

Levitas, 1998

Room argued that the first three aspects have to some extent been explored in more recent studies of poverty, and in so far as social exclusion focuses on these, it does not represent a significant departure from the past. However the move from a distributional to a relational focus is a significant change in emphasis. Social exclusion focuses on relational issues: inadequate social participation, lack of social integration, discrimination and prejudice and lack of power. The discontinuity in relationships with the rest of society is also seen as a distinct feature of social exclusion. Social exclusion implies continuity over time – it is more difficult to move in and out of social exclusion than it is to move in and out of poverty. In this sense it is similar to 'Hardship' as defined by Berthoud et al. (2004).

This analysis creates space for discrimination to be seen as a crucial dynamic in the understanding of exclusion – i.e. a focus on the excluders as well as the excluded. Room's approach is in some ways similar to that of Bourdieu's (1986) view of social capital. Unlike most US theorists such as Putnam (2000), who perceive social capital mainly in terms of community solidarity and support networks, Bourdieu views social capital as one of the resources which families deploy to ensure that their children have access to social networks and facilities which will maintain their advantage. Middle class parents use not only financial advantage to ensure their children can go to the best schools, but they also use their networks of acquaintances and knowledge of middle-class mores to ensure that their children know the right people and behave in appropriate ways with them. In this way middle-class families can perpetuate class positions over generations. This theory turns on its head the basic premise of the culture of poverty and underclass theories, i.e. that poor parents are somehow deficient in their ability to provide their children with the resources to engage fully in mainstream society. On the contrary, Bourdieu asserts that affluent parents and communities unfairly use their position of power and knowledge to ensure that their children maintain privilege.

The Culture of Poverty

In contrast to the stress theories of poverty and parenting, the 'culture of poverty' hypothesis (Lewis, 1966; Bertrand et al., 2004) points towards the persistence of poverty and low achievement across generations, and asserts that parents living in poverty form a different 'culture' from middle-class parents. It is this culture, rather than effects of material deprivation itself (or the stress of living in poverty) that influences outcomes for children. The culture of poverty involves *low expectations* for children, harsh or inconsistent punishment, an emphasis on conformity rather than individual attainment, and the use of physical rather than verbal methods of discipline. The culture of poverty theory asserts that this parenting style is transmitted through the generations, and thus creates barriers to children emerging from poverty. The implications are that reducing parental stress by raising income or improving the environments of poor parents will do little to produce positive outcomes for children. The aim should rather be to break the culture of poverty by changing the attitudes and parenting styles of materially deprived parents (Fram, 2003). Culture of poverty theory is similar to the underclass theories, but differs in that the culture of poverty is deemed to be a feature of all materially deprived communities, not just a section of the lower classes as asserted by underclass theorists.

Culture of poverty theories have a long history. Perhaps the most well known early exponent of this view was Bernstein (1960, 1974) whose work was concerned with the different patterns of speech between working-class and middle-class parents. According to Bernstein, working-class people use a *restricted* code whereas middle-class people use an *elaborated* code, and these codes are learned by children from their parents when they learn to speak. Familiarity with elaborated code was seen by Bernstein to provide middle-class children with access to educational success. Ermisch et al. (2001) provide a more recent example of a cultural explanation of poverty. They consider that children living in poverty are not only likely to be poorer in resources but also to have fewer opportunities for success. This is because of intergenerational transmission – for example their families have lower expectations of work and education.

Yaqub (2002) analysed data on the persistence of poverty over the lifetime in several countries and found that children's class, education and health correlate strongly with that of parents and siblings. He suggests that socio-economic background influences lifetime attainments, but stresses that outcomes are not determined by childhood experiences alone. Resilience and Plasticity (i.e. the ability to undo psychological or social damage) can counteract the effects of poverty at any point in the child's lifetime. Individuals' lifetime incomes are not correlated with their annual incomes until they are in their 30s, indicating that until this age people can change their trajectory.

An analysis in the UK of data from the longitudinal National Child Development Study (NCDS) of children born in 1958 (Hobcroft, 1998), found that poverty and social exclusion usually persist during the lifespan, and that the main predictors of adult outcomes were childhood poverty, family disruption, contact with the police, educational test scores and father's interest in schooling. Despite the finding of continuity, Hobcroft warned against interpreting his findings as meaning that a disadvantaged background necessarily determines the future for children. He concluded:

> There is huge scope for many, if not most, individuals to escape from the patterns and tendencies observed. An important potential area for further research is to examine more closely the characteristics of individuals who escape the general tendencies (Hobcroft, 1998, p. 95).

Another facet of the culture of poverty theories is the finding that most parents seem to replicate the basic parenting style that they had experienced as children (Chen & Kaplan, 2001). However there have been no studies of the styles of parents who experience very different socio-economic conditions from their children (e.g. parents who were very poor as children but who become affluent as adults). Thus it is still not clear to what extent these inter-generational similarities are a factor of learned parenting behaviour as opposed to responses to the environment. Research evidence has not given particular support to the culture of poverty theory. In the 1970s Keith Joseph, then education secretary and mentor to Margaret

Thatcher, initiated a whole programme of research in the UK. He was determined to break the 'cycle of poverty' and commissioned research to find out how this could be done. However the research showed that people living in poverty tended, as a whole, to be just as connected to mainstream values and mores as middle-class people (Smith, 1992). More recent research in the USA (Bertrand et al., 2004) confirms that people of low SES are not very different in their weaknesses and biases from those of the middle class.

NEIGHBOURHOOD POVERTY

While the influence of individual or family poverty on negative outcomes has received much consideration, more recent attention has been directed to ways in which neighbourhood poverty influences families and child development (Jencks & Mayer, 1990). Focusing too narrowly on family poverty fails to take into account the ecological context within which the family lives. Deprivation is caused not only by insufficient personal resources but also by unsatisfactory community resources such as dilapidated schools, remotely sited shops or poor public transport, which reinforce and perpetuate household poverty (Robson, Bradford & Tye, 1995). The identification of insufficient community resources has been highlighted in UK government documents aimed at developing ways to help families living in poverty (DETR, 1997).

Jencks and Mayer (1990) outlined five major theoretical models by which the characteristics and behaviour of neighbours are thought to influence child outcomes (summarised in Box 2.2). Some focus more on the behaviour of neighbours and others on the financial capital within families and locally in the neighbourhood.

The contagion, collective socialisation and institutional models lead to the prediction that a mixed community with some affluent neighbours would enhance child development through direct and indirect benefits of socialisation and resources. The competition and relative deprivation theories suggest that competition from, or comparing oneself to, more advantaged neighbours would be detrimental to impoverished families and children due to feelings of anomie, rejection and failure. Indeed, in uniformly deprived communities residents may gain strength from each other if there is social cohesion. Some studies are now trying to clarify this but it remains open to debate whether it is advantageous to 'gentrify' previously disadvantaged neighbourhoods. The relative balance of families who are poor or affluent has been studied in relation to child outcomes such as academic achievement but with few conclusive findings (see Chapter 4 for a fuller discussion of this).

One recent British study has looked at the relevance of comprehensive neighbourhood poverty for parenting. Ghate and Hazel (2002) surveyed a random sample of 1,754 parents living in poor environments about their parenting style, the range of problems they faced and difficulties with children and family. They divided the poor environments into three degrees of poverty. Although not all risk factors were positively associated with increasing neighbourhood poverty, some were. An important factor relating to parental malaise was the degree of

---

Box 2.2   Theoretical models linking community poverty to child outcomes

The *epidemic or contagion model* assumes that behaviours are learned or copied. The presence of anti-social neighbours or youth can spread problem behaviours such as substance abuse or delinquency. Positive behaviours can spread in a similar manner.

Collective socialization highlights the importance of adult role models in the community such as other parents, relatives or neighbours who may socialise towards acceptable success, rather than anti-social behaviour, depending on the local social norms and the extent of anomie. Additionally, these other adults can adopt a supervisory or monitoring function to control negative behaviour.

The *institutional model* proposes that adults from outside the community working in schools, the police force and other institutions can influence child outcomes depending on how skilled they are, their interaction with the children and the resources they provide, e.g. quality of education and policing.

Competition theory is most closely linked with poverty and emphasises the importance of resources and the potential impact if neighbours have to challenge each other for scarce resources. This would increase the likelihood of an 'underclass' emerging, composed of residents with the fewest resources (Wilson, 1987).

Relative deprivation theory proposes that individuals judge their position in society in relation to neighbours. Those with fewer resources are likely to be demoralised if neighbours appear to be more affluent. Bradley & Whiteside-Mansell (1997, p. 15) note that 'Being poor when all around you are poor and when living in a culture where material goods are given only moderate value means one thing. Being poor when many around you are not poor and when material possessions are highly valued means quite another'. In fact families experiencing 'personal' poverty in relatively affluent communities may be at particular disadvantage if they are subject to negative labeling by their more affluent peers.

Jencks & Mayer, 1990

---

area-level poverty: the poorer the area, the more likely parents were to have mental and emotional problems. Additionally, on various counts, the greater the degree of objectively measured area-level poverty, the more likely parents were to rate their area as a 'bad place to bring up a family'. Because they only studied parents in poor environments, and the vast majority of parents in these neighbourhoods were themselves poor, Ghate and Hazel could only partially address the question of whether it is worse to be a poor parent in a poor area than a poor parent in a more affluent area. However their overall conclusion was that the balance of evidence was that *'parenting in poor environments is a more "risky" business*

> ## Box 2.3   Models of the moderating influence of community poverty on child development, focusing on resources and relationships
>
> *Institutional resources model* refers to the quality, quantity and variety of community resources designed to influence outcomes through recreation, socialisation, educational, health and employment opportunities. This would include resources such as libraries, parks and community centres.
>
> *Relationships and ties model* highlights the importance of family attributes such as parental physical and psychological health, social networks, parental management strategies and the quality of the home environment.
>
> *Norms and collective efficacy model* refers to formal and informal institutions and the degree to which residents' behaviour is monitored and controlled. This model also includes influences such as peer groups and threats from the neighbourhood such as violence or illegal substances. A further benefit of positive collective socialisation derives from creating structure and routines that guide behaviour.
>
> Leventhal & Brooks-Gunn, 2003

than parenting elsewhere, and it gets riskier the poorer the area' (Ghate & Hazel, 2002, p. 101).

Drawing on the work of Jencks and Meyer (1990) and other sources, Leventhal and Brooks-Gunn (2003) proposed three models whereby the effects of neighbourhood on child and youth outcomes are moderated (summarised in Box 2.3). However, it must be noted that it is still not clear whether these are neighbourhood effects or the effect of individual deprivation or indeed of community of interest. We need to find out whether new mothers will mimic the routine of their neighbours in areas where the majority of parents have a particular routine for their children. At the moment it is presumed that this takes place, but there is little evidence to back up the idea.

Mechanisms of Neighbourhood Poverty Influence

Neighbourhood economic disadvantage has been linked to a variety of negative outcomes such as 'smoking, drinking, long-term illness, female heart disease and infant mortality rates' (McCulloch, 2003, p. 1425). Ross et al. (2004) cite a recent study demonstrating a three-fold risk of coronary heart disease in poor people living in impoverished US neighbourhoods compared with richer residents in affluent neighbourhoods. The community influence on health will be compounded by the patterns of eating by neighbours and friends, the types of food outlets available to buy ingredients or ready-made meals, and by the extent to which healthy lifestyles are discussed or not by friends and family (or can be afforded).

Research identifies some of the mechanisms through which deprivation exerts an effect on health, e.g. stress, stigma and feelings of powerlessness, hopelessness and fatalism (Cattell, 2001). Besides having a direct impact on health these psychological correlates also influence health indirectly through unhealthy life-style choices. In the UK, the rising proportion of the population below the poverty line has led to a sharp rise in health and developmental inequality (Jack, 2000) reflected in higher rates of ill-health and mortality among the poor. While it could be argued that this finding is simply the summation of many individuals living in poverty, there are community influences on behaviours such as smoking. Living in a community which accepts smoking in public, in restaurants, or in the presence of young children, by the simple proportion of smokers who then set the 'rules', will serve to compound the influence of individual behaviour. In a different community, where there is much discussion of health risks, where some institutions take the lead in banning smoking, and where there is a general move to deny smokers the right to smoke in front of whomsoever they please, then the individual is more likely to attempt to control their smoking. Those communities that took the lead in banning smoking from public places were generally not the most impoverished, but the most affluent (such as the exclusive suburb of Boston, Brookline, one of the first to ban smoking in restaurants, in the mid-1990s).

McCulloch and Joshi (2001) refer to the increasing polarisation of wealth at the local level in Britain that has led to the development of urban communities of concentrated poverty. These areas of concentrated disadvantage are characterised by deprivation and social exclusion 'providing a fertile environment for the mushrooming of social problems' (Cattell, 2001, p. 1502). A similar phenomenon is currently occurring in London, albeit on a less extreme scale, with better-off families moving to the suburbs to escape perceived problems associated with poor schooling, rising crime levels and 'abysmal transport', accompanied by an influx of large numbers of immigrants and ethnic minorities (http://www.migrationwatchuk.org) leading to commentary in the press from both the left and the right (e.g. Johnston, 2005; Phillips, 2001).

The difference between being a poor individual or living in a family defined as poor, and the double experience of living in poverty while being surrounded by poverty, has been Wilson's ongoing theme with particular reference to disadvantage suffered by minority families. However, Weatherburn and Lind (2001) challenge the assumption that economic stress in the community directly motivates individuals to commit crime (see Chapter 10). Using evidence from aggregate-level studies they show strong positive associations between economic stress and child neglect (US Department of Health and Human Services, 1988) to support their claim that economic and social stress exert their effects on crime by disrupting the parenting process. This in turn makes children more susceptible to anti-social influences from peers in the neighbourhood leading to higher levels of crime.

These models build on the work of Jencks and Mayer (1990) by incorporating additional, important factors relevant to the impact of neighbourhood conditions on child and youth outcomes such as parental health, parenting style and the impact of parental networks, as well as the quality of resources and monitoring. They highlight that children's experiences of poverty are not universal but rather contingent upon the particular ecological niche inhabited by the child. A constellation of factors combines to produce a particular outcome for a particular child.

SOCIAL DISORGANISATION

In their classic study of delinquency, Shaw and McKay (1942) argued that structural features of urban communities such as poverty, population mobility and ethnic heterogeneity impeded communication and obstructed the quest for common values. This in turn led to cultural diversity with respect to non-delinquent values and the attenuation of mainstream cultural values. A more recent re-working of these themes (Sampson & Groves, 1989; Sampson, 1992) highlighted social disorganisation of a community. This refers to conditions where the behaviour of community members is not effectively controlled and the community does not share a set of common goals or values. Without this social organisation within a community it is predicted that there will be a range of parenting problems (such as child abuse) and more delinquent and criminal behaviour.

As with many theoretical constructs, social organisation and social disorganisation represent different ends of the same continuum (Bursik, 1988). Socially organised communities are characterised by positive (i.e. mainstream) norms as well as by mechanisms of control to enforce these norms. In contrast socially disorganised communities are typified by chaos and social disorder. The key indicators of social disorganisation are summarised in Box 2.4.

Box 2.4 Key elements of social disorganisation in communities

Public incivilities. Public incivilities encompass both physical and social signs of a community in decay. Signs of physical disorder include noise, dirt, graffiti, abandoned or run down buildings, whilst social disorder is evident in troublesome neighbours, public drinking and people hanging around on the streets (McCulloch, 2003). Drawing on Wilson's 'Broken Window' theory, Cohen et al. (2000, p. 230) posit that disordered environments signal that behaviours usually considered unacceptable 'can be perpetrated without fear of consequence'. Not only do incivilities suggest that residents are no longer able to enforce control but in some instances more formal controls such as policing and the judicial system have become ineffective.

Lack of collective efficacy. Social disorder signals a violation of shared norms prompting many residents to withdraw from the community due to fear and mistrust (Aneshensel & Sucoff, 1996). This fosters feelings of alienation, powerlessness, anxiety and depression, which in turn lead to further withdrawal. Social networks begin to weaken, breaking down cohesion. Where high residential instability and heterogeneity prevail, this further contributes to the weakening of social ties and trust. The community's sense of collective efficacy declines as residents come to believe that they no longer share common values and norms and are unable to enforce sanctions or effect change. This breakdown in cohesion and collective efficacy can have serious negative consequences for children and youth as an important mechanism of control evaporates.

Lack of informal social control. Informal social control is a central dimension in the measurement of structural social organisation or disorganisation (Bursik & Webb, 1982; Sampson & Groves, 1989). A key component of informal social control is the collective supervision a community exerts over antisocial behaviour of youth, peer groups and gangs through monitoring and surveillance. Informal social control requires a shared sense of norms that value protecting neighbours from criminal victimisation as well as a willingness to act on these norms (Nash & Bowen, 1999). Highly disordered communities with low levels of collective efficacy or perceived norms may discourage residents from attempting to implement control of youth due to feared retaliation and lack of support. This may be reflected in detrimental outcomes for child and youth socialisation, evident in a rise in delinquent behaviour.

Fragmentation and weakening of neighbourhood institutions and services. Kornhauser (1978) argued that the instability and isolation of community institutions are also particularly relevant to social disorganisation. When links between community institutions (such as health, education, police and social services) are sparse, the capacity of a community to defend its local interests is weakened. A weak community organisational base also serves to attenuate local social control functions regarding youth, and disrupts provision of basic services to residents. Further, a lack of political commitment and the withdrawal of residents from local organisations may be reflected in a deterioration of existing institutions and facilities.

Breakdown of traditional family structure and function. In a review of factors associated with weakening communities and their impact on families, Barry and Garbarino (1997) cite research highlighting poverty, female-headed households, and failure to complete high school, unemployment, and reliance on welfare. They point to difficulties in meeting developmental needs for children and youth reflected in increased child abuse and neglect, as well as increased adolescent childbearing and suicide rates.

In contrast to theories such as Wilson's (1987) 'underclass' model that emphasise the structure of the community shaping its values, social disorganisation theorists place more weight on community organisation being determined by characteristics such as the prevalence and inter-dependence of *social networks* in that community. Social disorganisation theorists perceive the community as a complex system of reciprocal friendship and kinship networks, and informal ties rooted in family life and inter-generational socialisation processes. This approach is similar to the arguments being made currently by psychologists who stress the importance of parents and children in shaping the environment, in the same way that the individual creates his or her own ecological niche in the family (Dunn & Plomin, 1990). While there is a focus on ways that communities shape individual development, there is equal, or even more, emphasis placed on the values of community residents, their behaviour both within the home and in the wider community, and the community is very much the sum of these parts, shaped by its residents.

SOCIAL CAPITAL

One of the most important ways that social disorganisation influences health and well-being is through its impact on social capital. Social capital refers to the values that people hold, the resources that they can access through relationships and reflects a shared sense of identity, common values, trust and reciprocity (Edwards, Franklin & Holland, 2003). This aspect of community has emerged as one of the most popular exports from the sociological realm into a wide range of literature concerned with families and children (Coleman, 1988), with dire warnings of what will become of a society that lacks this attribute (Putnam, 1993, 1995). However, it has roots going back many decades to the writing of Marx and Durkheim (Portes, 1998).

The essence of social capital is in its *potential* for support, which is generated through relationships and participation in groups. Social networks are conceptualised as if they were investment strategies, allowing group members to draw against available resources accrued as a result of past obligations fulfilled for other network participants. Coleman suggests (1993) that the norms and expectations of a community, particularly an informal community, rely on social capital arising from dense social networks that have continuity over time. Communities lacking social capital will not be able to reinforce social norms, resulting in further social disintegration and negative outcomes for families and children.

Distinctions are frequently drawn between different kinds of social capital: bonding, bridging, and linking (Putnam, 2000; Wiles, 2004; Woolcock & Naryan, 2000). Bonding social capital is more inward-looking, focused on experience and familiarity, essential for 'getting by' (Wiles, 2004). It exists in horizontal relationships/networks between family members, close friends and ethnic groups. Bonding strategies build trust and cooperation among individuals and *within* communities. In contrast, bridging social capital is more relevant for 'getting ahead'. It is also a horizontal link, but it exists *across* ethnic groups, across other communities or with work associates and employers. From a community development perspective, bridging strategies break down barriers between groups and communities and enable collaborative action on shared objectives (SPNO, 2002). A third type – linking social capital (also known as 'scaling up') – is not so widely used. Really a subdivision of bridging capital, it is said to provide a vertical link between social classes or to the wider world. Scaling-up strategies connect communities in collective action for social change and development at the policy and/or systems levels (SPNO, 2002; Wiles, 2004).

Bonding is likely to emerge most strongly from more homogeneous stable communities, whereas one would be more likely to find bridging social capital in heterogeneous communities, with affluent and disadvantaged living in close proximity. Rural neighbourhoods are likely to be high on bonding but lower on bridging, and urban communities the opposite, high on bridging but low on bonding. Linking social capital allows communities of any mix to create their own movement, as a result of community action. The mix within a neighbourhood need not be solely in terms of affluence or social class, but may be a mix of ethnic or religious groups, or the relative balance of younger and older residents.

In an exploration of families and social capital, Edwards et al. (2003) comment on differences between bonding and bridging capital in relation to families in communities. The former operates more often at family level and its function is to invest in children's futures. It generally brings together individuals who already have some commonalities. From this perspective, changes in family structure, e.g. single parenthood, would decrease social capital available to the family with poorer child outcomes. Bridging social capital, as proposed by Putnam, refers to the ability of a community to create links with organisations and institutions and between individuals who do not necessarily have anything in common, for the benefit and the improvement of the community. It strengthens 'weak ties'. It follows that communities low in social capital will not be able to enforce norms or maintain resources necessary for the health and well-being of residents.

Social Capital and Socialisation

Coleman (1988) has refined the idea of social capital as it applies to the socialisation process. His formulation provides a conceptual link between the attributes of individual actors and their immediate social context. The characteristics of family or community members, their strengths and weaknesses, are known as the human capital their income and other material resources the financial capital and their environment is the physical capital. Social capital is defined by function rather than form (Coleman, 1988; Furstenberg & Hughes, 1995), lodged in individuals or in the physical environment, but within 'family relations and community organisations that are useful for the cognitive or social development of a child or young person' (Coleman, 1990, p. 300).

An individual creates an investment through involvement in social relationships and the resulting social capital (obligations, expectations) may be drawn upon to enhance children's opportunities. The influence is predicted to take various forms. Social interactions of parents may enhance the child's social skills, thus furthering their chances of success with peers and other adults. Alternatively, parents' friends may provide additional sources of information and help regarding schoolwork. Finally the parents' social contacts may enhance their own well-being, which in turn will promote children's development, although it may be argued that this kind of activity could harm children if the parent spends less time in the home (Buchel & Duncan, 1998).

It has been argued that this theoretical model may be particularly useful for understanding the different outcomes for children from disadvantaged communities, in that parents with less abundant economic and human capital resources may still use them efficiently. A number of studies have applied this theoretical formulation to child outcomes. Furstenberg and Hughes (1995) suggest that separate elements of social capital (e.g. parents' resources within the family, their social network, their embeddedness in the community) might be related to different areas of child success and should be studied separately.

Social Capital and Social Networks

Social disorganisation is said to prevent the establishment of social networks necessary for the generation of social capital. Networks are weakened or prevented from forming by residential instability, heterogeneity and withdrawal from the community due to feelings of fear, mistrust and suspicion. Williams (2003) highlights a number of additional factors which are obstacles to the formation of networks, including 'time famine' in families arising from work demands, the demise of the extended family, rapid family formation and disintegration, poor housing estate design and loss of public spaces.

Social capital can be generated through formal and informal networks and can operate at both individual and collective level. In a typology of social networks based on two impoverished neighbourhoods, Cattell (2001) found that a sense of control, higher self-esteem, hopefulness, health and enjoyment were associated with what she termed 'Networks of Solidarity'. These networks were characterised by strong personal ties as well as participation in community organisations. In contrast, individuals from 'Socially Excluded' networks tended to be marginalised and more likely to display feelings of anxiety, depression, hopelessness and fatalism as well as physical symptoms. High levels of social capital were available to those in networks of solidarity due to a density and variety of relationships and resources, while socially excluded networks were low in social capital due to a paucity of relationships and resources. In line with Jencks and Mayer's (1990) theories of community influence, individuals with a narrow range of reference groups felt themselves to be in competition with those perceived as somehow different and were critical of those receiving greater benefits.

The relationship between personal characteristics and available networks is, however, complex. Several studies have noted that individuals with certain types of extravert personality are better able to develop networks with neighbours (Barnes, 2004; Ghate & Hazel, 2002), and these individuals may be less likely to find themselves in disadvantaged communities (Barnes, 2004). Thus the driving force comes from the people themselves, wherever they happen to be, rather than networks of support creating the wellbeing. This model is in line with an economic analogy of social capital – i.e. that the more you have, the more you can generate.

The differences that individuals bring to their communities are illustrated by these quotes from mothers in the Families and Neighbourhoods Study, discussing their own personalities in relation to getting to know other parents in their neighbourhoods (Barnes & Baylis, 2004, pp. 57–58).

> [What about the people, do you find it friendly here or not?] We're not that way inclined. We tend to keep ourselves to ourselves. Us being friendly goes as far as saying hello to neighbours, but I'm not the sort who would socialise with my neighbours just because they were my neighbours. But yes, they're friendly enough, just to say hello to, but that's as much as we want anyway (disadvantaged rural area).

[Have you developed friendships with parents at school?] I'm a bit picky about who I choose to come to my house or to know where I live. I'm not having irate parents knocking on my door, or even parents knocking on my door every 30 seconds, 'Can I borrow a loaf of bread?' I won't be doing that (disadvantaged rural area).

[So you've made some friends then?] Lots of friends. And even before that, I was really good at making friends. I used to chat with lots of parents, I did know a lot of the parents before (disadvantaged inner-city area).

[Have you got involved in any school activities?] No, I'm not one for that. Some people help out at school fetes and things, but that's not me! (disadvantaged town).

[Is it a friendly place then?] Yes, people talk to you in the street, don't get me wrong! But that's just me, I don't want to mix (disadvantaged town).

[So how friendly is it around here, generally?] Well I find it really friendly, but then I am quite a friendly kind of person, I'm quite outgoing, so I don't have a problem around here (advantaged city suburb).

I'm quite a shy person so I find it very difficult to like jump in there head first saying, 'Hello, my name is Susan'. But I don't do too bad, I'm getting there (advantaged city suburb).

What this study also found was that parents in an affluent neighbourhood were on average substantially more extravert and agreeable in their personality traits than those in three disadvantaged areas, and that one small rural disadvantaged community was typified by a significantly higher proportion of people with less agreeable and outgoing characteristics than all of the other areas studied. This highlights the importance of knowing not only about the level of poverty in a community but also about the individuals who make up the area (Barnes, 2004).

Finally, it must not be thought that social capital is necessarily always a 'good thing'. Negative forms of social capital have been described (Portes, 1998). The same strong ties that bring benefits to members of a group equally bar others from access. This happens most commonly in strong ethnic communities, but it is also emerging in 'gated communities' (see 'Environmental theory and defensible space' in this chapter, below). Successful members of the group may be held back by claims from others to give assistance. Group participation may also give rise to demands for excessive conformity, thereby restricting personal freedom. Finally, group solidarity may be motivated by adversity or opposition to mainstream society, linking this with collective negative socialisation and with anomie of a community. Ethnographic studies of youth involved in drug-dealing in New York have recorded how youth are prevented from escaping into a more legitimate lifestyle (Williams, 1990). Similarly, children growing up in a family with criminal parents, immersed in subcultures that may have very strong social capital, may find it hard to pursue academic qualifications or traditional employment.

Social Capital and Policy

It has been argued that the current emphasis in the UK on 'social exclusion' brings a shift in focus from poverty, a distributional issue, to that of relational issues such as inadequate social participation, lack of social integration and lack of power (Room, 1998) as typified by a lack of social capital. This has much in common with the theoretical constructs and processes identified by developmental psychologists explaining successful adaptation of children at risk of long-term disadvantage (Rutter, 1983), and also echoes the approach to development formulated by Bronfenbrenner (1979).

Wilson (1987) posited that members of the underclass do not have sustained contact with individuals and institutions representative of mainstream society, or with friends and relatives in more stable areas of the city or suburbs. The same has been argued with regard to the UK (6, 1997) where geographical location dictates what communities can provide residents (McCulloch, 2003). Housing policies concentrate low-income families together, and place them on the same training schemes, thus reducing the likelihood of developing social contacts and networks in the wider society.

Despite the usefulness of social capital as a mechanism to explain the relationship between community disadvantage and outcomes, the concept is subject to criticism. Cattell's (2001) comparison of two deprived neighbourhoods in East London revealed that social capital can exist in poor communities. Further, even in areas with low overall social capital, a segment of community characterised as high in social capital can arise, spurred on by social consciousness and the need for action through participation.

Edwards et al. (2003) highlight critiques of social capital as an answer to exclusion and deprivation. Some criticism relates to a failure to acknowledge that deprivation results from structural features such as racism, sexism and classism. Moreover there is a concern that a social solution to the issue of poverty is being sought instead of one that addresses economics. As Cattell (2001) points out, addressing exclusion cannot be dealt with only by fostering social capital through relationships but necessitates a measure of financial redistribution as well. The New Labour Party's conservative focus on the traditional family as the source of social capital is criticised on the grounds that it ignores positive experiences of children in alternative family structures (Roseneil & Williams, 2004).

Finally, it has been argued that social capital should not be applied to communities at all since it was originally constructed as an individual level attribute although it has been used increasingly as a characteristic of a community or even a nation (Putnam, 1996). Portes (1998) suggests that it should be retained principally as a characteristic of an individual or family to avoid circularity, but that these individual-level variables could be aggregated in order to describe community members.

ENVIRONMENTAL THEORY AND DEFENSIBLE SPACE

All the preceding theoretical formulations take as their basis people in communities and their attributes or disadvantages. However communities (at least territorial ones) also exist as physical entities and the built environment is receiving more and more attention. In urban areas levels of crime and disorder have been associated with the ability of residents to define the boundaries of their own living space and defend those boundaries. While initially applied to delinquency and crime, the extent to which families can create safe spaces for their children has great relevance to family functioning.

Defensible space (Moran & Dolphin, 1986; Newman, 1972) summarises those features of the environment (real barriers such as walls, gates, bars, lighting) that allow residents to maintain control over their own living space, both indoor and outdoor, as well as to facilitate social interaction. Defensible space features often overlap with territorial markers such as symbols of protection (dogs, alarms, neighbourhood watch signs) and 'personalisations' such as decorations. These markers are expected to enhance social cohesion, allow for more social control and reduce the likelihood of social disorder. It is predicted that in areas where the housing has more defensible space there will be less crime and a greater sense of attachment to the community. More transient than territorial markers are signs of incivilities (e.g. litter, graffiti, dilapidated property) that have been linked with social disorganisation in a community, with fear of crime (Perkins & Taylor, 1996), and with less attachment to the community by residents (Barnes McGuire, 1997a).

Recent research suggests that the extent to which residents appropriate public space is related to safety and community cohesion. Brunson, Kuo and Sullivan (2001) found that feelings of safety were related to the frequency and duration of residents' use of near-home space in low-income public housing developments. Both safety and community cohesion were associated with territorial appropriation of near-home space, which took the form of intervening in the event of illegal or destructive activities, care-taking actions, feelings of ownership and frequency of monitoring. Thus, it appears that the ability to exercise informal social control is an important aspect of defending one's own and communal territory. Whether greater use of public space was due to feelings of safety or safety arose as a result of residents' actions is open to interpretation. The authors suggest that territoriality and positive outcomes may have a mutually reinforcing effect.

This aspect of the community may influence community cohesion in an adverse manner, however. While territorial markers and defensible space allow residents to exercise control (Newman, 1972), too much safety may lead to greater social isolation in the same way that tightly meshed social capital *within* a community may restrict activities beyond the community. Gated communities have caused a considerable amount of controversy. The greatest number of these can be found in the USA but walled and gated developments are not just an American phenomenon; they can also be found in South America, South Africa, the Middle East and Southeast Asia and to a lesser extent in Europe, Canada, Australia, New Zealand and the UK (Blandy et al., 2003). One could argue that calling them communities is inappropriate. Even within the gates there is not necessarily a sense of community beyond the sense of 'keeping other people away' and in particular keeping out crime, while those the 'right' side of the gates become less and less part of the wider community within which their residences are placed. The conclusions reached by Blandy et al.'s review support this notion.

Research showed that motivations for living in a gated community are primarily driven by the need for security and a more generalised fear of crime. Importantly there was no apparent desire to come into contact with the 'community' within the gated or walled area (2003, p. 3).

Conflict between neighbours and the general feeling that gated community residents do not want to know their neighbours suggests that gated communities do not represent a new form of communitarian living (2003, p. 5).

They have been criticised not only for promoting a separatist kind of society but in particular for the likelihood of increasing segregation in communities, much of which in the USA is also racial segregation (Blakely & Snyder, 1997a; 1997b). Blakely and Snyder comment:

Suburbanization has not meant a lessening of segregation, but only a redistribution of the urban patterns of discrimination. Gated communities are a microcosm of the larger spatial pattern of segmentation and separation. In the suburbs, gates are the logical extension of the original suburban drive. In the city, gates and barricades are sometimes called "cul-de-sac-ization," a term that clearly reflects the design goal to create out of the existing urban grid a street pattern as close to the suburbs as possible (1997a, p. 2).

Exclusion imposes social costs on those left outside. It reduces the number of public spaces that all can share, and thus the contacts that people from different socioeconomic groups might otherwise have with each other. The growing divisions between city and suburb and rich and poor are creating new patterns which reinforce the costs that isolation and exclusion impose on some at the same time that they benefit others. Even where the dividing lines are not clearly ones of wealth, this pattern of fragmentation affects us all (1997a, p. 2).

We must also remember that the reasons for gating are not always entirely, or even primarily, the laudable reasons of crime and traffic control. Hopes of rising property values, the lure of prestige, and even the desire to build barriers against a poorer neighborhood or one of a different race are also common reasons behind gated communities (1997a, p. 3).

However, in the UK it has been argued, based on some examples in London, that gated communities can in fact promote race relations and increase community cohesion (Manzi & Smith-Bowers, 2005). Manzi and Smith-Bowers report that gating can encourage people to stay where they live rather than moving to more affluent neighbourhoods and abandoning areas entirely to people suffering multiple deprivations, and that resident associations can provide links across tenures and make neighbourhoods less segregated than they would be without gating. One of the report's authors commented:

Seeing gating as the antithesis of social cohesion ignores the much more complex relationships between individuals and their environments. Undoubtedly, gated communities represent a choice to exclude others but, as a club good, they may also represent a more positive model of housing development.

Policy-makers should consider how issues of segregation can be balanced against the need to develop consumer choice and potentially increase social cohesion by providing new forms of sustainable communities, instead of railing against privatism, isolationism and particularist interests. (University of Westminster, 2004 http://www.wmin.ac.uk/lrfg).

It is clear that perceptions of defensible space may be important in understanding how residents define their community, thinking about a smaller area as their 'neighbourhood' when there is more crime and disorder around them (Barnes, 2004). This will have implications for the extent to which the community can have an influence. By defining a smaller area, families will stay in their homes, or conduct activities at a distance from their local neighbourhood, which may impair the likelihood of developing social networks locally. The community is thus relevant in its absence, though this is likely to interact with individual factors such as a parent's personality, their gender, and both the age and gender of their child or children.

PSYCHOLOGICAL SENSE OF COMMUNITY

Psychological approaches to community have paid most attention, not to the structural aspects of the community, but to residents' perceptions of their community and the extent to which they express satisfaction. This could be associated either with fellow residents and community members, or with the structural characteristics of the area. 'Sense of community' is an emotion-laden construct that captures the social processes promoting cohesive and supportive communities (Cantillon, Davidson & Schweitzer, 2003), but a low sense of community has been related to both poor physical and poor psychological health (Ross et al., 2004).

While much of the literature assumes that there is a specific and relatively easily identifiable territory (such as a small town or one sector of a city) to which perceptions can be attached, McMillan and Chavis (1986) present a theoretical model of sense of community which is said to be equally applicable to both territorial and relational communities. They use the construct of community originally posited by McMillan a decade earlier (1976) as 'a feeling that members have of belonging, a feeling that members matter to one another and to the group, and a shared faith that members' needs will be met through their commitment to be together' (cited in McMillan & Chavis, 1986, p. 9). Four elements of a sense of community have been described (summarised in Box 2.5).

One aspect of a theoretical debate that is touched on frequently is the difference between the individual-level construct of social support and the systems-level construct of a cohesive or supportive community. Felton and Shinn (1992) suggest that social support and social networks are in fact extra-individual, but have usually been operationalised as individual-level concepts. Consequently, they maintain, the importance of groups and settings has been diminished. They emphasise that sense of community should be thought of at the extra-individual level, demonstrating how a community, whether it be a neighbourhood, a school, a workplace, or any other setting, may be experienced as supportive without having to identify individuals who create that environment. Feelings such as alienation and loneliness are not necessarily the result of an individual's personality type or inadequate social skills. While loneliness implies a failure on the part of the individual, they suggest that it may equally, or more often, represent failure of the community as a system.

> ## Box 2.5   Elements of sense of community
>
> *Membership* includes boundaries (who is in and out), emotional safety and security, a sense of belonging or identification with the group, personal investment and a common system (e.g. rite of passage, language, dress, gestures).
>
> *Influence* is said to be bi-directional. Members are attracted to a group they can influence but group cohesiveness is contingent on the group's ability to influence its members.
>
> *Integration* takes place through fulfilment of needs, with a strong community helping members meet each other's needs.
>
> *Shared emotional connection* is expected to take place after social contact with others over events that have some relevance to the community members and to the related honour, or humiliation, given to members for their actions.
>
>   McMillan, 1976

CULTURE, RACE AND ETHNICITY

An important way in which neighbourhood effects can be mediated is through culture or ethnic group, while these may also represent a community over and above any neighbourhood effect. This has been studied in most detail in the USA. García Coll & Magnuson (2000) point out that recent attempts to understand this aspect of community stress the contextual effects of socio-cultural influences on child development, rather than assuming that there are universal explanations for child outcomes. They feel it is important to understand why children from different cultures respond differently in similar situations. Ogbu (1981) noted that valued child competency and behaviour is determined by the availability of resources and folk theories of child rearing that dictate customary parental practices. Historically however, in the USA, White Anglo-Saxon middle-class culture prevailed, failing to acknowledge cultural differences. Minority families not subscribing to such a culture were subject to admonishment with their children's behaviour seen as deviant or deficient in some way (García Coll & Magnuson, 2000). This is an example of symbolic capital, a form of social capital, in which certain ways of thinking and acting are legitimised and regarded as authoritative (Bourdieu, 1997, in Edwards et al., 2003).

Although families do have a choice of where they would like to stay there are large differences in the quality of neighbourhoods, linked to a certain extent to the concentration of families from ethnic minority groups with higher concentrations of Black families in impoverished neighbourhoods in the USA (López Turley, 2003). López Turley suggests that Black children in predominantly White neighbourhoods do not benefit in ways one might expect from the higher neighbourhood income in these areas, possibly because they are more likely to be influenced by Black friends.

Reasons for the concentration of ethnic minority groups in poorer areas are linked in the USA to past segregation as well as to an inability to move arising from financial constraints. Access to good quality health care, and to employment and education, are limited for a large proportion of ethnic minorities living in disadvantage (García Coll & Magnuson, 2000), which perpetuates the cycle of poverty. This pattern is likely to be found in most developed Western countries. For instance, in the UK the English Housing Conditions Survey conducted by the Office of the Deputy Prime Minister found in 2001 that minority ethnic households were nearly three times more likely to live in poor neighbourhoods than were White households (37% versus 10%; Quilgars, 2005). Thus any examination of the influence of neighbourhood poverty on children's development or on parenting needs to incorporate information about the ethnic mix in a neighbourhood in addition to the mix of rich and poor.

Beyond these considerations of the mediating role that the ethnic mix of a geographical community might have, ethnic or cultural groups represent communities in their own right. The sociologists Portes and Zhou (1993) consider resources within an immigrant's community as a most important factor in improving the chances of upward mobility. With support from their community, immigrants can protect themselves from discrimination and the threat of vanishing mobility ladders. Moreover, for the second generation, the ethnic community can be the means by which they obtain both economic and moral support. For example, values regarding the importance of educational attainment and economic success can be maintained and transferred to the second generation (Portes & Zhou, 1993).

More importantly, ethnic communities are said to provide access to material and social resources for second-generation immigrants. Larger and longer-established groups develop distinct institutions and organisations which then provide support and economic opportunities. Material and social resources in the form of social capital are embedded in the social relations of the community. The successful facilitation of social capital impedes downward mobility. Thus, second generation persons unable to access appropriate economic resources from society more widely can utilise their social resources and networks to improve their chances for social mobility (Portes & Zhou, 1993). These researchers suggest that the ethnic community's social capital is at times more important than human capital in explaining why some second generation groups do better than others economically.

In a review of literature pertaining to immigrants to Australia from Western Europe, Giorgas (2000) concluded that ethnic community formation has served as a positive strategy for immigrants in overcoming social isolation and economic difficulties by providing employment opportunities and a sense of familial surroundings within their own ethnic group. Social capital is more effective in ethnic community groups with stronger cultural boundaries and a collective sense of identity.

In a multicultural society like Britain or the USA it is important to acknowledge that cultural differences as well as race/ethnicity (which can sometimes be a marker for social exclusion) might mediate the effects of neighbourhood context. They can, nevertheless, also represent the cornerstone of community identity and provide strength in terms of social support and a sense of shared values which can be a positive influence for children and families.

Australian research (Marjoribanks, 1979, 1986, 1991) considered the relationship between family learning environments and school-related outcomes among Greek, Southern Italian and Anglo-Australian students. Both Greeks and Italians tended to have more supportive family contexts, expressed stronger aspirations as adolescents and had higher social-status attainment scores compared to Anglo-Australians, illustrating the pervasive influence of ethnic communities on the learning environments of school-aged children.

This pattern of variation between groups can be found in many countries. In the UK, where there are a number of substantial communities of families from the Indian subcontinent, their children perform well in school on average and progress into the labour market. This is in marked contrast to children (especially males) of Afro-Caribbean background who perform less well in public examinations and are over-represented in the unemployed populations (http://www.standards. dfes.gov.uk/ethnicminorities/). While many explanations for these differences focus on differences in family structure and expectations, there are also community-related explanations to consider.

CONCLUSIONS

Increasing polarisation of wealth has led to areas (communities) of concentrated poverty characterised by multiple disadvantage, where many residents may live their lives without employment (the underclass). Commentators from both ends of the political spectrum (and many in between) have suggested that individuals with certain characteristics such as disengagement from mainstream society come to live in neighbourhoods that are increasingly excluded from any benefits that society might offer. We see later in this book that efforts have been made to lessen or even eradicate social exclusion, and that these efforts are increasingly being directed not at individuals but at communities.

Some theories (e.g. culture of poverty, contagion, collective socialisation, social disorganisation) place more emphasis on individuals shaping their communities while others (e.g. defensible space) argue that the communities can shape residents. What has yet to be agreed is whether it is better for communities to be heterogeneous to improve life chances for children and their parents. To achieve bridging social capital a mixed community is desirable, though bonding capital is more likely in homogeneous areas, also favoured by proponents of relative deprivation theory, who predict that a uniformly disadvantaged neighbourhood may be more supportive for residents than a mixed community. Competition theory also predicts poorer outcomes when some residents are affluent, with the formation of an 'underclass'. However, if the whole community is socially excluded then there may be little likelihood of gaining the resources (particularly inward investment) that are needed for progress. '

Social disorganisation and social capital theories place more emphasis on residents' social networks, institutional links and community cohesion and less on the structural or financial aspects of a community. These and community decay are seen as consequences of the actions of the residents and institutions in a community. Individuals in the community create social capital through involvement in social relationships and the resulting social capital (obligations, expectations) may be drawn upon to enhance children's opportunities. Although social capital is a useful mechanism for explaining the impact of neighbourhoods it has been criticised as somewhat simplistic. The theory of defensible space links the capacity for informal control with the ability to 'defend' one's territory. If residents cannot achieve this they will turn inwards rather than out to the community.

Considerations of a psychological sense of community and of the ethnic group as community are less bounded by geography than other theories but have generally not been considered in conjunction with explanations of community influences related to geographical community. Culture, race and ethnicity in particular may mediate the effects of neighbourhood poverty as well as being communities themselves, and this merits further attention both in research and when interventions are planned.

3

ASSESSING NEIGHBOURHOOD AND COMMUNITY CHARACTERISTICS

Understanding the influence of neighbourhood and community on families and children hinges on accurately measuring and assessing the neighbourhoods in which they reside and the communities to which they belong. As discussed in Chapter 1, the concepts neighbourhood and community may, but do not necessarily overlap. Because these terms are often used interchangeably, it is critical to be explicit about what is being measured at this ecological level. This chapter examines the various approaches and methodologies that have been utilised in measuring and assessing these constructs. Greater care and attention has been devoted over the years to developing measures of child, parent and family attributes than to developing contextual measures of neighbourhood and community. This has stimulated a call for the development of 'ecometrics,' involving improved measures of and methods for studying neighbourhood and community contexts (Raudenbush & Sampson, 1999). This chapter will propose a multi-level, multi-perspective and multi-method approach to understanding communities and neighbourhoods. The chapter focuses on neighbourhood as the geographically-bounded context in which children and families live, but also draws in the concept of community, which may or may not overlap with neighbourhood boundaries. Further, the influence of neighbourhood and community is filtered through residents' perceptions and experiences of their physical and social surroundings. While other chapters in this volume (see Chapter 4) discuss the effects of neighbourhood and communities, this chapter is focused on how to measure and assess neighbourhood and community contexts.

DELINEATING NEIGHBOURHOOD AND COMMUNITY BOUNDARIES

Chapter 1 discussed the definitions of neighbourhood and community. This chapter addresses the need for delineating and measuring what precisely is meant by both constructs. It has been difficult to generalise across studies of neighbourhood effects on children and families and to amass a body of evidence because the unit of analysis has rarely been comparable across studies.

Geographical Neighbourhood

Neighbourhood, and its associated features, is often the primary independent (predictor) variable, seeking to explain the outcomes for children and families based on the geographic areas in which they reside. There are, however, several layers of potential discrepancies. First, even studies using administrative boundaries use a range of units in the USA from census-defined block groups or census tracts to zip codes or other administratively-defined units and in the UK from the smallest areas such as postcodes and census output areas and super output areas, through to city boundaries, local authorities, shire counties and Government Office Regions (http://www.statistics.gov.uk/census2001/op12.asp). Indeed, so complex is the system in the UK that the Office for Nation Statistics has written a lengthy, but very helpful *Beginners Guide to UK Geography* providing up-to-date information, explanation, maps and listings of all the main geographies used in UK statistical production (http://www.statistics.gov.uk/geography/beginners_guide.asp). It provides information about the different ways that geography is used, giving details (including maps) of ways that the country is divided by different authorities. Separate documents are available about the following geog raphies: administrative (e.g. counties, districts); postal (e.g. post code); health (e.g. Strategic Health Authority, Primary Care Trust); electoral (e.g. constituency, wards); and census (e.g. output areas). Despite (or perhaps because of) these complications in defining neighbourhoods, most of the available evidence about defining neighbourhoods or communities has been conducted in the US.

Administrative units are defined for different purposes than research and have not been thought through with any idea that data from different types of area may need to relate to each other, creating a number of problems. First, they will not correspond to other administrative boundaries, thus a school district may or may not correspond to a geographic unit such as a census tract (a US term similar to an electoral ward in the UK) or 'block group' (a group of streets). A local electoral ward will not correspond with police beat areas. Neither will correspond to school catchment areas. The school may indeed be at the core of a 'community' of parents, teachers and students, but may not correspond to the neighbourhood in which at least the parents and students live.

Second, administratively-defined neighbourhoods and communities may not overlap with resident perceptions of their neighbourhood boundaries or communities of interest. Third, residents may vary in the geographic area that they define as their neighbourhood (Coulton, Korbin, Chan & Su, 2001) or the network of individuals defined as a community. And finally, internal variability in how residents define their neighbourhoods and communities may be substantial and may occur for a number of reasons. Residents who provide a service or who have a business in the neighbourhood may identify a larger geographic area than residents who spend less time in the community. Planners may identify different boundaries than parents. Planners, for example, may include a playground while parents may draw a smaller area closer to home in which they can look out of their windows to observe their children. Children and their parents may also define their neighbourhood area and boundaries differently, thus compounding the difficulties of assessing neighbourhood influences.

Phenomenological aspects of the community require perceptions of its residents such as their judgments of community danger, or the idiosyncratic behaviour of residents (e.g. the density of acquaintanceship or local social involvement), to be assessed. When the views of residents, or their actual behaviour are used to generate a community construct, two methodological issues emerge. First, it becomes necessary to sample a representative cross section of the residents, the cost of which may preclude this strategy from many studies (White, 1987). Second, when talking to residents, the decision has to be made whether to tell them what geographical area to think about or to allow them to define their own community. If the latter course is taken, then it will be necessary to discover how respondents arrived at their definition. However, a recent Canadian study by Ross, Tremblay and Graham (2004) analysed health data based on natural and census tract definitions of neighbourhood. They reported similar findings across both analyses and concluded that census tracts (containing approximately 4,000 residents) are good proxies for natural neighbourhood boundaries.

Even if one defined a neighbourhood for respondents, and was able to draw on a large representative sample of area residents, assessing cognitive aspects or mental maps of communities is not straightforward. Each resident has a personal sense of boundaries that are meaningful but this may, in fact, include several different definitions of their territorial space depending on the context (Galster, 1986). Asked about their neighbourhood in relation to children parents might think in terms of the local school and its surrounding streets, but their neighbourhood as a context for adult social activities, political participation, or shopping may be much larger. The clarity of a community, the extent to which a community has meaning or identity to residents, may indeed be one of its most important characteristics that needs to be assessed. Their lack of agreement becomes the community description. For example, one would expect that social cohesion and neighbourhood attachment might be lower and social isolation greater in areas that are not clearly identifiable to residents so it is vital not to exclude those who answer 'I don't know' from surveys about communities. Ways in which residents define (or do not contemplate) their community require more investigation and, in particular, ways that they define the social and affective aspects.

Coulton and colleagues (2001) addressed the question of whether census-defined neighbourhoods differ from resident-defined neighbourhoods by comparing resident-drawn maps of their neighbourhoods to US census defined block groups and census tracts. The US census divides urban areas into census tracts, which generally encompass between 2,000 and 4,000 residents. Census tracts are determined by natural and political boundaries, and local history also plays a role in Census Bureau designations. Census tracts are divided into block groups, which are smaller units generally made up of five to ten city blocks. Coulton et al. decided to use block groups in their study of neighbourhood impact on child maltreatment because they assumed that block groups, being smaller, would more closely resemble the face-to-face contact often associated with neighbourhoods. The systematic examination of resident-drawn maps, however, yielded a different story. Neighbourhood residents drew maps of neighbourhoods that were four times larger than their respective block groups. Their drawn neighbourhoods approximated the size of their respective census tracts in square miles. However, while the size resembled the census tract, the actual area drawn encompassed at least two census tracts and three block groups. This study suggested, then, that one cannot assume congruence between census- and resident-defined geographic entities. As a further complication, even though the area in square miles resembled a census tract, even if not the resident's precise tract, there was variation among residents within each neighbourhood in the maps drawn. Alternative measures, then, need to be developed. One possibility employed by Coulton et al. (2001) was to identify the 'common area' as determined by the area included by a significant percentage of residents. A second measure used in the study was to find the average centre of each resident-defined neighbourhood and draw a circle from that point that was the average size of the resident-drawn maps.

Neighbourhoods also have been defined by virtue of how a geographic area is negotiated by pedestrians (Grannis, 1998, 2001). In a multi-city study in the US, a 'tertiary community' was identified as a grouping of city blocks that residents could traverse on foot without having to cross a major street. The meaningfulness of this geographic area as a neighbourhood was indicated in the finding that residents had greater interaction with others in their 'tertiary community' than with those who lived in proximity, but across these major streets that served as neighbourhood boundaries.

Another approach to census-defined units was taken in the US by the *Project on Human Development in Chicago Neighborhoods*. The project grouped 847 census tracts into 343 'neighborhood clusters' on the basis of common characteristics and profiles with the goal that these clusters be 'ecologically meaningful' (Sampson, Raudenbush & Earls, 1997, p. 919). This allowed not only for groups larger than census-defined block groups, but also for the delineation of neighbourhoods with characteristics in common such that they might be experienced more similarly by residents than strictly census-defined block groups. This strategy also allowed for the influence of contiguous neighbourhoods that have been found to affect neighbourhood outcomes for children and families (Coulton, Korbin, Su & Chow, 1995; Sampson, Morenoff & Gannon-Rowley, 2002).

It is also possible to allow respondents to be aware that they are defining the neighbourhood themselves. In a study of parenting in four communities in the UK (Barnes, 2004) respondents were asked, preceding questions about their perceptions of their neighbourhood, to show the interviewer what they saw as their neighbourhood on a map. They could either draw on the map themselves or, with the help of the interviewer, describe the roads that bounded their neighbourhood. The size described varied considerably in each of the communities, related both to the type of community and the characteristics of the respondents. For instance, those in a small rural town, and a disadvantaged part of a large town set in rural surroundings defined smaller neighbourhoods ($0.5\,km^2$ and $0.6\,km^2$ respectively) than residents of a disadvantaged inner city area ($1.5\,km^2$) while residents of an affluent suburb of a large city had personal neighbourhoods twice that size on average ($2.9\,km^2$). Preliminary analysis suggests that the size of their personal neighbourhoods was related both to feelings about the area (larger when feel more attached, more sense of belonging) and to personal characteristics (smaller when more 'inward irritability'; Barnes, 2005).

Non-geographical Communities

The decisions made about communities that are not geographical are more complex. One may find that one is part of a community just by the fact of one's birth if, for instance the community is defined according to membership of a particular ethnic group. Important communities of interest may show no geographic identity. Young people increasingly enter Internet groups for recreation or advice, and the 'community' may be anonymous. While we do not know the magnitude or scope, Internet sites dispensing advice and support are very active and may have supplanted other networks. As the next decade unfolds, the Internet is a force to be reckoned with as a 'community' in its own right and interventions have already taken place to use the power of virtual communities to enhance social capital in geographical spaces (e.g. Hampton & Wellman, 2003).

Implications of Delineating Neighbourhoods and Communities

The geographic definition of neighbourhood or community is only the starting point, and several related issues are important to understanding the impact on children and families. An important question is the meaningfulness of a neighbourhood designation to understanding the effect on children and families. For example, do resident-defined neighbourhoods provide better social indicators than census-defined neighbourhoods? As Coulton and colleagues point out, 'The more important question for researchers, though, is whether census geography yields social measures that are similar to the neighborhood reality for residents' (2001, p. 381). Their study compared census-defined (both block groups and census tracts) and resident-drawn neighbourhood units on a set of social indicators that are often used in research to characterise neighbourhoods. These indicators included population, female-headed households, unemployment rate, poverty rate, crime rates and teenage pregnancy rates. Social indicators varied by whether census tract, block group, or resident-defined measures were used, both across neighbourhoods and across social indicators. Analyses indicated that there was agreement between resident-defined and census-defined areas on important indicators such as poverty rate or female-headed households, but less on crime rates or rates of teen childbearing. The findings, then, yielded a rather mixed picture, but strongly suggested that the delineation of the neighbourhood unit has an important impact.

Particularly relevant to understanding the impact of neighbourhoods and communities is that children and families themselves provide an important source of variability. Research on child development generally seeks parental and caregiver perspectives. Research on neighbourhood and community effects on children and families follows this model in that if resident perceptions are sought, it is parental perceptions of neighbourhood and community context that are seen as the locus of neighbourhood impact. That is, what aspects of neighbourhood context promote better parenting, which then presumably results in better child outcomes? In contrast to a focus on parents and caregivers, inclusion of the child's viewpoint in research and policy has been a major thrust of the interdisciplinary Childhood Studies approach (e.g. James & James, 2004; James & Prout, 1990). Parents and their children may perceive neighbourhoods quite differently (Burton et al., 1997). Spilsbury (2002a) expanded on Bryant's (1985) neighbourhood walk methodology to study children's perceptions of neighbourhood. Preliminary analysis of neighbourhood boundary data suggests that parents and their children may differently define several aspects of neighbourhood geography, including the boundaries of their neighbourhoods and the areas in which children are allowed to be unsupervised or with friends.

That there are different perspectives on neighbourhood boundaries brings us to the question as to whether neighbourhood research would be more or less powerful if neighbourhood, as the independent variable, was defined variably by resident or resident status (e.g. child versus adult). Statistical techniques and Geographical Information Systems (GIS) programmes are sufficiently sophisticated to identify and analyse individually-defined neighbourhood entities. That is, a neighbourhood variable could be constructed for each resident. Analyses, however, would yield results with neighbourhood transformed into an individual variable. Further, resident-defined neighbourhoods require commensurate adjustments in outcome measures. Some outcome measures, particularly those measures involving administrative data, may not correspond precisely to resident-defined neighbourhoods (Coulton et al., 2001). While some administrative and census data are available for small areas such as blocks, output areas or postcodes, other data would have to be averaged and estimated across resident-defined areas. If, however, the resident-defined neighbourhood did not conform even to street blocks or postcodes, the analysis would be compromised. This might mean that meaningfulness in the independent variable could compromise the ability to measure dependent, or outcome, variables. We note that neighbourhood measures can also be used as mediating or moderating variables, and the same concerns would apply. The Coulton et al. study (2001) elected to use measures of resident congruence on neighbourhood geography rather than individually-defined neighbourhoods. Future research should actively experiment with how to design and implement studies and interventions that accommodate variation in neighbourhood designations. Much more attention should be directed to how to employ multiple measures of neighbourhood: census defined, resident-defined, individually-defined, and measures of resident-defined agreement.

MEASURING ASPECTS OF NEIGHBOURHOODS AND COMMUNITIES

Once there is clarity on precisely the neighbourhood or community context being measured, a second major issue in assessing the impact of neighbourhood and community on children, parents and families is what features of neighbourhood or community to assess. What is it about neighbourhoods and communities that we expect to influence those living in them? Bronfenbrenner expanded his vision of an ecological perspective to encompass neighbourhood ecology as both experienced (1979) and as objectively measured (1988). The influence of neighbourhood and community has been assessed using both structural features of neighbourhood that are available through census and administrative data sources and through examining resident perceptions of their neighbourhoods and communities. Conceptualising neighbourhood and community features that can affect children and families as structural or perceptual does not preclude overlap in their effects or privilege one over the other. Indeed, structural features of neighbourhood can powerfully influence residents' perceptions and views of their neighbourhoods. Similarly, a neighbourhood that is viewed negatively by its residents may not elicit the investment of population movement or resources that could improve structural features.

Structural Features of Neighbourhood and Community

Interest in structural features of neighbourhoods and communities as affecting children and families arises from social organisation theory and research. As discussed in Chapter 2, Wilson (1987) in particular is credited with pointing to how the concentration of poverty in US cities over the past several decades, and the resulting isolation of inner city children and families from mainstream economic activity, has led to negative consequences and outcomes for these urban populations. Disinvestment and population movement have resulted in an emerging 'underclass' in which poor parents, usually single mothers, live in areas with the highest rates of negative social conditions. Rapid structural change has led to diminished social organisation in many communities and it is these neighbourhood and community conditions that pose a high risk for negative outcomes for children and families.

Structural features of neighbourhoods and communities can be measured using census data as indicated in Table 3.1. While this table refers to the US census most of these indicators can be found in census information collected in Western European countries. These structural characteristics of neighbourhoods can then be examined for their ability to explain child and family outcomes that are also available from administrative data linked to geographic areas. There are examples of these outcome measures in Table 3.2.

Aggregate statistical measures of neighbourhood conditions have contributed to understanding the relationship between poverty and related structural conditions and negative outcomes for children. These analyses, in which neighbourhood is usually represented by census-defined units, are powerful in their large sample size and more generalisable findings. They also employ data that are readily available, making replication feasible. On the other hand, statistical analyses at the level of the census tract or electoral ward cannot elaborate the processes involved as neighbourhood residents negotiate their living circumstances.

Table 3.1   Indicators of community structure from US Census Data

Variable	Definition
Poverty rate	% poor persons
Unemployment rate	% residents unemployed
Vacant housing	% vacant housing units
Population loss	% population loss from last census
Movement	% residents who moved in past 5 years
Tenure <10 years	% households in current residence less than 10 years
Recent movement	% households that moved in past year
Family headship	% households with children that are female-headed
Child/adult ratio	# of children (0–12)/# of adults (21+)
Male/female ratio	# of adult males (21–64)/# of adult females (21–64)
Elderly population	% of population over 65 years of age
Percent Black/African-American	% residents classified black/African-American
Contiguous to concentrated poverty	Contiguous to poor or non-poor tracts (poverty rate 40%): 0=borders no poor tracts, 1=borders one or more poor tracts

Source: Coulton, Korbin, Su & Chow (1995).

Related to structural features of neighbourhoods, direct observations provide another means to capture physical and social features of neighbourhoods. The most systematic of these 'windshield' methodologies has been employed by the *Project on Human Development in Chicago Neighborhoods* (Sampson & Raudenbush, 1999). Block faces (each side of a city block) were videotaped as a slow-moving vehicle drove through the neighbourhood. The project collected these data on close to 24,000 block faces. Through this methodology, various features of order or disorder can be independently and reliably coded. The project has validated measures of physical disorder (e.g. empty beer bottles, abandoned cars, graffiti), social disorder (drinking in public areas, prostitution, loitering adults) and alcohol and tobacco presence. There is also the capacity to construct measures of public social interactions (Sampson, Morenoff & Gannon-Rowley, 2002).

A similar method, but based on observers walking through areas, has been used in evaluations of community interventions described in Chapter 7. An inner city area comprising five census tracts in inner city Boston was observed in the evaluation of *Dorchester CARES*, a child abuse prevention initiative (Barnes McGuire,

Table 3.2   Outcomes measurable in US census-defined areas

Variable	Definition	Source
Child maltreatment rate	Children reported as maltreated/1,000 population children (0–17 years of age)	County Department of Human Services
Violent crime	FBI index crimes against persons/1,000 population	Police data
Drug trafficking	Drug arrests/1,000 population	Police data
Juvenile delinquency	Juvenile filings/1,000 teenagers (12–17)	County Juvenile Court
Teen childbearing	Births to teens (12–17)/1,000 teen females (12–17)	Birth certificates, State Department of Health
Low birthweight births	Low birthweight (<2500 gm) births/1,000 live births	Birth certificates, State Department of Health

Source: Coulton, Korbin, Su & Chow (1995).

1997a). More recently a large number of deprived areas in England that are locations for *Sure Start local programmes*, aiming to enhance the health and development of children aged 0–3 in deprived areas, are being observed on several occasions, both to demonstrate change in the neighbourhoods themselves (Barnes et al., 2003, 2004) and to explain any changes over time in child development and parenting (http://www.ness.bbk.ac.uk/documents/Methodology.pdf).

Perceived Features of Neighbourhood and Community

It is also important to understand how neighbourhood residents and community members perceive and experience the neighbourhoods in which they live and the communities to which they belong. Furstenberg (1993), for example, illustrated how parental perceptions of their neighbourhood surroundings can have a dramatic effect on parenting strategies. A major issue in assessing resident perceptions of neighbourhood is the unit of analysis. Are resident perceptions of neighbourhood an individual measure or a true measure of neighbourhood and community? Efforts to capture resident perceptions of neighbourhood and community have relied on two basic approaches: standardised interview instruments and ethnographic or qualitative approaches.

Standardised Interviews

Several measures have been developed (or modified from other measures) to test the basic theory that community social organisation or disorganisation has an important impact on neighbourhood children and families (Barnes & Shay, 1996; Coulton, Korbin & Su, 1996; Earls et al., 1994; Sampson et al., 1997; Simcha-Fagan and Schwartz, 1986). These studies have been aimed primarily at crime, delinquency and child maltreatment (see Chapter 4 for a discussion of findings on neighbourhood effects). While findings vary somewhat, these studies coalesce around the idea that residents perceive characteristics of their neighbourhoods that explain outcomes for children and families.

Simcha-Fagan and Schwartz (1986), for example, used both neighbourhood structural factors and resident perceptions of neighbourhood to identify three orthogonal 'neighbourhood super factors,' the first and third of which predicted community rates of delinquency. These factors were: community organisational participation (average parental educational level, community level organisational involvement); informal structure (residential stability, informal neighbouring, local personal ties); and community disorder – criminal subculture (low community attachment, low network size, anomie, social disorder, conflict subculture and illegal economy). A shortened version of the Simcha-Fagan and Schwartz scale was developed for a study of community and child abuse (Barnes & Shay, 1996; Earls et al., 1994), this time yielding four factors defined theoretically and confirmed by factor analysis: attachment and belonging to the neighbourhood; local social networks; perception of fear and crime; and physical and social incivilities.

The survey measure developed by Coulton, Korbin and Su (1996) sought neighbourhood perceptions of parents and caregivers of young children living in census-defined block groups with either high or low rates of child maltreatment reports. They argued that the psychometric properties of a measure of community need to be presented on the basis of an aggregation of its residents. Interview scales and items were assessed as to their individual and aggregate reliability. Promising levels of aggregate reliability were found for measures assessing neighbourhood facility availability, usage and quality; block level participation in activities; expectations of retaliation for intervention with others' children; neighbourhood quality; neighbourhood mobility; positive change; disorder; victimisation; and neighbourhood identity. Relatively high generalisability coefficients mean that residents observed and assessed these neighbourhood conditions similarly. Thus it was possible, using a generalisability model, to measure aspects of neighbourhood by aggregating the scale scores of a sample of residents. However, measures of neighbourhood interaction and most of the dimensions involving intervention with children, while internally consistent with the individual, could not be measured reliably using the average of residents' responses to these questions. One possibility is that some incidents are not observed frequently enough for residents to gain a neighbourhood level perception, so responses are based more on their own personal behaviour than on knowledge of the community as a whole.

A few measures have been designed to assess community social capital. More often it has been inferred from information about family activities and summed across community members. Furstenberg and Hughes (1995) assessed 'social capital in the community' by asking parents of African American teenage mothers about their involvement in schools, church and other community activities. They were also asked about four hypothetical situations and whether any community members would be available to offer support; generally, whether they thought the neighbourhood a good place for children to grow up. A similar approach was taken in analysing the US Panel Study of Income Dynamics (Boisjoly, Duncan & Hofferth, 1995). Questions were asked about a friend or relative nearby who could help in a serious household emergency, and one who could offer an emergency loan of several hundred dollars. This was examined according to neighbourhood poverty (% of non-elderly poor). It appeared that high levels of neighbourhood poverty, rather than isolating families, led to greater access to friendship networks. In both studies, however, social capital was measured at the family level and then related to characteristics of the neighbourhood, rather than access to community social capital being assessed at the community level.

In a major step forward, Sampson and colleagues (1997) coined the term 'collective efficacy' as a measure of neighbourhood, aggregating resident responses to five-point Likert scales composed of questions to tap 'informal social control' and 'social cohesion and trust'. This measure of 'collective efficacy' mediated associations between neighbourhood structural factors (concentrated disadvantage, immigration concentration and residential stability) and measures of community violence.

Finally, Sampson and Raudenbush (2004) suggest that previous work on resident perceptions of neighbourhood has ignored an important perspective. As discussed in Chapter 2, the 'broken windows' theory (Wilson & Kelling, 1982) makes a compelling argument that even minor signs of disorder and disarray can precipitate a slide towards increasing crime and deterioration of neighbourhoods. So-called bad elements move into these neighbourhoods assuming that the current residents have little regard for their surroundings as evidenced by such indicators as broken windows, trash and other signs of disregard. Sampson and Raudenbush (2004) argue that what has happened is that the increasing concentration of poor and minority families in disinvested neighbourhoods has resulted in a perception of crime and disorder. It is not simply that residents report on what they observe. Rather, their perceptions are driven by bias and racial prejudice. They go on to cite the work of Massey and Denton (1993) on segregated US cities, and note that these beliefs are not simply irrational, but:

> The rational basis of these beliefs lies in a social history of urban America, which links geographically isolated ethnic minority groups with poverty, economic disinvestment, and visible signs of disorder (Sampson & Raudenbush, 2004, p. 336).

Thus, they argue that neighbourhood social structure is a more powerful predictor of perceptions of bad neighbourhoods than are observable neighbourhood conditions. This argues for the inclusion of larger societal issues as impacting resident perceptions.

Unfortunately, much work remains in the development of measures of neighbourhood perceptions. There has been a tendency for neighbourhood research to use project-developed interviews and the development of standardised measures has lagged, even though the items on various instruments are often similar. While more general measures of neighbourhood are an important area for future research, progress has been made on constructs of interest. A notable example is the construct of 'collective efficacy' identified through resident interviews (Sampson et al., 1997).

Ethnographic or Qualitative Approaches

Studies of neighbourhoods have also involved qualitative or ethnographic methods. The apparent fluidity of psychological perceptions of community has led some researchers to move towards more open-ended assessment methods. Hedges and Kelly (1992) conducted focus groups at ten different locations throughout the UK, asking the participants to explore the extent to which they could define an area to which they felt they belonged, its size and key features and the factors contributing to community loyalties. Puddifoot (1994), also in the UK, assessed community identity by five questions about the community's name, feelings of belonging, reasons for belonging or identification with the community and ways in which the community does, or does not, have its own identity. Brodsky (1996) conducted open-ended interviews with women living in a disadvantaged area of Washington DC, asking what issues they had to cope with, what and who helped them cope, and whether they considered themselves successful, extrapolating their psychological sense of community from transcripts. These more flexible strategies may be particularly relevant in situations where the residents have a psychological sense of community that is essentially negative, characterised by feelings of alienation from their surroundings. For example, Brodsky (1996) argued that the dimensions of community satisfaction proposed by McMillan and Chavis (1986) had negative meaning for the single mothers she interviewed. Their sense of resilience and coping was associated with a negative psychological sense of community, discounting their families from membership of, or identification with, the local community. They asserted that the neighbourhood neither influenced them nor fulfilled their needs, and that they did not have a shared emotional connection with neighbours (Brodsky, 1996). She argued that psychological sense of community (Glynn, 1986) should be conceptualised as bipolar, that instead of thinking about having or not having a positive sense of community, either a positive or negative sense of community was possible. This makes the construct much more comparable to social organisation/disorganisation.

Ethnographic descriptions of communities and neighbourhoods have provided in-depth, contextual understandings aimed specifically at eliciting the perspective of those being studied. Ethnographic work can be broadly defined to include a range of methodologies from open-ended interviews to participant observation in which the ethnographer lives and participates in the context being studied. Ethnographic studies most often involve a relatively small number of individuals within a circumscribed geographic location or social network and they often provide insights that elude statistical measurement. At the same time, questions about the representativeness of the neighbourhoods and individuals who live there, and the difficulties of replicating labour-intensive ethnographies challenge the generalisability of ethnographic findings. Even though some ethnographies have been carried out in neighbourhood contexts, few have sought to directly compare the effects of differing neighbourhoods on children and families.

Anderson (1990, 1994), while not comparing different neighbourhoods, describes two distinct and competing sets of roles for teens within neighbourhoods, a more conventional middle-class 'decent' role and a 'streetwise' role. Bourgois (1996) took up residence with his family in an urban US neighbourhood known for drug use. By living locally with his wife and young child, and immersing himself in the rhythms of daily live, Bourgois gained substantial credibility with neighbourhood residents and was able to observe on the ground the efforts of parents to raise children in the midst of drug trafficking. Similarly, the classic ethnography of Stack (1974), in which she lived in an impoverished urban African-American US neighbourhood, allowed her to become a participant in a social network of African-American poor women. She exchanged babysitting and had access to patterns of child care that would not have been accessible to someone not living and participating in the community.

Few ethnographic studies have directly compared neighbourhoods. A notable exception is the work of Furstenberg (1993) on parenting strategies in neighbourhoods that pose different risks for children. To identify these patterns, ethnographers spent time with parents in neighbourhoods with differing profiles of risk. Korbin and colleagues conducted ethnographic research in Cleveland, USA specifically designed to compare across neighbourhoods. While ethnographers did not live in the census tracts, they spent substantial time visiting neighbourhood institutions, such as churches, libraries, recreation centres, block groups and other naturally occurring sites for neighbourhood interaction. They also conducted open-ended ethnographic interviews with 'knowledgeable neighbours' who seemed to be involved in their communities and willing to participate in interviews (Korbin & Coulton, 1997). In one comparison of European-American and African-American neighbourhoods, the ethnography sought to explain an aggregate finding across all residential census tracts in the city of Cleveland that impoverishment had a weaker effect on child abuse reports in African-American than in European-American neighbourhoods. Ethnographic data pointed to the importance of the social fabric in accounting for this difference.

Multi-method Approaches and Challenges in Assessing Neighbourhood Effects

Only occasionally have multiple methods, multiple perspectives and multiple levels been applied to understanding the impact of neighbourhood and community on children and families. For example, only a few studies have incorporated both ethnographic and structural approaches, for example, the work of Garbarino and colleagues (Garbarino & Crouter, 1978; Garbarino & Kostelny, 1992; Garbarino & Sherman, 1980), Korbin and Coulton (1997) on child maltreatment, and Maccoby and colleagues' (1958) study of neighbourhoods with varying rates of juvenile delinquency.

A critical direction in neighbourhood research is the increasing reliance on research designs and analytic techniques that allow for testing of theories across multiple ecological levels. Raudenbush and Sampson's (1999) call for 'ecometrics' represents a growing trend to give as careful attention to development of neighbourhood and community measures and analyses as has been devoted to the development of individual measures.

Some challenges in interpreting neighbourhood and community findings remain in assessing neighbourhood effects on children and families. This list is not exhaustive and each of these challenges is worthy of a full discussion on its own. First, the 'ecological fallacy' argues against assuming that characteristics identified at the aggregate level necessarily apply to individuals. Second, many relationships identified at the aggregate level could alternatively be individual level influences that show statistical correlations at the neighbourhood level. These correlations may occur because of a third issue, selection. That is, individuals may sort themselves into neighbourhoods or communities based on their own tendencies or proclivities towards certain behaviors. A fourth issue is that neighbourhoods or communities have been treated largely as isolated units, but may be powerfully impacted by conditions in contiguous areas.

SUMMARY AND FUTURE DIRECTIONS

Neighbourhood and community research is at an interesting and important threshold. The first challenge is to more clearly define and operationalise what, precisely, is meant by these terms. In recent years there have been a number of innovative efforts to more systematically define what is meant by the geographic neighbourhood, though community retains a somewhat broader definition that can incorporate social ties and common interests not bounded by geography. Neighbourhood and community may or may not overlap, but it is important that research and programmes are clear in their definition of the neighbourhoods in which children and families live and the communities to which they belong. Research has begun to address the tension between administrative units, such as census-defined areas, and resident perceptions of their neighbourhoods and communities. Further, it has been increasingly recognised that because residents vary in their identification of neighbourhood and community boundaries innovative analytic strategies must be developed. Administratively-defined units are useful because of the range data that is often available. Nevertheless, resident perceptions of neighbourhood and of community are necessary for these units to be meaningful. Less work has been done on the child's perspective of his or her neighbourhood and community and this is an important area for future work.

The second challenge is to more clearly delineate what it is about neighbourhoods or communities that we expect to affect children and families, and how to measure these constructs. Research has focused on the structural characteristics of geographically-bounded neighbourhoods as well as resident perceptions of neighbourhood conditions as associated with a range of child outcomes. Both structured instruments and ethnographic approaches have been applied to identifying resident perceptions of their neighbourhoods and communities. Methods for direct observations of neighbourhood physical and social properties are also being developed.

The third challenge is how to analyse and interpret the complexities of the relationship between neighbourhood and community on the one hand, and child and family outcomes on the other. Newer analytic tools, such as hierarchical linear modeling, have increasingly made it possible to assess the contributions of multiple ecological levels in explaining child and family outcomes.

There has been a resurgence of interest in neighbourhood and community contexts as important, but perhaps still poorly understood components of an ecological model of human development. This chapter has outlined the progress, issues and challenges in assessing neighbourhoods and communities. The next chapter will consider the evidence for neighbourhood and community impact on children and families.

4

THE INFLUENCE OF NEIGHBOURHOOD AND COMMUNITY CHARACTERISTICS ON FAMILIES AND CHILDREN

Past literature on the relationship of neighbourhood and community to children and families yields a myriad of findings, some congruent, some contradictory.

> Ideally, science is about finding simple and elegant solutions to complex problems. It often seems, however, that social scientists do just the opposite: making seemingly simple matters more complex (Furstenberg et al., 1999, p. 214)

When framing the question of whether and how neighbourhood and community factors influence children and families, one could easily argue that it is the question that is exceedingly complex and calls for new models and approaches. While Chapter 2 discussed the theoretical orientations that link neighbourhood and community context with child and family outcomes, and Chapter 3 discussed how to assess neighbourhood and community, the current chapter draws together the research evidence that neighbourhood and community can be linked to child and family outcomes. The purpose of this chapter, then, is not to revisit or reorganise past research. There are many excellent reviews of these findings (e.g. Ellen & Turner, 1997; Leventhal & Brooks-Gunn, 2000; Sampson, Morenoff & Gannon-Rowley, 2002). Instead, this chapter will explore the pathways and mechanisms by which neighbourhoods and communities are thought to influence children and families. As discussed in Chapter 3, it is important to be clear on how the neighbourhood or community is defined, as well as what aspects of the neighbourhood or community are being assessed.

EFFECTS OF NEIGHBOURHOOD CONDITIONS ON CHILDREN AND FAMILIES: THE CASE OF CHILD MALTREATMENT

Research on the influence of neighbourhood and community structural factors on children and families has not surprisingly indicated that disadvantaged neighbourhoods carry with them profiles of high crime and disorder, drug trafficking, low social cohesion, over-representation of single mothers and concentrated disadvantage. These factors are, in turn, associated with a range of adverse outcomes for children, including juvenile delinquency arrests, teen pregnancy, school drop-outs, low birthweight and child maltreatment. These associations of structural factors with child outcomes have been found in various studies, though findings are sometimes mixed or inconsistent across studies. In addition, the processes by which neighbourhood structural conditions result in adverse outcomes for children and families remain less well understood than the associations. The case of child maltreatment is used as an illustrative example.

The impact of neighbourhood conditions on the extent of child abuse and neglect is supported by several studies that have documented variation in reported rates of child maltreatment across neighbourhoods. Early work by Garbarino and colleagues sought to document the processes by which an ecological framework (Belsky, 1980; Bronfenbrenner, 1979; Garbarino, 1977) would translate into actual outcomes for children and families. Child abuse and neglect was not seen as isolated behaviour, but 'child maltreatment is an indicator of the overall quality of life for children and families' (Garbarino & Crouter, 1978, p. 607). Later work has supported this view in finding that the same structural characteristics that explain neighbourhood variability in reported child maltreatment rates also explain variability in other adverse outcomes and conditions for children, including low birthweight, teen pregnancy, juvenile delinquency and violent crime (Coulton et al., 1995).

Garbarino's (1976) study in New York State found that socioeconomic and demographic conditions explained (statistically) the variability in child maltreatment report rates across counties. Results of the New York study suggested that child abuse and neglect occurs when parents experience socioeconomic stress without a counterbalance of social support. This hypothesis was tested in a subsequent study of a single county in Nebraska (Garbarino & Crouter, 1978), divided into 20 'subareas' defined by prior city planners as well as being divided into 93 census tracts. Both census and survey data were available. Variation in child maltreatment reports was related to socioeconomic, demographic and economic factors, with economic factors accounting for 62% of the variance for 'subareas' and 38% for census tracts. The combination of residents' perceptions of their neighbourhoods with socioeconomic variables explained 66% and 41% respectively of the variability in maltreatment rates in subareas and census tracts. Garbarino and Crouter's study (1978) also pointed to an important process mechanism by showing that, in areas experiencing socioeconomic stress, institutions and agencies were more likely to be the source of child abuse reports, while in areas with higher socioeconomic profiles, reports were more likely to come from known individuals in the social network such as family, friends and neighbours. This finding in the Nebraska study (Garbarino & Crouter, 1978), of the importance of the social fabric, was expanded in the next study of child maltreatment in Chicago's neighbourhoods (Garbarino & Sherman, 1980). A multiple regression analysis to identify variations in neighbourhood rates of child maltreatment was used to select two neighbourhoods for in-depth study. They were matched for socioeconomic status, but one was at low-risk for child abuse reports and the other at high-risk. In-depth interviews with families and various key informants (mail carriers, school personnel, etc.) yielded a picture of the low-risk neighbourhood as one with a significantly stronger social fabric than the high-risk neighbourhood. The design of this study, combining aggregate and in-depth approaches, has served as a model for subsequent multi-method studies of neighbourhood impact (e.g. Korbin & Coulton, 1997). It is likely that the impact of neighbourhood-level poverty interacts with family-level circumstances.

Garbarino (1985) argued that, while rich people can better afford to live in a poor neighbourhood because they can purchase schooling outside the area and travel to other shops, poor people rely more heavily on the social resources of their ecological niche for support, encouragement and feedback. Emotional support, in the form of close contact with friends and family, has been associated with nurturant mothering even in communities with high rates of poverty and violence, possibly due to the effect that support has on enhancing maternal psychological well-being (Ceballo & McLoyd, 2002). Barry and Garbarino (1997) point out that since children's later development depends on parental skill and effectiveness in their first few months of life, it is important that support be provided for parents from the start. Chapter 7 describes some initiatives that have taken this approach as a way of enhancing outcomes for young children and their parents.

Findings on the importance of socioeconomic conditions have been replicated in a number of studies in the USA. In Spokane, Washington, 43% of the variance between neighbourhoods in Child Protective Services reports could be accounted for by average income in the community (Deccio, Horner & Wilson, 1994). An examination of child abuse cases in Chicago, for children born from 1982 to 1988, found that the extent of community poverty was significantly associated with rates of child sexual abuse, physical abuse and neglect (Lee & Goerge, 1999). The communities in question were the Chicago Community Areas, with an average population of 37,000. Using a regression model that took into account maternal age, child sex, birth order, race, birth year and region, it was found that the extent of community poverty had a similar effect to maternal age. For instance, neglect and sexual abuse quadrupled in those communities where 40% or more families were living in poverty compared with areas where the rate was lower than 10%; and physical abuse was more than three times as likely to occur in those communities.

Patterns of child abuse between neighbourhoods have recently been examined in a study of a cohort of children in Britain. The Avon Longitudinal Study of Parents and Children (ALSPAC) comprises 14,256 children born in three health districts of Avon, where about 7% of children live in deprived inner-city areas. Results from the ALSPAC study indicate a strong, significant association between child maltreatment and area poverty; the greater the level of deprivation, the higher the risk of maltreatment. Children living in council-owned homes compared to those in owner-occupied homes were seven times more likely to suffer abuse. The researchers suggest this finding is possibly due to direct effects arising from the stress of living in poor housing as well as an indirect reflection of neighbourhood quality. Further, children whose fathers were unemployed were twice as likely to appear in the register. It was proposed that this derived from material deprivation and lack of father's self esteem due to unemployment, as well as from increased paternal contact. Family mobility and weak social networks were also significant predictors of abuse, whilst maternal employment was a protective factor (Sidebotham et al., 2000, 2002). Differences due to race or ethnicity were not reported, due to the small numbers of families from minority ethnic groups in the study.

Research findings on neighbourhood deprivation coincide with a body of evidence linking family poverty with increased rates of child maltreatment (e.g. Gelles, 1992; Pelton, 1981). Low income, defined as less than $15,000 per annum, is strongly associated with all forms of abuse, and further, control for income is likely to diminish or remove differential rates according to race, at least in the USA (Cappelleri, Eckenrode & Powers, 1993).

Debate persists as to whether poor and ethnic minority families are over-represented in official child maltreatment reports because of increased stress or increased scrutiny, or a combination of both. Low social class and minority status are among the prominent sources of a bias towards over-reporting of child maltreatment (Hampton, 1987; Lindholm & Willey, 1986). In neighbourhoods with a high proportion of families living in poverty there may be particular efforts to focus on child maltreatment, over and above particular attention being paid to families thought to be at high risk. Notably, in the *Sure Start Local Programme* areas in England, the proportion of children identified as potentially at risk and placed on the child protection register has risen twice in the first three years of the programme's operation (Barnes et al., 2004, 2005b), changes that have not been reflected overall in England. While one of the initial aims of the programme was to reduce re-registrations on the Child Protection register (see Chapter 7 for more details), paying attention to specific neighbourhoods has had the effect of increasing rates, at least in the short-term.

Racial and geographic disparities in child maltreatment reports are even more evident using a life table approach. A study tracking children until their 10th birthday in one US city found that child maltreatment reports were three times higher for urban than for suburban children, and 33.4% of African American children versus 11.8% of White children were reported for substantiated or indicated abuse by the time they were 10 years of age (Sabol, Coulton & Polousky, 2004). On the other hand, data collected from parents in the ALSPAC study, via questionnaires, suggested that many instances of child abuse, particularly emotional abuse, had gone undetected by authorities, and that awareness of emotional abuse remains low, with society tolerating and accepting it as normative (Sidebotham et al., 2000).

In a study that refined the description of community characteristics using administrative and census databases, Coulton and colleagues (1995) used Principal Components Analysis to identify three factors that explained 78% of the variance between census tracts in child abuse rates. The first and largest factor, 'impoverishment', included the poverty rate, unemployment rate, vacant housing, population loss and female-headed families, indicating the manner in which lone parenthood is inextricably linked with poverty. The second factor, 'child-care burden', included the ratio of children to adults in the community, the ratio of females to males and the percentage of the population that was elderly. The final factor, 'instability', included the proportion of residents who had moved in the previous five years, the proportion who had lived in their current home for less than 10 years, and the proportion who had been in their home for less than one year.

These three factors were used in a regression analysis to predict neighbourhood child maltreatment rates, created by geo-coding each substantiated or indicated report for one year and dividing the rate by the population of 0- to 17-year-olds in that tract. The rate per census tract was a conservative estimate in that each child involved in multiple reports was only entered once. Each factor was related to maltreatment rates, with impoverishment and child care burden having the greatest predictive power. The concentration of poverty in the wider area, assessed by noting whether or not the tract was contiguous to another census tract of concentrated poverty, was also related to higher child maltreatment rates independent of the three indicators of community social organisation. There was also an interaction between impoverishment and instability, with the effect of instability falling as the effect of community impoverishment rose. Since impoverishment and child-care burden also had significant predictive power in relation to drug crimes, violent crime, juvenile delinquency, teen childbirth and low birth weight, the authors suggested that child maltreatment is embedded within a wider set of community forces (Coulton et al., 1995).

These aggregate analyses of the impact of structural conditions on child maltreatment rates were linked to an ethnographic study (Korbin & Coulton, 1997). Neighbourhoods with 'high' or 'low' rates of child maltreatment were identified for an in-depth ethnographic study that involved interviewing 'knowledgeable neighbours' and visiting various institutions in the census tracts, including recreation centres, block group organisations, grocery stores, libraries and any other institutions that families and children were likely to frequent. The ethnographic study was able to shed light on the processes behind the associations of neighbourhood structural conditions with various adverse outcomes for children. The factor termed 'child care burden' could easily be assumed to indicate that mothers were shouldering the burden of care for too many children in the absence of men and elders in the tracts. The ethnographic interviews and observations, however, suggested that the real impact of 'child care burden' was reflected in neighbours' concerns that they were unable to manage the behaviour of other people's children. This is similar to Sampson and Raudenbush's finding in the Project on Human Development in Chicago Neighbourhoods (1997), that collective efficacy was important in differentiating the quality of neighbourhoods for children and families.

The Cleveland study on the impact of neighbourhood factors on child maltreatment (Coulton, Korbin & Su, 1999) used both official reports and a self-report measure of child abuse potential (Milner, 1994). Neighbourhood structural factors explained variation in child abuse reports, but child abuse potential showed only modest neighbourhood effects, and was more evenly distributed across neighbourhoods. Two alternative explanations are possible. First, it is possible that neighbourhood conditions have less effect on the potential for abuse than on the possibility that the potential will be expressed as an abusive act. When the child abuse potential is evenly distributed across neighbourhoods but the report rates differ, this suggests that neighbourhoods may act to prevent actual child maltreatment among populations with similar predilections. Alternatively, neighbourhood processes may affect the recognition and reporting of child maltreatment more than its actual occurrence. This suggests that, in addition to looking for neighbourhood as a contributory factor to the occurrence of child maltreatment, there may be processes of increased recognition or bias that influence neighbourhood differences in reports (Sabol et al., 2004; Sampson & Raudenbush, 2004).

Multi-level Analyses of Neighbourhood Conditions

Understanding the influence of neighbourhood and community within an ecological framework necessitates a consideration of the transactions, or interactions, across ecological levels (Cicchetti & Lynch, 1993; National Research Council, 1993). A study of low birthweight and neighbourhood conditions in Baltimore, USA, found that living in a poor, disinvested neighbourhood could reduce the protective effects of some individual-level factors, such as prenatal care on birth weight, as well as increasing the negative impact of risk factors such as low education (O'Campo et al., 1997). Similarly, in a study of child maltreatment in Cleveland, USA, adverse neighbourhood conditions exacerbated the effects of individual-level risk factors (violence in the family of origin) and weakened the effects of protective factors (educational level of parents). These two studies suggest that research should approach the complexity of neighbourhood effects by seeking to illuminate interactive effects and transactions across ecological levels.

The studies described above link neighbourhood structural factors and social disorganisation to child abuse and neglect as an illustration of how neighbourhood and community variables affect children and families. At the same time, neighbourhood and community factors affect how parents respond to negative environmental factors. These responses are reflected in parental management strategies, both positive and negative, discussed in the next section.

NEIGHBOURHOOD OPERATING THROUGH PARENTS AND FAMILY MANAGEMENT STRATEGIES

One way to look at neighbourhood and community influences on children and families in an ecological framework is to see how contextual factors influence parenting, which in turn has an effect on children. One UK study of four neighbourhoods, three deprived and one affluent, found that there were strong relationships between neighbourhood features and neighbourhood-level parenting, but not necessarily such clear relationships with family-level behaviour (Barnes, 2004). The importance of including information at the individual level (e.g. personality) was also noted. Social disorganisation was assessed, as were feelings about neighbourhood quality, attachment to the area and residents' perceptions of the local consensus both about parenting and about the likelihood that unrelated adults would intervene with local children (informal social control). The study found that feelings of attachment, and ratings of the neighbourhoods as a good place to raise children, were strongly associated with low levels of crime and disorder, and also with the extent of local networks of friends. The extent to which the respondents had more positive views about local parenting and expected more informal social control was also related to their own participation in social activities with neighbours and in exchanging favours. Specifically, more informal social control was expected, and there was more consensus about parenting, more local monitoring and less retaliation in the face of control, when there was more local neighbourly exchange and socialisation. Neighbourly interaction was also highly (negatively) related to the extent to which local children, youth and parents were expected to retaliate aggressively if children were controlled by neighbours.

Discipline used by families was largely unrelated to neighbourhood characteristics, but more closely related to child behaviour problems, adult personality characteristics, parents' own experiences of discipline as children and to parental mental health problems. Maternal depression was, nevertheless, related to local networks and to attachment to the neighbourhood, suggesting that there are complex inter-relationships between social processes in the community, interacting with individual vulnerability, which then influence parenting behaviour. The only direct relationship between neighbourhood and harsh parenting was that more verbal and physical discipline was reported in the area with the highest level of crime and disorder (an inner-city neighbourhood), compared to equally deprived but more suburban or rural settings.

Poverty, danger and inadequate public resources undermine positive parenting practices (Pinderhughes et al., 2001). Osofsky and Thompson (2000) posit that overprotective and authoritarian parenting may result from community violence accompanied by a breakdown in protection traditionally offered by other resources such as schools, churches and community centres. In an attempt to ensure the safety of their children, parents may adopt strategies ranging from increased monitoring and restriction of freedom to the use of punishment. Specifically, it has been suggested that parents within dangerous urban neighbourhoods may use physical control to ensure their children's safety, to a level that others may define as excessive (Ogbu, 1985).

One of the reasons why parents adopt these sometimes harsh strategies is the breakdown in collective socialisation accompanying disorganisation. O'Neil, Parke and McDowell (2001) found that mothers who perceived greater social disorganisation in their neighbourhoods, in the form of more child-related problems, danger, crime, poverty and less social control, exercised greater restriction over their children's behaviour. Less adult supervision was reported where mothers perceived more available child-focused resources (parks, libraries, sports teams, after-school care), or where children were perceived to have greater social involvement in neighbourhood activities and with other adults.

Similarly, Rankin and Quane (2002), studying a group of African American mothers, showed that youth were more exposed to negative peers in neighbourhoods with lower collective efficacy. However, monitoring by mothers in these neighbourhoods was associated with fewer child behaviour problems and greater social competence reflecting the protective effect of this strategy. They suggest that parents were responding to disorganisation rather than to disadvantage.

Further findings from this study indicated that there was also higher parental monitoring in neighbourhoods with higher collective efficacy, signalling shared norms and values. The authors point out that monitoring can be viewed either as a function of living in a socially organised neighbourhood, or as a response to disorganisation conferring protective benefits against disadvantage and negative peers (Rankin & Quane, 2002).

In a review of contextual factors shaping parenting practices, Kotchick and Forehand (2002) record that the use of physical punishment by African American parents has been reported as greater than that of other American parents including Europeans, Asians and Hispanics. This apparent racial difference points to the fact that, compared to other families, a greater proportion of African Americans is likely to be living in socio-economically disadvantaged neighbour-hoods. Indeed, in a recent study examining factors associated with parental warmth, the use of appropriate and consistent discipline and harsh parenting style, initial findings that African American parents tended to be less warm and more inappropriate and inconsistent in disciplining their young children disap-peared once neighbourhood contextual factors were added to statistical models (Pinderhughes et al., 2001).

An analysis of interactive effects between race and danger showed that parental warmth was, in fact, lower for European American parents in the above study. The authors suggest that African American families living in deprived areas have already experienced so many stressors that the impact of danger carries very little weight. Interactions between race and locality and child behav-iour problems indicated that African American urban parents and European American rural parents experience higher rates of child behaviour problems linked to less appropriate and inconsistent discipline. Unfortunately this study did not include an African American rural group for comparison.

Armistead et al. (2002) compared a sample of urban African American mothers with a similar sample living in rural areas and found greater risks and higher monitoring rates present in the urban sample, suggesting more environmental risks for urban compared with rural children. Monitoring strategies mentioned included keeping children inside for most of the day except for school attendance, and not allowing children to leave home unless accompanied by an adult. Percep-tions of danger were not related to parental warmth.

Some studies have found links between parental mental health and negative parental management strategies, e.g. maternal depression has been identified as a reason for lower levels of monitoring (Jones et al., 2003). The researchers suggest that inadequate parental monitoring is associated with higher child behaviour problems leading to increased maternal depression. Hill and Herman-Stahl (2002) however suggest that it is social disorganisation that leads to maternal depression as a result of perceptions of lack of safety. Feeling that the neighbourhood is unsafe, mothers may vacillate between control and permissiveness, resulting in inconsistent discipline. And further, due to stress mothers may react unpredictably, hostilely or by withdrawing from the child. Alternatively, hostile control may be an attempt to protect the child from danger. These authors found no relationship between perceptions of safety and maternal affection.

What these studies show is the protective effect that parental monitoring provides under deprived and uncertain neighbourhood conditions. The fact that maternal affection is generally not impacted by neighbourhood conditions nor by the use of seemingly harsh parental strategies strongly suggests that these parental monitoring strategies do not reflect an intention to be harsh or harmful but are aimed at protecting children.

NEIGHBOURHOOD AND COMMUNITY OPERATING THROUGH SOCIAL CAPITAL AND COLLECTIVE EFFICACY

Sampson (1992, 1997b) has argued that community disorganisation is of primary importance to parents because of the role it plays in facilitating or inhibiting the creation of social capital, and that lack of social capital is one of the primary features of socially disorganised communities. He proposes that closure or connectedness of social networks among families and children in a community provides children with the norms and sanctions that could not be brought about by a single adult. Drawing on the work of Furstenberg (1993) in Philadelphia, he noted that skilled parents are likely, in optimal circumstances, to develop links both within and beyond the community. However, whether skilled or not, those living in the poor, unstable and socially disorganised neighbourhoods of North Philadelphia tended to adopt an individualistic style of parental management, disconnected from the community and low in social capital. Families in the socially cohesive South Philadelphia neighbourhoods were more likely to form local friendships, share responsibilities with other families and support each other. Thus, parents in South Philadelphia were able to draw on existing social capital in their communities and, in doing so, to create a source of social capital for children and youth in the form of collective socialisation.

Sampson, Raudenbush and Earls (1997) elaborated upon these ideas with the concept of 'collective efficacy' which reflects social cohesion among neighbours and their willingness to act in the common good, particularly in response to neighbourhood children. Neighbourhood structural factors (concentrated disadvantage, immigration concentration and residential stability) explained 70% of the variance in collective efficacy. Collective efficacy was related to decreased neighbourhood violence and mediated the effects of structural features on measures of violence in the neighbourhood. Collective efficacy (Sampson et al., 1997) and social capital (Subramanian, Locher & Kawachi, 2003) have emerged as constructs that can be reliably measured as a neighbourhood-level factor accounting for child and family outcomes.

Furstenberg and his colleagues (1999) have illuminated the multi-faceted relationships between neighbourhood context and 'family management' strategies. They depart from a reliance on the traditional, most often studied attributes of parenting, dimensions such as warmth, authority and discipline. Instead, they extend the focus of parent-child studies beyond the parent-child dyad and the family, to the relationships between the quality of the contexts in which families live (including neighbourhood and community and related institutions – schools, social agencies, workplace) and 'family management' strategies. The latter include

> Both in-home practices designed to develop children's capacities to manage the world outside the household and the strategies that parents employ to cultivate, oversee, and influence the external world in which children participate (Furstenberg et al., 1999, p. 218).

The overall conclusion they reached was that strategies within the family, such as the style of discipline and control or the amount of involvement with children's activities, were influenced more by family- or individual-level characteristics, while the manner in which families reacted to the outside world was influenced more by the nature of the local neighbourhood.

Statistically speaking, there was more variability within census tracts (similar to electoral wards) than between tracts in the psychological family factors such as warmth, autonomy and styles of discipline. While Furstenberg and colleagues propose that these findings suggest local neighbourhoods are less relevant than 'in the heyday of community studies in sociology' (1999, p. 153), the study nevertheless pointed to important relationships between the composition of the neighbourhood (the structural characteristics) and social process factors. For instance, parental restrictions on teenagers were greater in neighbourhoods with more minority residents (African American or Hispanic), and both parental investment and restriction were lowest in the poorest White neighbourhoods. There were also interactions with the parents' own characteristics. The most restrictive parents were those with the least education in neighbourhoods with the lowest levels of social capital, but even in the worst neighbourhoods parents with higher education were the least restrictive. The researchers' major conclusion about the relationship between family and neighbourhood was that neighbourhood institutional connections and social networks were of most importance when both the family and the neighbourhood were relatively advantaged. In contrast, parental investment in and restriction to the family setting were the most common family strategies when both the family and the neighbourhood experienced disadvantage.

Revisiting the findings of the Philadelphia study, Furstenberg (2001) reiterated that there was little evidence to support the idea that greater cohesion, better resources or higher levels of behavioural problems in a neighbourhood are related to individual or family well-being. However, he noted the benefits that derive from high social capital in the form of resources such as after-school care and recreational facilities permitting parents to entrust their children's well-being to community co-socialisation processes that foster pro-social child behaviour and further community cohesion and organisation. Whilst living in socially disorganised communities with low social capital does not predict a negative outcome, Furstenburg (2001) acknowledged that parents often try to channel their children towards resources in other communities to improve life chances. Clearly, the recognition by parents of the benefits to be derived from additional resources (human and material) may shape parental management strategies.

Research also has identified a relationship between individual and family factors and outcomes on the one hand, and neighbourhood and community influences on the other. Some research has linked restrictive parenting with dangerous neighbourhoods. For example, recent findings by Gutman, Friedel and Hitt (2003) suggest that the effect of restrictive parenting may be mediated by parental depression and exacerbated by the dangerous neighbourhood. It would appear that depressed parents lack the energy required to exercise appropriate management strategies. Economic factors beyond parental control may also impact on parenting strategies. Bradley and Corwyn (2002) noted that poor parents are less likely to be able to purchase cognitively stimulating materials such as reading and learning materials or to afford educational and cultural events. They are less likely to regulate time spent watching TV and more likely to have lower expectations of their children. Other researchers have suggested that parental education may be the predominant factor explaining aspects of children's behaviour such as the amount of reading or TV viewing (Bianchi & Robinson, 1997). Another study found that although quality of home environments did not mediate neighbourhood effects, mothers higher in human capital (better education), social capital (partnered) and financial capital (better housing), provided more cognitively stimulating home environments for their children (McCulloch & Joshi, 2001). These findings suggest that parents low in personal sources of social capital such as education and skills, as well as in financial capital, lack the ability to provide enriching environments for their children. This appears to support Furstenberg et al.'s (1999) contention that neighbourhoods are perhaps less important than previously thought. However, lack of personal capital on the part of parents may place them in neighbourhoods with lower levels of social capital, and these families and their children then face a double burden of poverty. The review by Leventhal and Brooks-Gunn (2000) has shown that children can do well in affluent areas when exposed to positive role models, resources and good education. Thus the quality of the neighbourhood should not be discounted.

The Child's Perspective on Social Capital

A core assumption about neighbourhood and community quality is that in situations of high social capital or collective efficacy, neighbourhood adults will assist children should they need it. This has been largely explored from the perspective of adults and their willingness to aid neighbourhood children. However, a study of 100 adults and 60 children between the ages of seven and 11 in Cleveland, USA, found there was no necessary congruence between the children's reports of help-seeking and provision and those of the adults:

> The responses of both children and adults allow us to paint a picture of a negotiation, a dance. A "positive" outcome depends not only on adult provision of help, which is rooted in social capital and collective efficacy, but also on children's agency (Spilsbury & Korbin, 2004, p. 202).

Children out and about in their neighbourhoods are in a bind. They recognise that there are situations in which they may need adult help. At the same time, they have been warned by parents, teachers and the media to fear and avoid unknown adults. To resolve this bind, children expressed a strategy for determining which adults are likely to help but not harm them. Known adults were the preferred choice. Women were preferred to men, and women with children, preferably with a stroller, signaling their status as mothers, were viewed as particularly safe choices.

Multiple perspectives that include both children and adults are needed to understand neighbourhood processes that influence children and families. Children have contributed meaningfully to community concerns, such as programmes concerning health (e.g. Morrow, 2001), the design of play spaces and physical attributes of the environment (Francis & Lorenzo, 2002; Hart, 1997; McKendrick, 2000). Thus, adults who direct their efforts to improving neighbourhoods and communities without inclusion of the perspective of children and youth may be 'dancing alone' (Spilsbury & Korbin, 2004, p. 203). This is discussed in more detail in Chapter 8, which looks at children's involvement in their communities.

ALTERING COMMUNITY INFLUENCES ON FAMILIES AND CHILDREN BY MOVING THEM FROM IMPOVERISHED NEIGHBOURHOODS

One of the ways to scientifically assess neighbourhood effects without being limited by selection effects would be to randomly assign families to neighbourhoods. As implausible as such a quasi-experiment seems, a few studies have been able to approach these conditions. In the Gautreaux Assisted Housing Program (Rosenbaum, 1991), close to 4,000 families from Chicago's housing projects were given the opportunity to participate in a project designed to give them the chance to move to new and subsidised housing in the suburbs or better areas of the city proper. Once families agreed to participate, they were assigned to housing as it became available, without being able to choose their new location. Positive outcomes were found for those families who were relocated to suburban areas. Parental employment improved as did some indicators of child well-being. For example, high school drop-out rates for the teens who moved to the suburbs were one-fourth of those who were assigned to city residential areas, and college enrolments doubled (Kaufman & Rosenbaum, 1992). What these findings do not elucidate, however, are the mechanisms by which these differences came about. Mothers in the Gautreaux programme attributed their children's success to better schools and safer neighbourhoods, but these are speculations and the various options were not presented to them systematically. Other possible mechanisms could be at the level of the neighbourhood, with affluent neighbours providing greater support for local institutions; at the parental level with parents striving to give their children more support commensurate with the greater support they observed in the new environment; or at the level of the child, with children themselves altering their behaviour or their motivation in light of the new environment. The study is consistent with the work of Leventhal and Brooks-Gunn (2001), who propose that the presence of more affluent and employed neighbours has a positive effect on children (Leventhal & Brooks-Gunn, 2001).

Moving to Opportunity for Fair Housing (MTO) is a research and demonstration project of the US Department of Housing and Urban Development. Low income families with children in five US cities (Baltimore, Boston, Chicago, Los Angeles and New York) were given the opportunity to volunteer for the project. Families were randomly assigned to one of three groups: (1) the experimental group that received housing subsidies and counseling to relocate to project-selected low poverty areas (<10% poverty); (2) a comparison group that was offered Section 8 housing subsidies to move into higher-rent housing in a location of their choice; and (3) a control group that was not offered any housing subsidies or vouchers.

Findings from the five sites and the overall evaluation have been somewhat mixed (Leventhal & Brooks-Gunn, 2003; Orr et al., 2003). Girls were more likely to stay in school and had lower rates of delinquency. Boys showed increases in several areas of academic achievement, but experienced an increase in behavioural problems. There was only marginal improvement in schools attended, but a decreased risk of being the victim of a violent crime. Employment outcomes for adults have not shown statistically significant improvement. Evaluating these findings involves some methodological limitations in that, for example, families in the control group did not necessarily move to a particular place as opposed to simply a low-poverty area, and not all families in the experimental group actually relocated to a low poverty neighbourhood (Coulton, 2004). Effects of neighbourhood on achievement outcomes appeared to be partially mediated through school safety as well as time spent on homework. Not every family offered the opportunity to move to a better neighbourhood took advantage of the project, and it is possible that some of the effects could be due to unmeasured family variables (Leventhal & Brooks-Gunn, 2004). Families who did move appeared to enjoy the benefits of greater social organisation in the form of perceived safety and opportunities.

Although both the Gautreaux and MTO studies have demonstrated some positive outcomes, additional research is needed to discover exactly how the composition of neighbourhood influences children, parents and institutions. Further, it is not practical or feasible to relocate very large numbers of impoverished families, and even if it were possible, some families would be unwilling to move. Less drastic approaches to community improvement, specifically aimed at better child outcomes, have shown very promising results. These will be discussed in Chapter 7.

CONCLUDING REMARKS

It is important to understand the current state of knowledge about the relevance of neighbourhood and community to families and children, so that further research can clarify unanswered questions and interventions can be designed accordingly. Aspects of the community are increasingly being used to explain differences in child development outcomes and differences in parenting behaviour, and 'the study of neighborhood effects, for better or worse, has become something of a cottage industry in the social sciences' (Sampson, Morenoff & Gannon-Rowley, 2002, p. 444). The results of neighbourhood and community studies have been mixed. There have been promising results for relationships between neighbourhood structural factors and adverse outcomes for children, and between the presence of affluent neighbours and positive effects on child and adolescent outcomes. Moreover, the effects of neighbourhood residence have been indicated by the naturally occurring quasi-experimental relocation of families. Nevertheless, several studies have found that variation within neighbourhoods exceeds that between neighbourhoods, thereby yielding results that show less of an effect of neighbourhood conditions than was anticipated (e.g. Cook, Shagle & Degirmencioglu, 1997; Coulton et al., 1999; Furstenberg et al., 1999). Not all theoretical approaches have been applied to all family issues but some clear patterns are emerging. While much of the research is exploratory, using developing methodologies, what *is* evident is that some community characteristics *do* have (cross-sectional) associations with child and family outcomes, and that major alterations in community characteristics can have far-reaching implications for the health and well-being of residents. The few studies that have used a multi-method, multi-level approach have suggested that it is the interactive effects and transactions across ecological levels that hold the most promise for elucidating these very complex relationships.

5

CHILDREN AND YOUNG PEOPLE IN COMMUNITIES

INTRODUCTION

This chapter examines children's and young people's experience and use of space and place in their communities. Since the post-war period there has been a lively and imaginative body of literature on children and their communities, in particular the urban environment. Key areas of research have included: children's cognitive mapping (Lynch, 1977; Matthews, 1992), children's use of streets, recreational and play space (Bunge, 1973; Hart, 1979; Moore, 1986) and more recently geographers are widening their perspective on children's geographies to encompass the social, imaginative and familial as well as the physical (Aitken, 1994; Holloway & Valentine, 2000; Philo, 2000); moving to new domains such as the navigation of information technologies (Valentine, Holloway & Bingham, 2000), the after-school play group (Smith & Barker, 2000) and birthday parties in commercialised leisure centres (McKendrick, Bradford & Fielder, 2000).

Research on children in their community context takes place against contradictory discourses about the state of children in the public arena. On the one hand there is the view that childhood is becoming *too controlled*, that contemporary children have lost their freedom to play outside and roam around, to just 'be children', that they are battery-reared rather than free-range, confined, chaperoned, escorted from one organised play activity to another – '*Minded out of their minds*' (Hugill, 1998). On the other hand, there is the contrasting view that children, particularly youth, are becoming *uncontrollable* and threatening, in need of containment, zoning and policing, for instance, through more responsible parenting and, in severe cases, curfews. Whatever the public mood or discourse, the difficulties that the urban environment creates for children continue to be hotly debated (Ward 1978). Similarly research is conducted against the process of urbanisation itself which typically has meant some loss of old play spaces (such as the alley-way, street or open green field) alongside the advent of new spaces. Throughout the twentieth century we have seen the creation of specialised theatres, museums, adventure playgrounds, city farms and leisure parks all designed with children in mind.

CHILDREN AND SPATIAL MOBILITY

Children's spatial mobility is an illuminating lens through which to examine the extent to which a local environment facilitates children's autonomous action outside of the domestic home. Spatial mobility is concerned with the freedom of children to walk, roam, generally move through the public spaces around them, whether in their everyday routines such as getting to school and back home again or for specific outings, for instance, to play in public places or to visit friends' houses. In neighbourhood contexts, children move in the company of other children or alone, accompanied by adults or independent and relatively free from adult supervision. It would seem that a basic principle of a 'just' city for children is that it enables the free movement of children through it (Amin, 2000). As Webber (1964, p. 64) has argued 'it is interaction, not place, that is the essence of the city and of city life'. This is echoed by the architect Richard Rogers in his analysis of urban renaissance in Britain during the late nineties: 'The city is, first and foremost, a meeting place for people' (Urban Task Force, 1999, p. 26). Indeed a 'successful' urban child might be expected to be an active navigator through the multiple settings of modern cities. Similarly high levels of child mobility could be seen as an index of a child-friendly neighbourhood. So what does empirical data tell us about children's and young people's experience and use of space and place in their communities? How do contemporary children get by in their everyday life – how do they get to school, visit friends or play outside? This chapter explores the extent to which it is possible for children to exercise independence in their everyday lives in communities: how do they use space and place outside the home; when are they able to travel alone or is their movement generally bounded by adult surveillance? There is increasing awareness of the diversity of ways in which children use their local environments, and of course children do not form a homogeneous group, as experience varies by age and gender in particular as well as according to personality and family rules.

The chapter also examines the negotiation processes which take place between children and parents about how children may interact with their local environment, looking at how parents shape children's geographies and how children manage the restrictions placed upon them by their parents. Children's spatial lives are bound up in a web of personal emotional biographies and family practices, as well as local environmental features and parenting norms. Legitimate parental concerns to protect and promote child well-being are constantly calibrated against real and imagined environmental risks, from routine traffic and 'stranger danger' to climate hazards. For instance, in Punch's (2000) ethnography of children's lives in rural Bolivia, she found that strong river currents in the wet season were a major parental fear, substantially restricting children's routine mobility outside the home. In a different context, the first wave of bombs on the London transport system in 2005 prompted public debate on the limits of children's spatial movement in the city:

> Stockwell station is somewhere I go a lot. My family use it all the time too...Yesterday's event was another in a series that is transforming Londoners' familiar home patches into alien, unfamiliar territory...I have just texted my daughter suggesting she walks home from school (Coward, 2005, p. 20).

Transition from Home to the Neighbourhood: Stepping Out

Typically, children's early exploration of places outside the domestic home occurs under adult guidance, shaped by local cultural traditions and societal norms. For instance, in the Newsons' community study of 600 children growing up in Nottingham, England, in the early 1960s they found that by four years of age children are beginning their first steps outside:

> At four he will rarely be allowed to wander unaccompanied more than a hundred yards or so from his front door, for fear of accident. If there is a back yard or a traffic-free "front", he may be told to keep within it, or go no further than the few feet of pavement immediately outside. Children with gardens have similar restrictions (Newson & Newson, 1968, p. 51).

Whereas four-year-old children were generally not allowed to cross roads, particularly busy roads, a majority of mothers (79%) reported allowing their children other independent actions in their local neighbourhood, such as going down the alley way or up the street to a shop on their own, or to buy an ice-cream from the ice-cream van parked outside the home. These early independent behaviours were slightly more common in working-class neighbourhoods, although not significantly so, as most mothers felt their children needed encouragement to have experiences of purposeful independent action.

> The other week I gave her threepence and told her to go and buy herself a lollipop. But she said "No, you come Mummy." She was a little bit nervous and shy. And I made her go. I said "All right, Beverley, we won't have an ice-cream," and walked away, and she did get it on her own (Newson & Newson, 1968, p. 74).

However, in working-class neighbourhoods, the Newsons noted that children were used frequently by adults to 'run errands' either to deliver messages to nearby neighbours, particularly for households without telephones, or to 'pop down to the shop' for a packet of tea. Clearly the demise of corner shops close to home, alongside the practice of car-based supermarket shopping or home delivery, has reduced one naturally occurring opportunity for young children to display purposeful independent action outside the domestic home. However, even if local shops were more prevalent, in today's climate of fear for children's safety it is unlikely that four-year-olds would be sent on errands.

In the rural communities she studied, Punch also found that from five years of age children were assigned family work tasks outside the immediate domestic surroundings such as fetching water or moving animals. These activities were actively promoted by parents, who were in constant negotiation with their children about the balance between play and work.

> Adults in Churquiales often use a well known local superstition called the duende (dwarf) as a control mechanism over children's time to persuade them to work more and play less. In particular, this tactic is used to encourage them to come straight home from school rather than stopping and playing along the way (Punch, 2000, p. 51).

The interaction of place, parenting and children's spatial movement is further illustrated in Huttenmoser's (1995) study of five-year-old children and their families living in contrasting neighbourhoods in Zurich, Switzerland. Huttenmoser tracked the duration of time children spent playing outside in the immediate living surroundings to their home, for instance, on the front steps or in the street. In this middle/upper middle class urban sample, he found that young children were less likely to play outside when the local environment had heavy street traffic, where the home was aligned to a main street, or where there were obstacles close to the house entrance. As Chawla and Malone (2003) argue, there is a strong sense in which 'children live in the local' and that, even from a young age, the quality of children's immediate home environment is crucial in facilitating access. However, Huttenmoser found that the extent of young children's spatial mobility was not only driven by physical factors. He observed less unaccompanied play where mothers were more restrictive and controlling of children's mobility, parenting behaviours which are clearly psychologically and culturally driven. Traffic-calming measures were a key policy recommendation from this study, although he also suggested that parenting approaches may develop independently of local environmental factors or improvements.

Moving Beyond the Immediate Home-place

In contemporary urban contexts, the beginnings of significant *unaccompanied* movement out of the domestic home and its immediate surroundings occurs from the ages of eight or nine years (often later for girls), and is greatest when children are in the company of other children (Matthews, 1992). Comparing a group of six- to eleven-year-old children living in an English suburban estate, Matthews (1992, p. 21) noted: 'the greatest jump in children's range came between the ages of 8 or 9, when parental constraints became sufficiently relaxed to enable children to wander freely within the confines of their suburban estate'. In O'Brien, Jones, Sloan and Rustin's (2000) British study, by the last year of primary school (age 10/11 years) a significant majority of the children living in London and Hatfield (between 56% and 86% of the sample) reported a fair degree of independence in their daily life – being allowed to go without an adult to the local shops, to play out on the streets, to walk alone to a friend's house and to go to and come home from school. Many British 10/11-year-olds in the last year of primary school are beginning to explore their neighbourhood more independently, moving further away from their home base and starting to do new things, often in preparation for the move to the 'big' secondary school.

Ambivalent feelings about independence were commonly expressed by O'Brien et al.'s (1999) 10- and 11-year-old interviewees. Whilst it was 'cool' to be 10 or 11 and a relief that adults had started 'treating me like a real person – not a baby', it was also 'scary'. Children often moved around their neighbourhood in groups for companionship and sometimes protection: 'If I'm hanging about with friends then I'm okay 'cos I know if I get into trouble then they're gonna, they're fast runners they can run to the police or something' (Boy, 10 years, White, outer London). Getting about the city by foot was exciting but often meant careful watchfulness. Some children in this study showed high levels of self-reflection about the contradictory feelings attached to autonomous spatial movement. Reflecting on the first time he walked to school on his own, an 11-year-old boy reported:

> I've always been walking to school, even when I was young. [Can you remember how old you were when you first did that on your own?] Seven . . . The first time I was a bit scared so I was running, but I tripped over so I just walked. [What were you scared of?] I don't know. I was just getting used to being on my own.

As children grow older generally they continue to increase their home range and reach out to the public spaces and places beyond the boundaries of the household (Moore, 1986). In this context the space beyond the apartment, house or garden, to the courtyards, streets, parks and the local greens become central sites of exploration and are important locations for the creation of confidence in being in the public arena for children, though they are also places that can create anxiety, especially in relation to the presence and behaviour of older and unfamiliar children, as these remarks by 12-year-olds demonstrate (Barnes, Baylis & Quinn, 2004):

> I'm not allowed to go to park by myself, but I'm allowed to go with one friend. (male)

> In the day it's safe (large open area), but in the evening there's quite a lot of teenagers. And people go on motorbikes there (male)

> [Do you go to the park?] Sometimes, yeah? Sometimes, like us, we go but if we go we've got loads of people with us, don't we? (female)

Different physical 'public realms' are offered to children by diverse spatial layouts, population density and the nature of the built environment itself. The relationship between residential setting, neighbourhood and children's outdoor play suggests particular layouts offer better opportunities for exploration and play, but there is by no means a clear consensus on these matters (Matthews, 1992). Studies of public housing estates in Britain indicate that low-rise, low-density layouts encourage more play in the nearby paved areas and streets (Coleman, 1985). Children who live in medium/mixed-rise developments are more likely to use for play stairways and places close to home offering potential security. Whilst high-rise homes are often associated with less outside play, there is debate about whether children are emotionally and socially inhibited by these residential settings, since children typically create imaginative informal sites and hidden places to play even in opportunity-poor environments such as 'waste' grounds (Hart, 1979; Moore, 1986).

Many writers have suggested that feelings of trust, belonging and mutual support amongst children are more likely to build up in a place where face-face contact on a regular basis is possible (Morrow, 1999). Such patterns of contact may be less likely in global cities, such as London, with their sheer vastness and social heterogeneity. In O'Brien et al.'s (1999) study, the very simple act of calling on a friend to play, a key activity in sustaining children's social relations and linking them to other children, was found to be less common in London when contrasted with rates in Hatfield, a lower-density new town outside London. In fact on most indicators, children's freedom to move around their neighbourhood was greatest in the new town. A higher proportion of children living in Hatfield said they were allowed to play out on the streets, cycle on main roads, go to the cinema or shopping centre further away from home and go out after dark.

These findings resonate with Kytta's (1997) comparison of eight- and nine-year-old children's independent mobility across an urban, small town and rural environment in Finland. Using children's diaries of daily journeys to and from home (e.g. crossing roads, cycling, visiting a friend), she found that the highest rates were for children living in rural villages, followed by those in small towns. In this relatively culturally homogeneous country, urban children reported the lowest number of journeys and urban parents were the most restrictive of child spatial mobility. Although the exact mediating mechanisms are unclear, it appears that the size and density of population in a neighbourhood, interacting with inhabitant and structural characteristics, creates differing frameworks for child mobility. It may be that in smaller, less dense neighbourhoods adults, and neighbours more generally, are enabled to promote a more supportive and vigilant local culture for children, the 'eyes on streets' perspective called for in Jane Jacobs' book (1961), *The Death and Life of Great American Cities*. In an ethnography of a small Canadian town, Prairie Edge, Bonner (1997, p. 191) suggests that small neighbourhoods enhance visibility and interpersonal accountability: 'A small town has the possibility of being a polis, a public space where one sees and is seen by others'. While small town culture can restrict individuality and enforce conformity, for instance, through gossip, it may provide a better neighbourhood context to facilitate children's public mobility, as Bonner (1997) puts it, *A Great Place to Raise Kids*. Diffusion of civic responsibility may be more likely in large and densely packed neighbourhoods, in line with diffusion of individual responsibility processes and low altruism often found in large group contexts. The creation of conditions of accountability and trust in larger urbanised neighbourhood contexts is a future challenge for urban planners and citizens alike.

School Travel

Getting to school is a central part of most children's daily life and, rather than the school buses common in the US, children in Britain either make their own way on foot or take public transport if their parents are unable to drive them. Being able to move easily from home to school and back again is an important indicator of independent mobility at a personal level for children and, in terms of urban design, high levels of walking to school suggest sustainable movement patterns.

Since the early 1970s, Mayer Hillman and colleagues from the Policy Studies Institute, London, have been examining levels of children's independent mobility, in particular travel to school. They have charted the decline in walking to school and the growth in car usage (Hillman, Adams & Whitelegg, 1990). Using a similar methodology and comparable neighbourhoods, O'Brien et al. (2000) found evidence for a continuation of these trends. The proportion of English primary children who walk to school has decreased even in the decade since Hillman et al.'s study (see Figure 5.1): only 54% of primary school children reported walking to school, in comparison with 70% in Hillman et al.'s study. Levels of car usage also increased over the period.

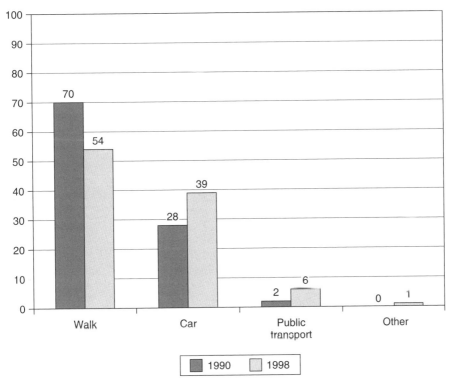

Figure 5.1 Mode of transport to school: trends over time (10/11-year-olds) (percentage)
Source: O'Brien (2000, p. 11).

More recent survey trends for British primary school children suggest slight decreases in the proportion of primary school children walking to school (51%), with a corresponding increase in those being taken by car (41%) (DTR, 2002).

The extent to which children can be free to take some of the school journey on their own is another dimension of independent spatial mobility. In 1970, 94% of children travelled unaccompanied to school (Hillman et al., 1990). This fell to 54% in 1990 and continued to fall to 47% in O'Brien et al.'s sample of similarly aged children (see Figure 5.2). Of those children who were accompanied by someone to school, 66% of the primary sample were accompanied by an adult. One in five primary school-aged children (21%) travelled alone to school.

This pattern suggests an increase in parental chaperonage but there are a set of complex reasons for the observed shift in school travel over time, including: the growth in car ownership and associated traffic danger; the variable quality and reliability of public transportation systems; the timing of the school day; and in the context of the growth of dual-earner families, the relative proximity of school, home and parental workplaces.

Research in London suggests that lower levels of walking and greater car use and accompaniment is most common in suburban families where car ownership is highest (Hood, 2004). Inner-urban, poor children are most likely both to walk to

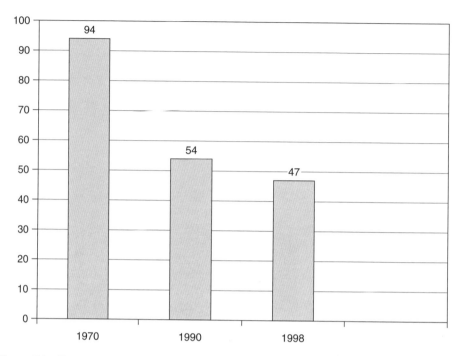

Figure 5.2 Percentage over time of children going to school unaccompanied by an adult (10/11-year-olds) (percentage)
Source: O'Brien (2000, p. 11).

school and to be unaccompanied. In the inner London context where educational standards across schools vary so much, there has been a decline in the numbers of pupils attending their local primary school, and this pattern has increased journey time to school and so reduced the option of walking. The growth in car use even for short journeys appears to be linked to time pressures in modern lives and to balancing the demands of work and child-care for women and men alike.

In the case of London, parental concerns about road safety during children's walks to and from school resonate to some extent with child pedestrian casualty data. In 2003 just under a third of child pedestrian casualty cases took place on the school journey, in comparison to a quarter in 1999 (Hood, 2004). Child pedestrian casualties were greatest for those living in poor neighbourhoods and for Black and ethnic minority children. The study by Roberts, Norton and Taua (1996) in New Zealand shows that poor children are exposed to more traffic risk than their prosperous peers. They suggest that it is this exposure which differentiates children in the social class groups and which is the explanatory factor in relation to child deaths from road accidents. After controlling for traffic volume and speed in their neighbourhoods, the risk of injury to children in families without a car was twice that of families with a car. Not only was it the fact that the poor children were more likely to walk to school and to cross more roads during the week that placed them at risk, but the greater use by affluent families of cars to transport their children to school also contributed to that risk while at the same time protecting their own children from harm.

PUBLIC PLACES AND SPACES

The types of places children explore and their mode of movement between places have also been subjects of much research. Studies have indicated that, when moving around public spaces, children notice the minutiae in a way adults do not, enclosed as they are in cars (Hart, 1979). In their study of young Danish children's perceptions of their neighbourhoods, Rasmussen and Smidt (2003) stress the physicality and bodily nature of children's interactions with their environment. Children between the ages of 5 and 12 years from diverse urban and rural neighbourhoods were asked to keep a weekly photo-journal, taking their camera with them to as many places as possible and collecting images of the places visited and the things they got involved in. Subsequently, Rasmussen and Smidt interviewed the children about their photo-journals and, using a phenomenological perspective, generated themes of significance from a content analysis (see Box 5.1). The themes displayed a remarkably wide range of naturally occurring places, spaces and activities showing the usefulness of this open-ended inductive methodology for capturing children's 'fourth environment' beyond the school, home and playground (Matthews, Limb & Taylor, 1997). The thematic range demonstrates how the concept of the neighbourhood, when viewed from these children's perspective, is a complex web of significant physical and social relations connecting material forms (e.g. earth mounds) to human actors (e.g. peers).

Box 5.1   Thematic Categories from Children's Photo-journals

Places used by children in the neighbourhood. Playgrounds, slides, earth mounds for the children to dig in, shacks, dens, handball goals, playing fields, old rowing boats, campfire sites, swings in trees.

Means of transportation used in the neighbourhood. Roller-skates, bicycles, home-made go-carts, sleighs, school bus, parents' car.

Nature spots and objects from nature. Trees, stone walls, flowers, herb gardens, fallow fields, the beach and sand dunes, wood chips.

Public buildings and places of cultural interest. Water towers, water tanks, building sites, corner shops, shopping centres, sports centres, the harbour.

Private buildings, places and areas. Single family houses and their gardens, holiday cottages, their patio.

Special persons with a connection to the neighbourhood. Park-keeper, shopkeeper, friends

Rasmussen & Smidt, 2003, pp. 90–91.

Rasmussen and Smidt argue that the realm of the senses is particularly important in understanding how children use their neighbourhoods. They posit that it is through bodily and sensory encounters with the physical environment that children come to embody the neighbourhood 'under their skin'.

> [the neighbourhood] is stored within the child's body as tactile knowledge and a "community of the senses". The body and its movements are vital building blocks in making meaning of the environment...Knowledge about the neighbourhood is therefore not always expressed in verbal language, but is rather expressed through a physical "know how", for instance about how to scale a tall fence, or the specific manner of climbing a certain tree, or a sense of which shortcut to choose between two locations when in a hurry (Rasmussen & Smidt, 2003, p. 88).

Geographers have tended to differentiate between children's *formal and informal* locations in the public realm (Moore, 1986). The former are planned and organised by adults for use by children, typically for play but increasingly for education (Smith & Barker, 2000), including parks, playgrounds and leisure centres; the latter are unprogrammed places and spaces, including small woods, alley ways and waste grounds. Some research has suggested that informal locations offer children a wider range of play settings for autonomous exploration (Hart, 1979), although recent studies show that commercialised and more organised leisure centres can also be stimulating places for children (McKendrick, Bradford & Fielder, 2000). For example, McKendrick et al.'s (1999) study of collective play spaces in the UK shows that some are child-centred, providing challenging play environments (e.g. imaginative soft play features for young children, rope ladders, slides and skate boarding for older children), and enable children to interact with each other in small and large groups. McKendrick et al. argue that, far from representing a gating and zoning of children's activities, these places signify 'an extension of children's environments in society...into domains and locales which were hitherto the preserve of adults' (McKendrick et al., 2000, p. 113). However, they also note that these new commercial public places for children 'to play' or 'have a party' may have risen, not only for child-centred reasons, but to meet changing adult lifestyle and parenting patterns (e.g. time pressures of dual-earner parents who wish to pay for a birthday party; a place for non-resident parents to take children on access visits; a place for children to play while parents exercise; a supervised safe place to play when the local street or park is perceived by parents as unsafe).

Others have raised concern about the quality of play spaces that are not organised around the child. Hughes (1994, p. 6), for instance, who defines play as 'behaviour which is freely chosen, personally directed and intrinsically motivated', laments the decline of urban parks and playing fields as spaces for children's play. He reminds us that there are some special parks with play equipment, for instance, Coram's Fields in central London, to which adults are allowed access only if they are accompanied by a child. The autonomous and self-directed nature of play was also fore-grounded in a recent UK governmental review of children's play *Getting serious about play*. In this consultation, play was operationally defined as '*what children do when they follow their own ideas and interests, in their own way and for their own reasons*' (DCMS, 2001, p. 6). Whatever position taken by commentators and researchers on play in public places, there is also stress on the importance of balancing agency with safety and quality. A recurrent theme is the lack of public play provision for disabled children, rural children and girls. More recently, as play and childcare have become interconnected in institutionalised settings such as after-school clubs, there have been recommendations that consultation with children about the nature of the provision be continuous:

> Understanding the temporal nature of children's culture is thus paramount if we are to engage with them in a process of consultation over their play needs and desires, and over the way the built environment of their out of school club is structured and decorated. Any true democratization of children's play spaces needs to reflect these ongoing developments within children's culture (Smith and Barker, 1999, p. 41).

Despite these anxieties, national survey data show that most young children engage in active play (defined as kicking a ball, running about or playing active games). The Health Survey for England (2002) found that 89% of 2–10-year-old inner-city girls and 87% of boys participated in active play and rates were higher for non-inner-city areas. However, levels of direct involvement in sport and exercise were a lot lower (41% and 38% respectively for inner-city girls and boys, with higher rates for those children not living in the inner city). Moreover, another recent UK survey (Children's Play Council with the Children's Society, 2005) has found that a minority of children (one-fifth) between the ages of seven and 14 years report playing outside for less than an hour a week. Also almost half of the whole sample (47%) reported avoiding playing outside because they did not feel safe, while 48% would do so if better facilities were provided. In this study, girls were more likely than boys to make safety their top priority, which may explain girls' lower use of public spaces such as parks and streets (e.g. Matthews, 1986; Karsten, 1998). In O'Brien et al.'s (2000) study, boys had greater freedom to roam and play out more independently than girls did. Boys were also more likely get around by bike and to be recent users of the local park. The importance of play and leisure in public places for children has been illustrated in longitudinal inquiries. Feinstein et al.'s (2005) study has shown, for instance, that taking part in sports or clubs during the adolescent period can have a beneficial impact on mental health and educational outcomes in later life.

Street Play and Hanging Out

Despite the emergence of new public spaces for children, particularly young children, there is general recognition that, in contemporary urban neighbourhoods, 'the street' is generally no longer as freely available as a play or hanging out space for children and youth. The loss of the street as a domain for unstructured space free from adult regulation and supervision is a significant transformation in children's lives. Reflecting on children's street play in the 1950s and 1960s, Iona and Peter Opie (1984, p. vi), for example, noted that 'there is no town or city known to us where street games do not flourish'.

> When children play in the street they not only avail themselves of one of the oldest
> play-places in the world, they engage in some of the oldest and most interesting of
> games, for they are games tested and confirmed by centuries of children, who have
> played them and passed them on, as children continue to do, without reference to
> print, parliament, or adult propriety (Opie & Opie, p. vi).

The speed at which street space for children's play has been lost is remarkable,
although there is some debate about when the significant downturn actually
happened. In her history of working-class childhood in East London during the
early part of the last century, Davin describes streets 'teeming with children':

> The street offered a range of pleasures: the company of other children and all the regular
> street games, for example. Smooth paving stones were good for marbles and "buttons"
> or hopscotch...If you could get a length of rope, you could fix swings from lamp-post
> to railing, or skip, or from the lamp-post bar twist two ropes tightly together and play
> "swing-twist-'em", clinging dangerously as the ropes untwined (Davin, 1996, p. 64).

Many of the street games she recounts could be observed until the 1930s when the
municipal park became the more favoured space for such vigorous physical play,
particularly for working-class children (Humphries, Mack & Perks, 1988).

Drawing on data from children and young people living in a working class
neighbourhood in an English town, Matthews (2003) suggests that any decline in
the use of 'the street' reduces children's opportunities for identity construction, as
'the street' is often a site where children can 'separate or engage in the processes
of separation' away from the adult gaze. Matthews uses the term 'the street' as a
metaphor to represent all outdoor spaces in the public realm, as well as to empiri-
cally chart children's specific usages and relationship to the local streets in their
neighbourhoods. Collecting data from 140 10- to 16-year-olds he found that, before
the age of 11 years, children use the street mainly for games, adventure and play.
As they get older the street becomes a central place for meeting friends and
hanging out, and by the late teenage years the street is important for excitement
and getting away from the 'humdrum' of routine life. Crucially, at whatever age,
the street is a place for children and young people to spend time together with
their peers away from their parents. Matthews posits that it is through their
different uses and occupation of street space, including their encounters with
adults, that young and older children, girls and boys, explore and come to understand their own present and prospective social relations and positions. In this
way, Matthews argued, the street is important for understanding how children
engage with their own growing up, suggesting that experiencing being in the
street is a central part of a young person's separation from childhood, supporting
their transition to adulthood.

> Knowing your place, that is, where and where not to go, what to do and when, is
> indelibly, yet invisibly, inscribed into the environment. Understanding the semiotics
> of the street is an important part of growing-up and for the youngest children many
> of these messages are inevitably acquired through the primary habitus of the family
> and transposed on. Heightening children's awareness to possible danger in order to
> prepare them for forays beyond the home is a formative aspect of socialisation
> (Matthews, 2003, p. 108).

This perspective resonates with Garbarino's (1978) long-held view that the neighbourhood provides children with an important opportunity to learn about social conduct, and as such has the potential to act as a key social support system. The view that street play and hanging out can have positive psychological functions for children is somewhat at odds with those who stress that the presence of children and youth on the streets is problematic and anti-social (as discussed in Chapter 10). Clearly, the sorts of behaviours children engage in when they are together in public places, and the sense in which these behaviours are perceived locally as pro- or anti-social, is crucial in making sense of these tensions. Governmental attempts to provide youth with places to go and activities to engage in (e.g. the recent Green Paper, *Youth Matters*; Secretary of State for Education and Skills, 2005) are attempts to create substitutes for 'the street'.

Clearly a more constructive cross-generational dialogue needs to develop to ensure that adults can encourage and facilitate legitimate child and youth desires to have a civic life outside of the home. The debate about loss of public space for child play and 'hanging out' has most salience for children living in poor neighbourhoods where levels of communal resources for leisure activities are typically low, and where sufficient parental economic resources are usually unavailable to purchase organised activities. Empirical studies of poor neighbourhoods have shown they are jointly characterised by high concentrations of children and low levels of local facilities and services.

In Power and Tunstall's (1995) longitudinal study of 20 unpopular social housing estates in the UK between 1980 and 1995, they found above-average concentrations of children. Children under 16 years of age made up close to one-third of estate residents at both time periods. As one adult resident observed: 'There seem to be hundreds of lads on this estate...The kids come out after 12 o'clock at night. The activity on this estate at 3am is tremendous' (Power & Tunstall, 1995, p. 20). The researchers noted that many of the youth were 'under-occupied' and recommended that, 'Unless local leaders have links both with young people and the police, the situation can easily explode, as it has on three estates' (Power & Tunstall, 1995, p. 73).

The importance of understanding children's and youth's perspectives is vital, as other studies have shown that one function children see of group congregation in public places is to protect themselves against other children. For instance, Skelton's (2000) study of working-class teenage girls in Wales shows how walking around in groups of three or more creates a sense of security amongst the girls, allowing them to 'have a laugh'. The streets of the Rhondda valley were places where different sub-cultural groups of children mingled and sometimes fought. Similarly, Taylor, Evans and Fraser's (1996) study of neighbourhoods in Manchester and Sheffield found that fear of harassment from other children, particularly older male children, was very common. The youth and children of their study developed elaborated vocabularies in daily interaction to differentiate themselves from other, disliked children:

In both cities, considerable energy went into the denunciation of other children as "townies". This particular construction of Other Children does not seem to involve any one fixed clothing preference (though baseball caps, sweatshirts and running shoes were important signifiers), style of speech or patterns of behaviour. It is rather more a general category of Otherness (an early adolescence "gallery of folk devils") to which feared or disliked other children are allocated in conversational exchanges (Taylor, Evans & Fraser, 1996, pp. 265–6).

Other research has shown the importance of parental strategies to protect children living in such distressed environments, for instance, older sibling supervision, avoidance of risky areas, promotion of strong supportive ethnic and religious networks and close monitoring and restriction of activities (Burton & Jarrett, 2000 for a review of the literature).

STAYING IN

The concept of community without propinquity, discussed in Chapter 1, is even more relevant to children and youth than it is to adults. They have grown up with an expectation that computers and especially the internet will offer many opportunities for social contact and leisure activities. The internet, mobile phones, digital TV and games consoles have transformed the way they use their leisure time. Texting and chat-rooms are for many an essential means of communication and social interaction.

Through the internet children are able to connect with other children and form virtual communities and neighbourhoods, for instance, through games such as 'RuneScape Community' http://www.runescape.com/. This game contains many of the elements of routine social interaction, for instance, users can create a 'friends' list (including 'real' friends) and an 'ignore' list for disliked characters they have met. The distinctive features of the Internet also allow children virtual global mobility as they can stay in their own 'world' or visit over a 100 other worlds to play the game. Similarly they can create their own personae (a unique anonymous name and set of physical features) to 'walk' around these spaces. After logging on, children can check if their friends are 'out to play', send them a private message, while at the same time viewing how many users are currently on-line. This may be up to 60,000 globally at peak times such as after school.

In a national survey of 1,511 9–19-year-olds who use the internet weekly, Livingstone, Bober and Helsper (2004) found that playing games was the most popular activity (conducted by 70% of the sample). However, as in other interactive realms, children use the internet in a diverse set of ways shaped by personal and structural characteristics. In their study children from lower socio-economic groups, and girls, had on average lower time online per day and years of internet use, and were more likely to self-rate as having lower internet expertise. Children from higher socio-economic groups were more likely to have a Broadband connection and be expert users and creator of websites. It was of note that middle-class children, especially girls, were most likely to be *civic-minded* in their use of websites (e.g. visiting charity, environmental and human rights sites). They suggest that children living in poorer households may have less access to the knowledge resources of the internet, and as a consequence be on the 'wrong side of digital divide', with the potential to be more disengaged from this form of social interaction.

As with the advent of television, there has been concern that children's use of the internet within the home will reduce their motivation to play outside, thus creating 'indoor children'. Reviewing the evidence, Valentine et al. (2000) suggest that, apart from a minority of heavy users, the more general pattern is one of complementarity: that is, computer activity is integrated into children's everyday indoor and outdoor interactions. In their own study of computer use both at home and at school by children in England (aged 11–16 years), they found that:

> Children use on-line spaces to find information to help them develop and enjoy their off-line, outdoor hobbies and to make on-line friends who share these off-line outdoor interests. While playing outdoors, children often talk about and share information they have gathered indoors on-line (for example tips about how to improve their surfing techniques) and develop friends through playing in public space with whom they may also communicate on-line (Valentine et al., 2000, p. 166).

In this move 'inwards' and 'inside' into the private sphere, children have the potential to shape their own personal places and identities within the home itself and in their movements between and perceptions of the inside and outside. Clearly, however, the quality of material and economic resources of the domestic space are important. Being home-based, chilling out, by choice in a spacious and IT-rich house is a world apart from potential social exclusion in an over-crowded, IT-poor flat. Local inequalities impact on and interact with the processes of globalisation represented by the internet. The growing importance of the home as a communication and play space for children, whether by choice, parental constraint or other factors, will most likely continue to develop. This lifestyle pattern puts pressure on the traditional layouts and space standards of conventional housing designs for families with children. City planners will increasingly need to re-conceptualise indoor as well as outdoor space requirements in the move towards child-friendly neighbourhoods.

PARENTING, CHILDREN AND YOUNG PEOPLE IN COMMUNITIES

Child and youth interaction in their communities cannot be understood without taking into account changes in family life and parenting. Since the 1970s, transformations in family structure, fertility behaviour and maternal employment have been notable features of change. Across the more affluent and industrialised areas of the world, in particular Europe, America and Australia, marriage rates have declined, non-marital unions have increased, couples are having fewer children, and maternal employment has increased creating a growth in dual-earner families (Adams & Trost, 2004; O'Brien, 2005).

The ageing of the population in the early part of the last century was initially the result of a fall in fertility, but as the century progressed both lower fertility and improved mortality rates were influential. For instance, population projections indicate that by 2016 for the first time in Britain the proportion of over-65-year-olds may be greater than the under-16-year-olds (Grundy, Murphy & Shelton, 1999). It is interesting that, at a time when children are increasingly coming under the academic spotlight, they are also becoming increasingly demographically rare, at least in the more affluent sectors of the world. Some commentators have suggested that this relative demographic rarity created the conditions for children becoming culturally more precious and 'priceless' in advanced economies (Zelitzer, 1985), and also contributed to the growth in more child-centred approaches to parenting. As Jencks (1996) has argued, children in the postmodern world come to signify adults' hope for and meaning in the future, not simply society's investment in the perpetuation of the human race and future workforce. In their historical review of parenting ideologies, Elizabeth and John Newson (1974, p. 80) concluded that, by the mid-1970s, 'Mothers and fathers have never in history been more conscious either of the complexity of their responsibilities or of the splendour of their rewards'. Since that time, there is some evidence that ideologies of intensive mothering and involved fathering have become even more normative and elaborated (Coltrane, 1996).

Moreover, significant demographic changes, such as more marital instability through increases in divorce and repartnering, and the growth of dual-earner families from the increase in maternal employment outside the home, have led to an increase in the amount of time children of all ages spend away from their parents. These structural changes add to the impact of industrialisation and mass schooling which initially began the move of parents and then children out of the domestic home for significant amounts of time during the day (Hernandez, 1995; Qvortrup et al., 1994). The associated rise in non-parental care through nurseries and other child-care organisational settings has been well-documented and has transformed children's lives (Moss & Penn, 1996). In some Scandinavian countries about 60% of children between the ages of one and six years spend approximately six to nine hours a day in institutional care such as day-care centres before they attend school (Kjørholt, 2005). Even though these centres are predominantly organised around child-centred pedagogies and are generally extremely well-resourced when contrasted to other European countries (Moss & Petrie, 2002), there is still debate in these countries and in others (e.g. Lareau, 2003; Nasman, 1994; Zeiher, 2003) about whether or not contemporary children's lives are becoming too organised.

Scandinavian scholars have been at the forefront of this dialogue about the process of 'institutionalisation' in children's lives, that is, the growing tendency for organisations rather than families to provide for the care and education of children (Nasman, 1994; Qvortrup et al., 1994). Within this debate the compartmentalisation of childhood is a strong theme, including the extent to which specialised children's institutions separate children off from adults and the adult world. For example, in her study of highly urbanised Berlin, Zeiher (2003) expresses concern that modern children are growing up in an urban context where they are ferried between dislocated 'islands' of activity. She suggests that many urban children spend too much time in child-specific institutions.

> Children spend much of their time within the confines of islands such as houses, day-care and recreation centre buildings, sports fields, and playgrounds, and they have to go on their own or to be escorted and ferried by adults between these urban islands (Zeiher, 2003, pp. 66–7).

Lareau's (2003) American ethnography of children's daily lives presents a powerful case that, far from being global, these patterns of institutionalisation are socially stratified. She posits that the hyper-orchestration of children's lives is more available to and more common among well-resourced middle-class families, and that it operates to actively foster or cultivate the child.

> The white and Black middle-class parents engaged in practices of concerted cultivation. In these families, parents actively fostered and assessed their children's talents, opinions and skills. They scheduled their children for activities. They reasoned with them. They hovered over them and outside the home they did not hesitate to intervene on the children's behalf. They made a deliberate and sustained effort to stimulate children's development and to cultivate their cognitive skills (Lareau, 2003, p. 238).

Although poor and working-class families share some of these parenting practices, Lareau suggests that the logic of child-rearing in these parents is characterised by a commitment to the accomplishment of natural growth.

> The working class and poor parents viewed children's development as unfolding spontaneously, as long as they were provided with comfort, food, shelter and other basic support... As with concerted cultivation, this commitment, too, required ongoing effort: sustaining children's natural growth despite formidable life challenges. Parents... organised their children's lives so they spent more time in and around home, in informal play with peers, siblings and cousins... adult-organized activities were uncommon (Lareau, 2003, p. 238).

While Lareau places a great deal of salience on socio-economic factors in shaping parenting practices (since the bottom line is that formalised children's activities can be expensive), she argues for an interactionist model, stressing the importance of the interlocking influences of educational and occupational biographies as well as material resources in determining eventual child-rearing preferences. It may well be that macro-social changes such as the decline in fertility also have a part to play, as they impact differentially on social groups. For example, the reduction in sibling numbers is generally more common in middle-class families, and may create more pressure for parents in these families to orchestrate and mediate contacts with other children outside the home in order to ensure peer companionship.

Other English studies (e.g. Barnes & Baylis, 2004; O'Brien et al., 2000; Valentine & McKendrick, 1997) have shown how familial practices are a crucial context for understanding children's geographies, not just through the dimension of parental control, but also through the emotional and cultural orientation embedded in intergenerational negotiation concerning children's access to public space. Case studies in these projects indicate that there are complex familial negotiations around 'letting go' and 'keeping close'. Both parents and children display emotionally active concerns about autonomy as well as dependency. For instance, in O'Brien et al.'s 2000 study, Clara, an 11-year-old white girl living in a 'safe' outer London suburb, never played outside unsupervised, was always accompanied to school and was never left alone at home. Nevertheless in her interview she described a very full life with many friends and a wide range of interests and passions (music, Brownies, swimming, dance and horse-riding). She loved her home with its range of possessions, garden, special places and spaces to make her own. Clara's parents, particularly her mother, carefully planned her daughter's activities and, whilst there was a degree of negotiation, possibilities of action were bounded by principles about proper and appropriate ways of life for a girl of Clara's social position (her parents self-identified as strongly middle-class). When Clara's mother was asked about Clara's childhood in comparison to her own, she reflected: 'It's a lot more protected, which I don't like, but I feel is necessary, more supportive, a lot more involved in what they do'. Clara's mother saw herself as more directly involved in explicitly shaping her daughter's life-world than she remembers experiencing in her own childhood. This mode of parental sponsorship, very similar to the style of concerted cultivation described by Lareau, served to create a closeted life style where Clara could be spatially segregated, chaperoned and organised to ensure the cultural reproduction of a particular form of middle-class life for a girl. In contrast to other children, Clara presented no significant concerns about her orchestrated and structured life, in fact quite the opposite; when probed more deeply about any frustrations she might have with not being able to go out alone, Clara responded by saying that 'I'd rather be safe'. It may well be that this form of cocooned movement through the city, alongside high levels of attachment to home, is but one of a range of adaptations particular parents and children make to getting by in a more insecure social world. Moreover, the general elaboration of the modern urban home, with its play spaces, global communication networks, pets, toys and music systems, has created a socio-sphere of enrichment rather than entrapment for many contemporary children, particularly children from materially advantaged backgrounds.

Parenting practices are also influenced by powerful media discourses about the potential dangerousness of neighbourhoods for children. In Britain contradictory media messages are common. For instance, on the same day that the Department of Environment and the Regions (DETR) announced measures to encourage more children to walk to school, some newspapers were highlighting the dangers of outside play. 'Parents told not to let children play alone' ran *The Independent* newspaper (20 July, 1998). Parents are often faced with sensationalised and ill-informed media, particularly after there has been one of the rare occurrences of child abduction and murder by strangers. Typically the media accounts emphasise children as vulnerable or too incompetent to negotiate urban space safely. In their attempts to protect and promote their children's well-being, it can be difficult for parents to know which way to turn.

In their study of four communities in England, Barnes & Baylis (2004) found that several issues, notably traffic, unknown adults and local older youth, were all a source of considerable concern for parents of children aged 11 to 12 years.

> Since the road's been opened both ends there's a lot more cars come flying down here now. My son's already been run over once, along the top, it broke his leg in three places. (rural area)

Children play in the garden and at friend's houses or vice versa. There's a pretty wood out the back here but I never go. You just don't know who's about down there. I wouldn't even go with the children, anything could happen. (town)

Teenage children, you hear rumours about what they are doing, shouting, swearing. Sometimes you hear that they're walking around with a knife in their hand, trying to be hard, I don't want my daughter going with people like that. (rural area)

For my son it's a concern about gangs of teenagers, gangs of boys, maybe if he's out by himself, especially if he's got a mobile phone on him or stuff like that. (city)

CONCLUSIONS

In this chapter we have shown the diverse ways contemporary children and young people use the public spaces of the communities in which they live. We have found differences linked to the particular 'place' characteristics of the local neighbourhood settings and variation by the individual characteristics of children themselves. We have also traced the growing importance of virtual communities for children and youth through their use of the internet.

In general, however, the immediate neighbourhood is very important to children and young people as they move with age from the home to the public sphere. Although few children and young people are spatially restricted, there is growing concern about the barriers which local neighbourhood infrastructures create for children's independent mobility. While new community, child-centred resources and facilities have emerged for young children to help compensate for the loss of traditional play spaces, high quality local neighbourhood amenities for youth are less common.

Empirical studies have also shown that children's spatial lives are bound up in a web of personal emotional biographies and family practices, as well as local neighbourhood factors. Children's spatial lives have been transformed both by the nature of urban living and by the relationships between the generations in both the domestic and the public spheres. With increases in marital breakdown and dual-earner families, children's family relationships have become less permanent and predictable and children are spending less time with their parents. Parenting norms stress the precious and 'priceless' nature of children and the importance of family quality time, and we see more visible concerns about protecting children from 'risk'. Clearly a holistic approach to children and community life must balance children's needs and desires to have an active civic life with parental needs and anxieties to promote and protect their welfare.

6

COMMUNITY INTERVENTIONS AND POLICY

The preceding chapters of this book have discussed the research that illustrates the importance of communities (both communities of interest and neighbourhood communities) for parents in different stages of the family life-cycle. In this part of the book we discuss community-level interventions: what they are, how they work and how effective they are in their impacts on the lives of children and their parents.

POLICY DEVELOPMENTS

There has been an enormous upsurge of interest in communities as objects of policy intervention over the last decade, and a corresponding increase in resources for community programmes. This interest has come from the political left and the political right, both sides of the political spectrum now emphasising community as a key aspect for social policy intervention and research (Somerville, 2005). However this has not always been the case; historically there has been ambivalence from politicians of all dispositions about community interventions.

From the point of view of the 'left', community interventions are attractive because they are seen as a means to empower the most vulnerable members of society. Many progressive organisations and initiatives such as trade unions and cooperative movements have historically begun with small-scale local community ventures. They offer the prospect of collective action by disadvantaged groups, and the potential to challenge established vested interests.

Despite this, there have always been elements of the left that are suspicious of 'community' and community interventions. Social inequality is caused by macro economic factors rather than local factors, and according to this view, the answers to the problems of poverty and disadvantage lie in more equitable distribution of resources at national and international levels rather than in social action at a local level. Thus the spatial concentration of poverty and disadvantage is viewed merely as a by-product of the larger social forces which lead to a lack of social mobility and reduced life chances for poor people. Consequently community intervention is at best a 'sticking plaster' rather than a cure, and at worst a distraction from the real policy issues of class struggle and economic re-distribution.

From the 'right' the attractiveness of community comes from the view that strong communities, supported by volunteering, will be less dependent on state intervention and welfare subsidies. The right is also attracted to the social control implicit in many community interventions. On the other hand the right is distrustful of any social or 'intermediate' institutions (Margaret Thatcher's famous dictum *There is no such thing as society* exemplifies this view), and views with suspicion any intervention that potentially undermines the market or labour flexibility.[1]

During the 1980s and early 1990s relatively little attention was paid to communities and neighbourhoods, but since the late 1990s there has been a huge growth in political and academic interest in neighbourhood and community in all English-speaking countries, and from governments of all political shades. This consensus has come at the same time as the increasing importance of family policy, and the belief that resources spent on prevention and early intervention (especially in relation to the early years) is justified and cost effective. The result has been the implementation of a large number of government-sponsored area-based initiatives around the world, aimed specifically at improving the lives of disadvantaged children. Some of the more important of these are discussed in the next chapters.

However, this political consensus exists only on a very superficial level, and there is still a great deal of debate about the purpose, value and objectives of these interventions. There is also continuing debate about the nature of community and at what level it is legitimate to intervene (see Chapter 1 and Shaver and Tudball, 2002).

There are a number of different approaches to interventions for communities and the most important differentiation from the point of view of families is between interventions at the *community level* and those that are *community-based*. Both of these provide services to vulnerable families in the community, and both are geographically based in the community, but they operate from different theoretical standpoints and have different aims and objectives. Community-level interventions are aimed at changing the community itself rather than helping specific vulnerable individuals or families. This type of intervention is based on the belief that social problems, especially those created by disadvantage, are best dealt with by 'capacity building' the community so that the community itself can better address social ills, rather than by identifying individuals with problems and providing services to them. Underlying this philosophy are a number of assumptions. First, it is assumed that people living in a 'healthy' or 'cohesive' community are more likely to be healthy themselves, and therefore less likely to need welfare support. As we have seen, there is now considerable research evidence for this belief (Curtis et al., 2004; McCulloch & Joshi, 2001; Vinson, 2004), although the relationship between individual and community attributes is not at

---

[1] In addition to these reservations both left and right are, of course, suspicious of those aspects of community interventions which are attractive to the other side. For example, the left is concerned that community interventions will be used to replace state-delivered services, and the right is concerned about money being wasted on initiatives that are a cover for left-wing political organisations.

all straightforward. The corollary of this is that alleviating some of the stress of living in an 'unhealthy' community would reduce the social problems of residents in the neighbourhood. There is less evidence for this, however. Whilst it makes sense to believe that improvements in neighbourhoods could result in concomitant improvements in the lives of children and parents, this is not necessarily the case, and even if the improvements have an overall benefit, there may be losers as well as winners.

Another assumption on which community-level interventions are based is that social capital, and in particular *collective efficacy*, is improved by the use of local volunteers to deliver services to those in need of specific or targeted help. Increasing voluntary participation is expected to facilitate community cohesiveness and reduce dependency on professionals. There is some evidence that a successful method for empowering parents is to help them develop from dependent service-users into volunteers or paid workers in the service, and ultimately to become involved in managing the service (Gibbons, 1992; Parsons et al., 2003).

The philosophy underpinning these interventions is that communities are best placed to identify their own needs and to create and manage the optimal local solutions to those needs. Outside intervention is desirable only to the extent that it helps the community develop its capacity to help itself. Communities that are able to develop the skills of local people and 'wean' themselves from dependency on state or professional intervention will be healthier and more resilient. Self-reliant, cohesive communities will be able to sustain improvements over time and will need less support as they become independent of the intervention. Community-level interventions are therefore always seen as relatively short term initiatives. The ultimate goal is to encourage self-sustaining communities. This is analogous to the benefits of self-help groups for individuals and also to the ideas underpinning bottom-up interventions to help the economic development of third world countries.

Since community-level interventions seek to change the community rather than individuals, their success is measured in terms of changes at the community level. In theory, individual children may not benefit from the intervention as long as changes in the community are evident. However most interventions are ultimately aimed at change in outcomes for individuals, while this may or may not have an impact on the community.[2] Community strength is generally viewed as a vehicle for changing individual outcomes rather than as an end in itself.

Community-level interventions are usually contrasted with *community-based* interventions (see Table 6.1). Community-based interventions aim to help individuals with specific problems or issues rather than to change the community. They are community-based (as opposed to being based in an institutional setting such as hospital or town hall) largely in order to increase accessibility and acceptability of the service by potential service users. These services are often characterised by

---

[2] For example the intervention may result in *displacement* rather than alleviation of a problem – young people may display antisocial behaviour in another area or in the home rather than in the community – and theoretically this would still count as a success for community level interventions.

Table 6.1   Comparison of community and community-based interventions

Identifying Features	Community level intervention	Community-based intervention
Aim	To change the community's attitudes or behaviour towards an issue	To help individuals or families at risk and support them
Consultation	Consultation with community before setup	Similar but sometimes sited in communities without consultation
Decision-making	Bottom-up and based on empowerment philosophy	Can be bottom-up or top-down
Outcome measurement	Outcomes are changes in community	Outcomes are changes in individuals or families
Methodology	Capacity-building essential	Capacity-building is a by-product of the service
Orientation	'Strengths' perspective	Can work with 'problems' as well as strengths

'drop in' or 'outreach' referral methods rather than referral from other agencies or professionals such as teachers or general practitioners (Gauntlett et al., 2000). They generally aim to provide services to people living in the immediate neighbourhood rather than having a broad geographical remit.

In practice community interventions are quite difficult to define and implement, partly because the notion of 'community' is so contested (as discussed above), but also because it is not easy to separate a community from the individuals who live there. In addition, many services offered by community-level interventions are also community-based, as will become evident from the case studies described below. Nevertheless, it is important to understand the nature of community-level and community-based interventions and the evidence base for their effectiveness.

COMMUNITY DEVELOPMENT

There are several types of community-level interventions, but the most established is the community development approach. Community development is a strategy to tackle social problems that engages community members so that they can develop their own approaches to resolving issues within the community. The community development approach has become an international phenomenon, although the form it takes differs in different parts of the world. In the USA it owes its origins to the Community Development Corporations – not-for-profit organisations involving a combination of public and private money and the involvement of local people (McDevitt, 1997; Twelvetrees, 1996). There is a strong tradition of community development in the developing world, especially in Latin America, Africa and the Middle East (Churchman, 1990), as well as in Europe (Chanan, 1992). For example, in France, the 'Specialised Prevention' movement emerged in the 1950s and 60s, initiated by voluntary sector groups at a local level but later to be given statutory footing and supported by public funds (Michel & Gelloz, 1997).

At the structural or methodological level there is an increasing policy emphasis on the involvement of community members in designing, managing and monitoring community-based government initiatives. Many such initiatives now require community members to be consulted about how government money should be spent and expect community representation on steering and management groups and in service delivery, monitoring and evaluation. Community development approaches are increasingly being used to address specific issues within communities such as drug abuse, anti-social behaviour, racism and child abuse (Gauntlett et al., 2000)

Community development projects in the developed world have mostly been aimed at tackling neighbourhood poverty and deprivation. In the UK the first major nationally co-ordinated initiative was the Community Development Project, which was funded by the Home Office in 1969 (Green & Chapman, 1992). With the advent of conservative, individualist governments in the UK and the USA in the 1980s and early 1990s, community development ideas lost popularity. But they have now re-surfaced in response to the communitarianism of New Labour, which emphasises participation and social inclusion as part of the solution to social ills (Craig, 1999). They have been given an added boost with the growing political consensus that locally determined solutions are the best way of running services. It must be noted that the political impetus, and most of the research literature in this area, is focused on geographical communities, but there is a real question as to whether (and how) communities of interest could become the focus of interventions.

Community development work involves workers bringing local people together, training them to develop their skills and understanding (termed 'capacity building') and funding projects (see Box 6.1). The scale of community development projects tends to be quite small. However, some initiatives involve a much wider remit including economic regeneration, health and social service development and housing. Additionally the concept of 'multi-level interventions' has been developed, so that problems are addressed at the individual level by specialist services and community-level interventions address similar issues at community level.

Box 6.1 Key principles behind community development

According to the Federation of Community Work Training Groups (2001), the key principles behind community development approaches are as follows:

Start from communities' own needs and priorities rather than those dictated from outside;

On tap not on top: giving leadership to people in the community and acting as a resource to them;

Work **with** people; don't do things to or for them;

Help people to **recognise and value their own skills, knowledge and expertise** as well as opening up access to outsider resources and experience;

Encourage people to **work collectively, not individually**, so that they can gain confidence and strength from each other (although this experience often benefits individuals as well);

Encourage community leaders to be **accountable**, and to ensure that as many people as possible are informed and given the opportunity to participate;

Recognise that people often **learn most effectively by doing** – opportunities for learning and training are built into everyday working;

Support people to **participate** in making the decisions which affect them and work with decision-makers to open up opportunities for them to do so;

Promote social justice and mutual respect.

The activities involved in community development initiatives are focused around:

- information gathering and dissemination;
- advocacy;
- community education;
- facilitating self-help groups;
- key service provision;
- network development;
- community organisation development;
- public awareness raising;
- lobbying;
- political action.

(FCWT, 2001)

PROBLEMS AND CONTROVERSIES AROUND COMMUNITY DEVELOPMENT PROCESSES

There are a number of tensions inevitable in the implementation of community interventions in general and community development initiatives in particular. Most of these problems will have to be negotiated at some stage in every intervention, and this process is often challenging and time consuming. Unless these considerations are factored into the planning of community intervention, it is likely that there will be frustration at the slow progress of the intervention in its initial stages.

Definition of Community

Perhaps because of the historical beginnings of community development in rural villages, the community development literature is relatively silent about the definition of community, and tends to see the objects of community interventions either as self-evident or as defined by the local population. However, as we discuss in Chapter 1, *community* and *neighbourhood* are contested terms and there is often conflict and tension, especially in urban areas, about the nature, size and location of the community. Area-based initiatives, for example, have tended to focus on administrative entities such as wards, districts, parishes or other local government boundaries (with some exceptions, including *Sure Start Local Programmes* in the UK and *Stronger Families Stronger Communities* in Australia). But these are not always recognised as neighbourhoods by local residents, especially in urban areas where boundaries are more fluid and communities tend to be more heterogeneous. This may not necessarily pose a problem, but there may be challenges, for example, to the legitimacy of community leaders if the nature of the community is contested.

One of the consequences of policies which focus intervention on very specific geographical entities is the *cliff effect*, in which significant resources are designated to poor wards or districts but equally poor families living just outside these boundaries are deprived of these new initiatives. Sometimes these effects can be beneficial and deliberate (if frustrating for individuals outside the area). For example, improvements in inner-city schools can result in more middle-class people moving into the community, introducing all the benefits of mixed communities. However there can also be deleterious effects such as natural communities becoming split and fragmented because of competition for the benefits of the intervention between families in different locations within the community.

Power Issues

Community development is based on the notion of transferring power from external authorities towards local people. However this can be challenging for both sides. Tensions and power issues are fundamental to community development, in particular the unequal power relationship which exists between the 'sponsor' or outsider, who has financial control, and the community members (Buysse et al., 1999; Stone, 1996). The sponsors may have a particular agenda or political issue which they wish to pursue with the programme, but there is no guarantee that this will be shared by the community. For example, the sponsor may wish to address the issue of child protection, but the community may prioritise anti-social behaviour by children as the most important issue facing them. The sponsor will then be left with the dilemma of either accepting the community's priority at face value or trying to persuade them that their priority is misconceived and that child protection should be a higher priority.

Another arena of power conflict can be the community itself. Communities are never homogenous or uniform, and there are often high levels of conflict between different sectors of the local community. Because of their focus on 'empowering the community', many community development approaches have neglected to explore intra community power issues. They assume that the community is 'an undifferentiated harmonious unit of co-operation which, with some external help and inputs, would readily flourish into the most effective means of co-operation and development' (Khan, 1998). However real geographical communities are usually characterised by diversity, and there are always different interest groups who may well identify different issues, problems and solutions.

A particular danger is that community participation often involves the most powerful members of the community and the less powerful may be marginalised in the process of implementing the initiative, even if they are the nominal beneficiaries of the programme (Herbert-Cheshire, 2000). One criticism of the Community Development Project, for example, was its lack of gender and race analysis (Green & Chapman, 1992). Often, community involvement means working with local groups who are already formed and who may represent a specific interest or have a particularly powerful voice.

On the other hand it is often important for the success of community projects that they engage with powerful forces in the community. These community leaders may be the only members of the community with the authority and the knowledge to make real changes, and ignoring or bypassing them can severely limit the effectiveness of interventions. At the very least, community leaders can undermine the intervention by failing to support it

These factors mean that community workers must walk a difficult tightrope between the different power interests within the community and those commissioning or advocating the initiative. Naïve idealism or uncritical support for less powerful groups is likely to lead to failure. Equally risky for community workers is creating the perception that they are over identifying with community power brokers.

Representational Issues

These are clearly linked with the previous issue. An assumption behind community development is that the whole community – including those who have not directly participated in the community initiative – will benefit from the impact of participation. This means that the community members who actively participate by volunteering for management committees and the like represent, to some extent, other members of their community. For participants to be representative of the wider community it is necessary that they are either elected by their community, or are similar to it in their characteristics and views, are able to identify with it and have its interests at heart (Churchman, 1990). In practice these criteria are seldom met. Few people are elected for this kind of role and participants often differ in many ways from the rest of the community.

Representational issues are complex. Often 'community leaders' or people from grass roots organisations are the first to become involved in new projects. They are thus representing different groups – their organisation and themselves as individuals. There are also big differences within groups. For example, in a Chicago-based project, community workers trying to contact the 'Asian community' found that it was not an entity but encompassed huge diversity, including members from seven or eight different countries. There were differences in language, in length of time lived in the community and in factors such as age, gender and political affiliation (Wynn et al., 1994; Chaskin & Garg, 1997). A similar debate has recently been raging in the UK about engagement with the Muslim community after the London bombings in July 2005. There are those who expect 'the Muslim community' to do something about members who are likely to become suicide bombers. Others wish to 'engage' with the Muslim community or its leaders to increase mutual understanding. But the Muslim community is composed of many different groups, split by age, gender, country of origin, etc., and there are no easily identifiable leaders who represent the community as a whole (Preston, 2005; Walker, 2005).

Conditions for Collective Action

Community development relies on collective action. However, collective action is not easy to mobilise unless the issue is already causing a lot of concern, and the community is in a position to act collectively. Community members are likely to co-operate only in particular situations and under specific conditions (Khan, 1998; Heaton & Sayer, 1992; Egil Wam, 1994), e.g. when they have a common interest and are convinced that this can only be met by acting collectively (Khan, 1998). The effectiveness of community development is to some extent dependent on the distribution of wealth and power within the community. Co-operative actions are much more likely to succeed in relatively egalitarian societies (Khan, 1998) and where people are faced with a serious common problem or threat. Success of action is also more likely where the community is relatively small and where networking between peer groups exists.

These issues pose challenges for community development approaches to confronting 'domestic' issues such as child abuse and domestic violence which, unlike crime, racism and drug misuse, do not take place in public spaces. Community action on behalf of children and families may therefore have to begin with a public issue which can easily be identified as a community (rather than a private) concern. A good entry point in mobilising communities is child safety, as it is viewed as relatively unthreatening (Egil Wam, 1994). Once networks have been established then it is possible to move onto more sensitive or more potentially divisive issues.

Empowerment or Co-option?

There is a controversy within the community participation movement about whether the community development process is one of empowerment or one of co-opting. This argument is especially prominent in relation to involving people in the running of their own services. Critics of this approach argue that, rather than encouraging community members to run services themselves, the focus of their involvement should instead be on campaigning about structural issues and better services. More radical criticisms of the community development process are that it is a way of justifying non-intervention by the state and ignoring more structural issues such as poverty. It can be seen as a way of pathologising communities and blaming them for their own failure. The 'self help' philosophy which underpins the community development process is also viewed by some critics as allowing 'government to creep away from their responsibilities under a cloak of local empowerment' (Churchman, 1990). This devolves the burden of responsibilities and places more emphasis on communities to tackle problems and help themselves.

Complexity and Timescale

The process of involving community members in the organisation and governance of a project can take many years (Chaskin & Garg 1997; Stone, 1996; Woodhead & Siddall, 1995). Projects such as these involve co-ordination across many different sectors and complexity becomes a real issue (Bradshaw, 2000). This is particularly true for projects which are comprehensive in their nature. In addition there is often little demonstrable outcome, at least in the early stages in terms of service provision or changes to the community, and this can lead to initial local enthusiasm waning.

PARTICIPATION AND INVOLVEMENT OF FAMILIES IN COMMUNITY INTERVENTIONS

The majority of community development processes have been aimed at empowering adults to take more responsibility for developments within the community. Where parents have been involved, it tends to be in their role as adult citizens rather than specifically as parents. Children have historically been left out of community development altogether. Indeed they are often viewed by the community as 'the problem'. They are seldom involved in decision-making themselves (Chapter 8; Kirby, 2000; Heaton & Sayer, 1992). More recent UK Government initiatives such as *Sure Start*, and the *Parenting Fund* and the *Stronger Families and Communities Strategy* in Australia require parents (and sometimes children) not only to be consulted about priorities, but to become involved in programme-development and management (Sure Start Unit, 2002; NFPI, 2004). However, this aspect of programme-development is still in its embryonic stages and is perhaps the least well-implemented aspect of these initiatives. Indeed the new children's centres (which are to replace *Sure Start* local programmes) place much less emphasis on parental involvement than their predecessors.

The classic conceptualisation of the degree of participation by community members in governance of community interventions is the *Ladder of Participation* (Arnstein, 1969) which is presented in Figure 6.1. 'True' participation is only

| Citizen control |
| Delegate power |
| Partnership |
| Placation |
| Consultation |
| Informing |
| Therapy |
| Manipulation |

Figure 6.1 Arnstein's ladder of participation
Source: Arnstein 1969.

achieved in a small number of community development projects (Buysse et al., 2003; Cannan & Warren, 1997; Parsons et al., 2003). Often parents in the most deprived areas require ongoing support, and the communities themselves require a great deal more capacity-building than is possible with most community development projects. Arnstein's ladder has been developed and extended by others, to incorporate the stage of the programme (Wilcox, 1994) and the type of participation (Attwood et al., 2003; Beresford and Croft, 1993), in order to provide a more nuanced view as to what kind of participation is best in different contexts.

There are key pragmatic issues which can provide barriers to participation. Some of these have been mentioned previously in relation to the conditions for collective action. Somerville's (2005) discussion of different forms of local democracy and participation identifies the complexities and difficulties involved in developing truly participatory community governance. Whatever structures or mechanisms are adopted, local oligarchies tend to develop. Barriers to participation can be purely practical, e.g. the lack of time participants have available, the problem of sustaining participation and the skills available. Barriers can also result from the lack of trust felt by communities. This is particularly evident in marginalised communities or where families have become disillusioned after being involved in a series of initiatives which they perceive to have demonstrated few benefits (Buysse et al., 2003; The Countryside Agency, 1998).

Reviewing the literature on community involvement in area-based initiatives, Burton and colleagues (2004) differentiate three different purposes for community involvement, and therefore three different types of outcomes that research should address. These are:

- Developmental outcomes – involvement facilitates successful implementation of the intervention.
- Instrumental outcomes – involvement benefits the community members themselves (either those who are actively engaged or the whole community).
- Due process – involvement is undertaken because it is seen as a good thing in itself or as a right, irrespective of any demonstrable benefits for implementation or impact.

They point out that there is a lot of guidance about good practice in this area, and also qualitative research about what stakeholders think is effective. However there is little rigorous research about effective methods for involving community members or about the effectiveness of involvement on the quality of services or on outcomes. Nevertheless they conclude that involvement is valuable and should, in principle, lead to improved services.

One of the key findings of the research is that those parents most in need of services are least likely to access them and are also least likely to become involved in volunteering or other community activities. Participation in community processes involves a degree of initiative on the part of parents as well as attempts by services to engage them. Fram (2003) in the USA and Ghate and Hazel (2002) in the UK both studied groups of materially disadvantaged parents, and found that those in most need were least likely to access support, either from formal services or from family and friends. Barnes (2005) found that parents tended to access community services such as family centres through informal networks, and that they were unlikely to go along unless they knew someone who was already involved. It may therefore be necessary to strengthen informal networks of information and support to involve the most 'hard to reach' families in community developments.

Several researchers nevertheless warn against a simplistic view that strengthening informal support networks would necessarily be the most appropriate response to service provision for these parents (Ghate & Hazel, 2002; Sheppard & Grohn, 2004; Thompson, 1995). Social networks can be conflicted and unsupportive as well as supportive, and Ghate and Hazel (2002) point out that informal support networks depend on reciprocity. Parents who are not able to reciprocate (e.g. because of personality or mental health problems) tend to be isolated from both formal and informal support, despite being amongst the most vulnerable members of society. Services which are able to reach out to these individuals can help in a way that informal support networks cannot. The optimal solution is for services to work alongside informal networks to provide appropriate support to parents in need. There is currently very little research evidence about how services can most appropriately engage with informal support networks to help the most vulnerable parents in a sustained way, and this is an important gap in the research literature.

Another difficulty is that parents with young children may not necessarily be motivated to become engaged in community activities. Barnes (2005) found that parents with young children (especially those in deprived communities) have a very low level of involvement in community activity and volunteering. This may well be because they are focused on looking after their children and do not have the energy, the resources or the will to become volunteers or sit on committees.

COMMUNITY DEVELOPMENT AND MAINSTREAM CHILDREN'S SERVICES

Another challenge for community development approaches to supporting children and families is the question of the relationship of these initiatives to mainstream services such as child protection, youth justice and child and adolescent mental health services (CAMHS) which are aimed at vulnerable children.

There may be a conflict between these specialist services and community development approaches – for example, they may compete with each other for resources, and there may be differences in ideology, issues around confidentiality and the role of service-users. On the other hand there is potential for these approaches to learn from each other. For example, by taking on a community development role, child protection workers can increase the trust communities will have in them. Establishing trust between child protection services and communities is one of the key challenges for children's services (Cooper et al., 2003). Current approaches to child protection are built around defensive practices based on risk-assessment, surveillance and monitoring. Child protection services which are felt to be 'owned' by the community are far more likely to be trusted by children and families involved in the services, and also by community members who are concerned about children's welfare. At the individual level a better understanding of a child/young person's community and of their context provides practitioners with a more complete understanding of each case, which should enhance their work. If this kind of information is routinely collected, child protection work can in turn enhance community development through better documentation of issues and by lending their support to local community rights groups (Hudson, 1999).

There are, however, problems involved in increasing these links. Community development may lack status and influence in relation to 'heavy end' services and be poorly integrated into their processes. One problem which may emerge is that 'mainstream' services tend to respond mainly to crises or urgent cases. This can lead to community development workers identifying cases of concern, calling in child protection services and building up resentments within communities (Hudson, 1999). The joint roles of investigation and community work can erect barriers between the community workers and the community volunteers, leading to breakdowns in the community development process. Another potential problem lies in the conflicts between different sections of the community. Youth or community workers may, for example, be identified with teenagers hanging around street corners and elicit the wrath of older community members.

Underlying these problems is the question of values and intended outcomes. Whilst community development and child welfare/protection share the ultimate goal of enhancing the well-being of children and families, their basic approaches to this aim are in tension with each other. Community development emphasises the positive capacity of community members, and is concerned with collective action. Child welfare, and especially child protection, focuses on risk and deficit, and especially in Anglo-Saxon child welfare systems is concerned with individual rather than collective issues (Cooper et al., 1997). Nevertheless there is an increasing emphasis on contextual and ecological factors to be taken into account, even in individual assessments. The *Framework for the Assessment of Children in Need and their Families* (Department of Health, 2000), which is the tool used by all welfare services in the UK (and increasingly in other countries as well), includes *Family and Environmental Factors* as one of its three domains.[3]

Community development approaches to addressing child welfare needs are still in their infancy, and it is still not clear to what extent the potentially competing needs of individual children and communities are better served by these approaches. Nevertheless the potential benefits of both community-level and community-based approaches to family welfare are considerable. They offer the possibility of an approach which moves beyond the identification, diagnosis and 'treatment' of individual problems to a much more holistic view of children and families in communities, building on their strengths and strengthening local support networks and collective efficacy whilst at the same time providing intensive interventions to those individual families who would benefit most.

POLICY DEBATES AROUND COMMUNITY INTERVENTIONS

The controversies around community interventions is not only about the tensions and challenges of implementation, but relates equally to the policy drivers behind the interventions and the 'real' motivations of policy-makers who advocate community approaches.

The first area of debate is whether communities are legitimate targets for social policy. The argument, stated above, that poverty and disadvantage are caused primarily by broad social and economic forces implies that the most appropriate policy tools for addressing these issues is for governments to tackle the causes of structural inequalities in society by focusing on taxes, benefits, jobs, interest rates and international trade. If these matters are resolved satisfactorily then there will be no need to apply 'sticking plaster' initiatives at the neighbourhood or community level. According to this view, there are no poor neighbourhoods as such, just poor people who happen to live in proximity to each other. The focus of policy should be to lift these individuals out of poverty by establishing an economy in which wealth is redistributed (Murtagh, 1999a).

The argument is made that community development is not a genuine devolution of power but a transfer of responsibility from the state to community (Herbert-Cheshire, 2000). An issue to consider is whether the individuals involved feel empowered by the process or overwhelmed by the added burden of

---

[3] The other two are *Child's Developmental Needs* and *Parenting Capacity*.

responsibility that is devolved. As with the power issues discussed above, in the case of developments in rural Australia Herbert-Cheshire (2000) points out that it is more likely that those who become involved will be the high status members of the community, while its most marginalised members are likely to become even more disempowered and reliant on other members of the community rather than on the state. In addition she believes that community development programmes, while being portrayed by politicians as being 'bottom-up' are in fact determined by policy-makers rather than the local population (Herbert-Cheshire & Higgins, 2004).

Gillies (2005) applies a similar critique to British policy. Like Murtagh (1999b) she argues that community interventions are a method for politicians to evade responsibility for wealth redistribution by effectively blaming parents and communities for the problems of poverty. However she accuses politicians of being *too* interventionist rather than the opposite. She accuses the New Labour Government of using such initiatives as *Sure Start* to dictate how poor parents should parent their children. 'Family Support' in this context is merely a more palatable way of packaging government's desire to dictate to parents how they should behave. Parental involvement in community development initiatives is therefore a method for co-opting poor families into the myth that improved parenting and community social capital are the solutions to the problems of poverty.

Alcock (2004) identifies the many tensions inherent in area-based initiatives, especially in relation to the participation of local citizens. These initiatives tend to explicitly or implicitly pathologise people living in disadvantaged communities by shifting the responsibility for addressing social inequality away from policy-makers towards community members.

Another factor mitigating against community interventions is the fact that, although poverty and disadvantage are geographically concentrated, this does not mean that all, or even most, poor or disadvantaged people live in disadvantaged neighbourhoods (Lee et al., 1995). Similarly, few neighbourhoods, no matter how deprived, will have only poor people living in them.[4] In addition, some problems (e.g. substance abuse, crime, smoking during pregnancy) are more geographically concentrated than others (e.g. Attention Deficit Disorder with Hyperactivity, ADHD; domestic violence), and so initiatives focused on poor neighbourhoods will differentially hit and miss different groups of disadvantaged families.

Thus area-based initiatives aimed at reducing disadvantage are inherently inefficient – they will always involve some 'false positives' (families who are not disadvantaged but who use the services provided by the initiatives) and 'false negatives' (disadvantaged families living outside the intervention areas who cannot access the services). Over time these problems are likely to grow for any specific initiative, because relatively well-off families who hear about improved

---

[4] The geographic concentration of poverty is different in different countries, however, and is more pronounced in the USA than in Europe or Australia.

services will have the resources to access them, whereas those poor families who are not targeted will continue to lack the capacity to access services.

A further issue is that some communities are not viable and interventions in those communities are bound to fail, wasting public money and potentially even doing damage rather than good. Glennester and colleagues (1999) suggest that interventions in some communities should involve 'managed decline' rather than subjecting those communities to multiple and expensive interventions which are bound to fail because there is no longer a basic raison d'être for the community to thrive.

So there are powerful arguments to eschew community interventions in favour of policies aimed at the macro level and at individuals. However, the alternatives to area-based initiatives have their own problems. For example, it may be true that the causes of devastation wreaked on communities when industries fail are global, but it is not usually possible to address the consequences for those communities by implementing macro-economic changes or by propping up failing industries. Technological changes and other forces will inevitably cause the demise of specific industries or whole sectors of the economy and communities dependent on those industries are bound to suffer. Governments must intervene to support those communities. But this is only one example of the need for community interventions. Most community interventions are focused on areas with long-standing problems and multiple disadvantages, rather than those facing a crisis because of a declining industry. The causes of this pattern of deprivation may be complex and involve a number of different policy areas such as immigration, housing, employment and transport, but the solutions may at least partly be addressed by community regeneration or by interventions.

Targeting interventions at individuals is also not necessarily effective or efficient. Some targeted interventions (e.g. employment training for the long-term unemployed) may be efficient – because the beneficiaries of the intervention are easy to find and the intervention itself is relatively straightforward. But most interventions aimed at parents and parenting are far more complex. Identifying those parents who need the intervention is likely to involve expensive assessment and complex interventions. In addition, families are far less likely to volunteer to participate in programmes which are seen as stigmatising. Community interventions can reduce the stigma attached to service-use and can reach out to those 'hard to reach' families which individually-targeted programmes are unlikely to serve.

Moreover, there are other benefits of community initiatives which could not arise from individually-targeted interventions. Smith (1999) gives the following reasons for the existence of area-based programmes over and above the rationale that they address community effects:

● Increasing polarisation gives a political and social justification for intervention.
● Spatial concentration of problems makes area-based programmes an efficient way of targeting resources.

Similarly, the cross-departmental review conducted in the US by the Committee on Integrating the Science of Early Childhood Development (Shonkoff & Phillips, 2000) notes that, because of their efficiency, neighbourhood-level interventions can be cost effective even in the context of a small amount of explained 'area effect' (Box 6.2).

Box 6.2   Why neighbourhood level interventions can be cost effective

- Focusing activity can make more impact than dissipating it.
- Area-targeted programmes can more easily adopt a 'bottom-up' approach which can result in more efficient identification of problems and delivery of solutions.
- Local programmes may lead to increased confidence and capacity to participate in the community.
- Area-based programmes may be used as pilots to inform changes in delivery of mainstream programmes.

In summary, community interventions are not a panacea for social problems. Nevertheless the benefits potentially outweigh the problems, and there is potential for community interventions to have broader positive impacts than individually-targeted services.

In the UK, for example, some interventions (e.g. *Sure Start*) are concentrated on small geographical entities (wards or neighbourhoods), whereas others (e.g. *Health Action Zones*) are aimed at whole local authorities or even regions. Consequently, as Lupton (2003) points out, measuring the effect of these initiatives has been complex and difficult, and the attempt to find 'area effects' has proved to be challenging and contested. This has fed into the debates about the rationale and effectiveness of area-based interventions.

These are telling criticisms of community interventions and in particular their requirement to consult, involve and empower local parents and children. There are ideological reasons for opposing many of the current developments as well as practical barriers to their implementation. But it could be argued that these critics go too far. By focusing exclusively on the communitarian or social control aspects of initiatives like *Sure Start*, the critics fail to see their potential for generating positive community effects, not always those the funders or commissioners are hoping to achieve. The criticisms focus on the policies, rather than the realities of how these initiatives impact on the lives of community members. It remains to be seen whether their response will be to become the sort of parents the Government wishes to promote.

It is unlikely that governments of any persuasion would invest large quantities of money in initiatives purely for altruistic reasons. Community interventions are funded because they are seen by politicians as a way of progressing their own objectives and policies. In addition there are genuine tensions inherent in any community-based or community development initiative. 'Empowering' or 'giving control to' the community – or to sections of the community such as children and parents – is not straightforward, and the evidence that empowerment leads inevitably to better services and improved outcomes is not clear cut. We are still at the relatively early stages of research in this area, and our understanding of these complex causal pathways is still embryonic – 25 years after Bronfenbrenner's original articulation of the ecological model. Nevertheless the values which drive community interventions are important and need to be sustained. Improving outcomes for children and families are the primary tasks of these interventions but they are not their only purposes. They are also attempts at delivering interventions which engage with and value the child, the family and the community in a manner that has not been achieved by most professionalised services.

7

COMMUNITY INTERVENTIONS AIMED AT EARLY CHILD DEVELOPMENT AND PARENTING PROBLEMS

EMERGENCE OF COMMUNITY INTERVENTIONS FOR FAMILIES AND YOUNG CHILDREN

Broadly speaking, throughout the developed world community interventions concerned with young children and their parents have had two principal aims: to improve children's physical health and development, and/or to reduce levels of child abuse and neglect. These aims are sometimes addressed together within one programme but the policy developments have tended to run in parallel. While not attempting to make a comprehensive list, this chapter describes a sample of such initiatives from the USA, Australia and Canada and the UK, to provide a picture of how different countries have tried to take early intervention strategies usually focused on specific children (e.g. low birth weight, with a handicapping condition) or specific families (e.g. single parent households, young parents), and offered them instead to geographical communities. This re-direction of services has evolved in part to avoid stigmatising, so that the effects of social exclusion (or being part of the 'underclass') can be ameliorated without having to be identified in such a way. They also came about as professionals and researchers realised how important community characteristics were for the development and well-being of children and families (as we have seen in Chapter 4).

Dating back to the popularisation of the now infamous 'It takes a village to raise a child' notion, used and abused by numerous authors[1] (e.g. Booth & Crouter, 2001; Clinton, 1996), there has been a growing emphasis on developing ways to enhance the role of the wider community in raising children and fostering their early development. Beginning in the late 1980s and early 1990s a

---

[1] A Google search for the phrase on 18 July 2005 produced 34,500 results. One site is devoted to librarians and others trying to finds its origins, without much success (http://www.h-net.org/~africa/threads/village.html).

number of Comprehensive Community Initiatives (CCIs), sometimes referred to as Comprehensive Community Based Initiatives (CCBIs), emerged in the USA (Connell et al., 1995). They were founded on two common principles: the need for the formation and strengthening of partnerships between families, governments, child welfare, family support, health and educational agencies and a number of other organisations; and the need to empower community members to participate actively in partnership with government and the professional sector, to promote healthier communities (Tomison & Wise, 1999). Most of these initiatives were also developed on the premise that the devolution of authority and responsibility from higher-levels to the neighbourhood or community (bottom-up) was a necessary aspect of the change process, and that this would enhance child and parental well-being (Kubisch et al., 1995).

Under the auspices of the US National Academy of Sciences (NAS) in 1992, and since 1994 as a policy programme of the Aspen Institute, a Roundtable on Comprehensive Community Initiatives has been in place. Now funded by a number of foundations the group currently has about 30 members who meet to focus on community development.

In the USA CCIs were developed to address a range of issues – teen pregnancy, youth employment and training, and crime prevention, as well as more broadly based empowerment zones and enterprise communities (Kubish et al., 1995). There was, however, a particular call, *Neighbors Helping Neighbors: A New National Strategy for the Protection of Children*, to address the problem of child maltreatment holistically by reorienting services to the level of the neighbourhood (US Advisory Board on Child Abuse and Neglect, 1993). This fourth report of the board went beyond previous documents by looking in more detail at how to change services for children and families. Recognising the complexity of the factors that lead to child abuse and neglect, the group took an ecological perspective, saying 'to better understand the problem of child maltreatment, one has to understand the environment in which so many of today's children are growing up' (p. viii). In addition to recommending that a national strategy must be comprehensive, child-centred and family-focused, the relevance of the wider community was noted:

> A national strategy must be neighborhood-based. In fact it must address the viability of the neighborhood itself. If we are to have healthy families we must become sensitive to the quality of the neighborhood environments in which our families live (1993, p. x).

> We must strengthen our neighborhoods, both physically and socially, so that people care about, watch, and support each other's families. Child protection must become a part of everyday life, a function of all sectors of the community (1993, p. 3).

Two additional reports on early childhood policy written at about the same time have also been at the heart of much recent work in the USA to develop early childhood community-development initiatives. One was produced by the National Commission on Children – *Beyond Rhetoric: A New American Agenda for Children and Families* (1991) – followed by a report from the Carnegie Corporation's Commission on Early Childhood, *Starting Points* (1994). The latter called for communities to be mobilised to support young children and their families, although it did not specifically identify interventions focused on communities (rather than specific children or families) as the way forward. Instead it called for parents (who do not necessarily have any free time for this kind of activity – Barnes, 2004) to become more involved in their communities, noting:

> Reversing the quiet crisis requires more than the provision of direct services to families, such as those described in the preceding chapters. It has become increasingly clear that we also need to support communities so that they in turn can strengthen family life (*Starting Points*, p. 86).

The report's authors refer to ecological research, indicating that a viable, sustainable habitat is crucial to the survival of a species (p. 87). Applying this to child development, they suggest that a family's effectiveness in childrearing is bolstered by the existence of a supportive social network including people beyond the immediate family. The report identified four main ways that a community could support young children and their families: (1) by providing parent education on topics such as family planning, prenatal health, and good parenting; (2) by broadening the range of good quality child care options and allowing parental leave; (3) by guaranteeing adequate health care, especially preventive services and those focused on injury prevention; and (4) by strengthening community networks and drawing together programmes into locations such as family centres.

Thus rather than suggesting particular programmes for families and young children, the emphasis was more on thinking in terms of the community, promoting a culture of responsibility and planning at the community level, to understand both vulnerabilities and strengths. The example is given of the *Austin Project* in Texas, where a plan for capacity building was developed that gave children aged 0 to 8 as the community's most pressing priority. Measurable goals were set in a five-year plan, including the reduction of infant mortality, increase in the use of nutrition programmes, better health care for infants and toddlers, improvements in the quality of child care, parent education and parent support (Carnegie Corporation, 1994, p. 89), very similar to many of the goals of later initiatives such as *Sure Start* in the UK.

In the UK developments have taken place slightly later, but a number of 'Area Based Initiatives' or ABIs have been introduced since the late 1990s by the Labour government. They have generally had a broader perspective than those in the USA, with a strong focus on narrowing the gap between deprived neighbourhoods and people and the rest of the country as a means of tackling social exclusion and delivering improved services (RCU, 2002). While the majority (e.g. *Neighbourhood Renewal Fund*) have concentrated on economic aspects of communities, a number are of particular relevance to young children and their parents. Most particularly, *Sure Start Local Programmes* were developed in 1999 (Glass, 1999) to improve the health and well-being of children aged 0 to 4 years and their families so that they would have a greater opportunity to flourish when they started school. This initiative was designed to be part of a seamless range of support for children at risk of social exclusion, linking up with the *Children's Fund*, launched in 2000 and intended to provide services for children aged 5 to 13 years (e.g. http://northamptonshire. childrens-fund.org.uk/), and with an additional initiative, *Connexions*, for ages 13 to 19 focused not on geographical communities but on secondary schools.

INITIATIVES PREVENTING CHILD ABUSE AND NEGLECT

NCCAN Pilot Projects

The USA has been at the forefront of developing comprehensive community-oriented frameworks for addressing child maltreatment. In 1989, the US National Center on Child Abuse and Neglect (NCCAN) began providing support for planning and developing nine model comprehensive community-based projects, to encourage community groups to work together to prevent physical child abuse and neglect. The projects were designed to be both community-based and comprehensive and to network with and encourage the involvement of many community service providers. They were spread throughout the USA: Boston, Massachusetts; Carolina, Puerto Rico; Chicago, Illinois; Columbus, Ohio; Fairfax, Virginia; Ithaca, New York; Philadelphia and Pittsburgh, Pennsylvania; and Portland, Maine (CSR, 1996).

Each of the projects was designed to encourage networking and to promote the involvement of many community service providers. In addition the overall approach was bottom-up; each could shape its own services based on the particular geographic, ethnic, demographic and economic context of each community. All nine included elements designed to enhance public awareness about positive parenting and positive family support; parenting education and support programmes, including home visitation; and community-based task forces that planned, developed, implemented and oversaw the projects. In addition, some awarded mini-grants to local community organisations that were conducting child abuse prevention activities.

A national evaluation of the initiatives (CSR, 1996) found that the local task forces were central to success in implementing the initiatives (see also Ball and the NESS Research Team, 2002, evaluating *Sure Start Local Programmes* in the UK). These groups generally met monthly and had full decision-making and policy-making responsibility. Not only did they guide and monitor activities throughout the grant period, they were also central in the task of mainstreaming – enabling the communities to sustain the programmes after NCCAN funding ceased. The emphasis was on cohesive, collaborative working relationships instead of the competitive relationships that often result from the initiation of new prevention efforts.

Most projects found that, to reduce resistance from other community constituents, they needed to stress the collaborative nature of the effort and to allow members to air their differences and find solutions. The community-based task forces were also necessary to establish a presence within the community, obtain referrals, reduce duplication of services and achieve community ownership of the projects. When the task forces included community residents, the residents benefited because they had opportunities to become leaders, and the projects benefited because they had input from the community, which helped them with programme-development and implementation. However, involvement of local community residents was not necessarily straightforward, particularly if the area was disadvantaged. These projects found that residents expressed discomfort and lacked confidence in their ability to participate with professionals to advance the project's causes, secure additional funding and effect community-level changes.

Case Study: Dorchester CARES, Boston, Massachusetts

Funded by NCCAN, the primary aim of *Dorchester CARES* was to increase protective factors in the community by organising and making available family strengthening services, increasing social support networks and increasing the level of social cohesion within the community by bringing together different administrative bodies to develop a comprehensive strategy for serving families. Through Coordination, *Advocacy, Resource development, Education, and Services (CARES)* it was designed to create opportunities for family members to become more competent, independent and self-sustaining, thus reducing the chances of child maltreatment taking place (Shay, 1988; 1995). Initially it was designed to operate in only one census tract but, after the first year of operation, the coverage was broadened to include five contiguous tracts, with a population of approximately 19,000 made up of just over 4,000 households (Barnes McGuire, 1997b).

The project was based to a large extent on Bronfenbrenner's (1979) ecological model of development, subsequent work conducted by Garbarino (Garbarino, 1985; Garbarino & Kostelny, 1992) and literature indicating that social support has powerful mediating influences on family functioning (Crockenberg, 1981; Dunst, Vance & Cooper, 1986; McCubbin et al., 1980). In particular Dunst, Trivette and Deal (1988) hypothesised that the mediating influence of social support on parenting attitudes is explained by three factors: the burden of care is shared; esteemed members of a social network serve as models, demonstrating effective and nurturing behaviour; and sharing the 'trials and tribulations' of childrearing with others helps break feelings of isolation and normalise difficult times.

The grant mandated the development of a community-based prevention alternative to the existing child welfare system, developing family-strengthening services through a collaboration of existing local agencies to maximise resources, reduce fragmentation and link children and families to preventive, culturally sensitive services in their own neighbourhoods. Using Bronfenbrenner's ecological framework, the various levels of services available to families in the targeted neighbourhoods were:

- at the central level, direct contact with the families;
- at the next level, the restructuring and co-ordination of available services within the community through the creation of an inter-agency team;
- at the macro level, the community's network of formal support, including schools, day care and *Head Start* programmes, churches, health centres, law enforcement, housing programmes, welfare, job training and economic development associations (Shay, 1995, p. 8).

Guided by residents' needs and building on existing resources within the target area, the collaboration offered a continuum of prevention services ranging from primary prevention through secondary prevention to tertiary services for families where abuse, or definite risk, had been identified. To coordinate this continuum, a multi-disciplinary, multi-authority team was established, including local community residents, health officials, social services staff, the programme staff and representatives from other voluntary services in the neighbourhood.

A qualitative evaluation of the organisational process (Mulroy, 1994, 1997) found that environmental forces both within and beyond the local community had an impact on the success of inter-agency collaboration. Within the first months of the project obstacles were identified. First, area residents reported in a needs-assessment survey that their greatest needs were not for traditional health and human services, but rather for food, clothing, drop-in child care and personal safety in a violent neighbourhood. In addition, it was found that the area was more diverse than had been anticipated, with many different concerns, ethnicities, cultures and needs. To intervene in a community one first needs to know about that community. Thus the steering group had to incorporate local concerns prior to addressing their principal aim of reducing child maltreatment.

The planned partnerships, between medical, educational and social support services took time to develop. There was some tension between human services professionals and the group about the focus on bringing in local residents as paid staff, and there were some issues related to the lack of differentiation between professionals and paraprofessionals. But overall this was perceived to be a strength of the service, contributing to a non-judgemental approach to families. Of particular relevance to the long term integration of funding for the project into that for mainstream services were: a shifting political climate, a competitive grants system at both the state and the federal level leading to members of the committee applying for the same funds, and tension within the group about the meaning of 'community-based' services. Nevertheless, unusually for demonstration projects, it continues to operate as the *Dorchester CARES Coalition for Families and Children*, designated in June of 1996 as a pilot for the Department of Social Services Community Connections Initiative (http://www.dcares.org/events/). This expansion of the original *CARES* collaborative includes a larger number of new agency and consumer partners but operates with the same founding principles, serving the same area.

However, examination of the process of implementing innovative initiatives is only part of the picture. It is also important to know whether there are any changes in the communities themselves. An impact evaluation was also conducted, to look in particular at changes over time in levels of social support in the local area (integral to the focus of the programme) and at changes in parenting behaviour (Earls, McGuire & Shay, 1994; Barnes McGuire, 1997b). The household survey was designed to find out about community residents – who they were, what they thought of the neighbourhood and what kinds of relationships existed between caregivers and children. The questions covered aspects of family life that were targeted for change (social support, discipline) and those thought to make families vulnerable (income, family size, maternal mental health). In the third year only, questions were included about respondents' knowledge and experience with aspects of the *CARES* project and its related programmes. Open-ended remarks about the project were also collected pertaining to the community-based approach (see Box 7.1).

Three successive waves of random household surveys were conducted in the target area, some of the findings demonstrating the difficulties of attempting to develop services to effect change in a community. For example, the neighbourhood was reported as increasingly dangerous across the three years, with a particular

---

Box 7.1   Comments made by local community members in Dorchester, Massachusetts, during random household surveys

They're very concerned about the community, very concerned people [the *Dorchester CARES* staff and volunteers]...I first started going there and on a Friday [for the food pantry] there would be a long line, standing in line to get the food, the line is like an hour-long line. I said instead of standing in line I'm going down there and ask them if they need a volunteer to help, so I ask them one day and they say 'Yes, you come down and help pack the food' and I said 'Okay' so ever since then I go every morning, Friday and I help bag up the food and pass up the food and it's been good for me.

Well, let's see, I think for them it's very good to see children, or to see people of color, that's a good thing, since we are not seen, at least in positive ways, on television, newspapers, and things like that. So they have neighbors who are working and doing things and successful and contributing to society, leading productive lives, and that's very important for my children to see. It's also important for them to see their mother and their father working to improve the community. They understand that you can't just expect somebody else to do things for you; you have to get out there and do it yourself.

Like whenever I needed them, they [*Dorchester CARES* staff] were all there for me. The health center, the home visiting nurse, they help me cope with a lot of problems...and if I don't have transportation they offer it to me...if I need to relax, they come right over and take over for me for a little bit...I don't feel all alone.

My second house...I came here [the settlement house where all the services were based] to have coffee and donuts. I stay here because I had no place to go. I bring my kids to school. Come back here, work and help. Work a little while, volunteer. First time I came here for take classes. Now I decided to go downstairs for volunteer. I do 'Parents CAN', 'Food pantry', I do a lot of stuff; to me it's my second house because I have friends.

Barnes McGuire, 1997b, pp. 113–114.

---

concern about the increased use of drugs and deterioration in the housing stock (Barnes McGuire, 1997b). However, even in that context, the extent of social support available to the families was found to have risen by a small but significant amount by year three. While the level of reported harsh physical or verbal discipline did not change significantly over the three years, levels were higher when there was more perceived danger and disorder (Earls, McGuire & Shay, 1994) and lower when social support was greater (Barnes McGuire, 1997b). Thus there were some indications that, over the long term, a strategy designed to enhance social support and social networks in a specified community could have the desired impact on rates of child abuse and neglect while also providing a number of intensive services directed at improving parenting (such as the Nurturing Programme, Bavlolek & Comstock, 1985). Unfortunately the evaluation did not continue for a sufficient time to look at this.

Case Study: Strong Communities, Greenville County, South Carolina

Developed and led by Gary Melton, one of the members of the US Advisory Board on Child Abuse and Neglect responsible for the *Neighbors Helping Neighbors* (1993) report, *Strong Communities* is a comprehensive, community-wide initiative to prevent child abuse and neglect. Funded by a sizable grant from the Duke Endowment it aims to build and strengthen community norms that will encourage neighbours to help each other by watching out for all children in the community, their own and their neighbours. It sets out to fully implement the *Neighbors Helping Neighbors* strategy (Strong Communities, 2005) starting from the premise that, to be effective, child protection must be a part of everyday life. The materials and services are designed to increase watchfulness and involvement by all community members so that eventually local children will expect that people they encounter are likely to be concerned about their well-being. Their literature notes that:

> Perhaps more than any previous initiative, *Strong Communities* is designed to mobilize the entire community in keeping kids safe. Unlike most of the compre-hensive community initiatives to prevent child abuse and neglect, our strategy is to build community itself, not merely to foster collaboration among community organizations.
>   Although human service agencies make important contributions to people in need, they are not the primary actors in *Strong Communities*. Instead, we are making help "natural" in the institutions of everyday life: businesses, churches and other religious fellowships, civic clubs, fire departments, municipal governments, neighborhood associations, pediatric and family health clinics, police departments, schools, and YMCAs and other family centers. We are also seeking thousands of volunteers to facilitate this mobilization and to provide direct support to families of young children (2005, p. 1).

The focus of *Strong Communities* is universal, for all those in the community and not only those considered to be vulnerable or at-risk. Two of its activities illustrate *Strong Communities'* overall goal to involve the wider neighbourhood in the well-being and protection of children, the 'Pledge Card' and 'Occasional Child Care' campaigns. The pledge card campaign is designed to raise awareness of children's needs by asking those who sign up to do four things: (a) to make the Golden Rule [Do unto others as you would have them do unto you] a principle by watching out for children in the community; (b) to do their best to notice and express caring when a child or a child's family has reason to rejoice, worry or grieve; (c) to learn the names of the children in the ten closest homes; (d) regularly to take time to help a family with young children. Occasional child care mobilises community members to alleviate the stress that socially isolated families can find themselves in, by working with volunteers in each community who are willing to offer occasional care for young children when their parents have a family emergency or an important appointment or simply need a break, or when ordinary care arrangements are interrupted by illness or resignation. In addition to programme-wide activities, *Strong Communities* employs community coordinators in each of its programme sites to assist local residents and existing organisations and institutions (e.g. churches, schools, business groups) in developing their own initiatives and programmes. In this way, *Strong Communities* will be able to document the various paths that communities take in building their capacity to protect children.

An evaluation of this initiative is underway, but as yet there are no reported results of the outcomes. However, with its location in a defined geographical area there is scope for demonstrating change over time not just in child abuse and neglect but also in a range of indicators of family well-being.

ENHANCING CHILD DEVELOPMENT AND PARENTING

Case Study: USA, Early Head Start

Much has been written about *Head Start* and its success in helping young children from low-income families to prepare for and cope with schooling, with results noted into adult life. However, in 1994 a new initiative – *Early Head Start* – was designed with a slightly different orientation, as a two-generation programme to enhance children's development and health, strengthen families and community partnerships and support staff delivering services to low-income families with pregnant women, infants, or toddlers. The crucial difference from *Head Start*, apart from its focus on younger children in the 0–3 age range, was the focus on developing partnerships in disadvantaged communities, although receipt of the actual services depends on enrolment of specific families within the community. At the beginning in 1995, there were 68 programmes, the number expanding by 1996 to 143 and, following legislation in 1998, to more than 600 programmes by 2002 serving over 48,000 children (US Department of Health and Human Services, 2005a). Grantees were required to provide child development services, build family and community partnerships and support staff, selecting from a variety of approaches. One could envisage them as halfway to a 'real' community intervention in that the services are only offered to a limited number of families from the community. Thus, while there is work to increase community partnerships between professionals and with voluntary agencies, only some families from the community can benefit directly (compare this, for instance, with the *Sure Start Local Programmes* in the UK – see the next section – where all families with a child 0 to 3 in specified areas were eligible for all services).

An evaluation was conducted focusing on 17 programmes. It defined the way they had implemented the service as one of three models: centre-based, providing all services to families through the centre-based option of child care plus other activities, offering a minimum of two home visits per year to each family; home-based, providing all services to families through the home-based option through weekly visits and at least two groups per month for each family; or a mixed approach, providing centre-based services to some families, home-based to others. The evaluation compared families randomly assigned to receive *Early Head Start* with other families living in the same communities, following up a sample of 3,000 across the 17 sites that included all three options until the children were three years old (US Department of Health and Human Services, 2001, 2005b).

The evaluation identified significant developmental gains for children at two years, with higher Bayley Mental Development Index scores, and fewer children below one standard deviation from the mean (which indicates at-risk for later school difficulties). The children also had better language development and were less aggressive, though no differences in on-task behaviour were found. The home environments were observed to be more supportive, mothers were seen as more responsive and affectionate and they had gained more knowledge about child development. They were also less likely to use physical punishment and in general used more positive discipline strategies. The specific impact depended to an extent on the type of approach taken, centre-based enhancing child cognitive outcomes more, home-based enhancing parenting, while the mixed approach was similar to the home-based, but with more impact on children's social and language development.

These impacts were sustained at three years (Love et al., 2002). Additional results indicated that there were positive impacts on parents' progress to self-sufficiency through education and training, fewer families had subsequent births and fathers were found to use less physical discipline and to be less intrusive during play. It was noted that, while some enrolled families did not receive any of the services on offer, many families sustained their involvement over the three years. Existing services were available for families not enrolled in the programme, but membership and the related outreach and home visiting helped to sustain involvement for *Early Head Start* families.

There were differences in the extent to which the programme was implemented, and those taking the mixed approach and implementing it fully and early achieved the most impacts. The proactive orientation of the programme was seen to be particularly beneficial for parents at risk for depression and for teenage parents. Unfortunately the evaluation does not report on the ways that professionals in each of the communities achieved greater collaboration. The focus of the evaluation was principally on comparing families enrolled and not enrolled in each of the communities.

While *Early Head Start* has some messages for interventions at the community level, it represents a community-based rather than community development programme (Gauntlett et al., 2000). There are a number of other initiatives that have made a concerted effort to offer services to communities, with community development as their overall aim, rather than enhancing the progress of families who happen to live in communities. Community development programmes tend to be characterised by a bottom-up approach, participation of community members, a strengths perspective and the development of empowerment.

Case study: USA, Success by 6, United Way

Historically, United Way *Success by 6* began in 1988 through a collaborative effort of local politics, local services and local money, bringing together the mayor of Minneapolis, the Honeywell Corporation, the Superintendent of Schools and the United Way. Over the next decade other communities around the country began to replicate what had begun there and in 1998, Bank of America announced a five-year, $50 million grant to the United Way of America to grow the number of United Way Success by 6 initiatives. It has grown rapidly with more than 350 community coalitions currently in place in the USA and in Canada, which plan and implement a number of strategies at both the system change and direct service levels. While each community's priorities are unique, key strategies usually include raising awareness, improving access to services and advocating for public policies that improve the lives of children and families, addressing the root problems in a community that prevent children from entering school prepared to succeed.

United Way's *Success by 6* has emerged as one of the ways that many communities in the USA (and Canada) are meeting the challenges laid out in the Carnegie *Starting Points* report (1994). Its overall mission is to encourage and facilitate collaborations and partnerships to bring together local community businesses, local government, service providers, advocates, educators and families to ensure that young children are born healthy, remain healthy, nurtured and ready to successfully enter school by six years of age. It is based on the belief that the period from birth to age six offers a crucial window of opportunity to establish a foundation for success in school and life, and that children in this age group are dependent on their parents to offer early learning experiences that prepare them to succeed in school (see Box 7.2).

Box 7.2   Principles of Success by 6

SUCCESS BY 6 VISION:

All children will enter kindergarten ready to succeed.

SUCCESS BY 6 CORE BELIEFS:

1. The period of life from birth to age six offers a crucial window of opportunity to establish a foundation for a child's future success.
2. Children 0–6 depend on their parents and caregivers for early learning experiences that prepare them to succeed in school – and life.
3. It's up to all of us to create communities and systems that support young children, their early learning and their families.

http://national.unitedway.org/sb6/

It has three major components, the first of which is the most clearly community-focused: strengthening the nationwide infrastructure of community and state coalitions to generate support, align resources and influence systems so that they have a high impact on parents of young children, increasing school readiness. Its other two components are equipping parents and others for action to stimulate early learning with a nationwide campaign to inform and motivate parents, relatives and family friends to stimulate early learning; and increasing the quality of early learning opportunities offered out of home by making it easier to find, select and offer higher quality early education programmes. Each *Success by 6* initiative is organised through a local United Way, and engages as community partners a variety of business, government and non-profit organisations. They are designed to generate long-lasting community change to support young children by bringing stakeholders together and galvanising communities to solve problems and create strategies for system and policy change.

However, there is unfortunately little evidence either nationally or locally about the impact of *Success by 6* on community connectedness. The type of information that is typically made available on the United Way and local websites concerns monitoring information about numbers of children and families involved (e.g. http://national.unitedway.org/sb6/outcomessb6/index.cfm) or the kinds of services that have been enhanced (e.g. http://www.successby6ottawa.ca/rc/obj.htm) rather than any evaluation of systems change or community collaboration.

Baltimore's *Success by 6* action plan for children and families describes a research design that does go beyond monitoring data on the children and families served (FLBCINC, 2001). Their evaluation framework is multifaceted, aiming not only (as most evaluations of services do) to provide information about the successes and challenges faced in implementing the interventions with interviews and surveys, and documenting outcomes for children in school, but also providing data on trends of child and family well-being across the city, based on a range of data that are comparable to those identified by Coulton (1995) as recommended community indicators. The indicators they plan to collect in Baltimore include low birth weight, pre-term births, infant mortality, accident and injury rates, child abuse and neglect reports and indicators of crime, school avoidance and school success. By compiling geo-mappable datasets (BCDC, 2003) they plan to identify any citywide improvements over time as well as those of individual communities that have been targeted for *Success by 6*. Their results have not been published but if initiatives are to be considered community interventions then it is vital that evaluations consider this type of strategy to identify change at the community level, in addition to (or as well as) progress for individual children or families.

MORE RECENT EARLY CHILDHOOD COMMUNITY INITIATIVES

In 2002, representatives from a number of early childhood, community-oriented, initiatives located in Australia, Canada, the USA and the UK came together to discuss how they were each working to develop, implement and evaluate community-based early childhood system-building initiatives (Halfon et al., 2003). Despite having its own unique social and political context, each country had recognised the importance of early development and had responded by developing and implementing comprehensive, community-based, early childhood, systems building initiatives.

> Perhaps the most striking similarity that emerged among the initiatives is the focus of policy change not on the individual and service-delivery level – nor simply on creating new programs (like *Head Start*) – but instead on the community level. In each case these new initiatives move beyond the idea that a single solution or innovative program will "fix the problem." What has emerged is the notion that, in order to build long-term and sustainable capacity for the health and development of all young children and communities, the focus needs to be at the community level and not solely or principally on individual efforts (Halfon et al., 2003, p. 54).

A review of some of those initiatives presents possibly more questions than answers when considering whether it is sensible to direct services at the community level if one wishes to enhance child development.

Case study: Victoria, Australia, Best Start

In Victoria, under the auspices of the Department of Human Services and the Department of Education and Training, *Best Start* was developed with the aim of improving the health, development, learning and well-being of all children across Victoria from pregnancy through to transition to school (taken to be children 0 to 8 years of age). The programme hopes to achieve this aim through supporting communities, parents, families and service providers to improve universal local early years service systems. The initiative's goals are better access to child and family support, health services and early education; improvements in the capacity and confidence of parents to be parents and of families to care for children and help them to enjoy parenting; and communities that are more child-friendly (www.beststart.vic.gov.au).

Local groups of parents, health and education early years providers and community leaders are expected to join together to form local partnerships to steer the development of *Best Start* activity so that they can evaluate new ways of connecting early childhood, social, health and education services to maximise child development opportunities. There are currently 11 demonstration projects, plus some additional projects focusing on Indigenous (Aboriginal) children and families.

One way that the project will be monitored is by the collection of a range of indicators. It has been recognised that, in order to demonstrate the effectiveness of a community-wide initiative – in this case the community is a whole state – one has to have consistent evidence available year-on-year. The programme has long-range goals, based on evidence that improvement in child health, development and well-being during early childhood are likely to impact on adolescents and adults by, for instance, reducing the likelihood of adolescent alcohol and drug use, juvenile crime, teenage pregnancy and increasing the likelihood of graduation from high school and subsequent employment. However in the short-term they have outlined the basis for an evidence-based data monitoring system for children and families that could have the capability of measuring the determinants of health and well-being of individuals and the population over time. A set of *Best Start* indicators has been designed to represent health issues for children from pregnancy though to transition to school around eight years of age, demonstrating both positive and negative factors of well-being. They include some that can be obtained from health databases such as births to teenage mothers, rates of breast-feeding and immunisations; some that education departments will record such as enrollment in preschool; and other information from surveys such as the time parents spend reading and parental literacy (Waters, Goldfeld & Hopkins, 2001).

While the evaluation plan is sound, it remains to be seen if the professionals on the ground enter all the necessary information. Other evaluations in the UK (e.g. Barnes et al., 2005b) have found that information about breastfeeding, maternal smoking and immunisations is patchy in data systems maintained by health visitors during routine child-health checks. Professionals sometimes consider it is more important to 'do their job' dealing with children and families, rather than completing what they sometimes see as unnecessary paperwork or computer data entry.

Case Study: Queensland, Australia, Pathways to Prevention

This initiative from Queensland is unusual in that it is designed to prevent the development of delinquency focusing on young children in their transition from home to school, between the ages of 5 to 6 years rather than at the age when delinquent behaviours become more common. It is based on a report to the Federal government, indicating that life transitions are important times of stress for families, but also important windows of opportunity for intervention (National Crime Prevention, 1999). Implemented in 2002, it is offered through seven primary schools in one of the most disadvantaged areas of Queensland, a community with high economic disadvantage and social hardship. There are no efforts to target 'at risk' children or families. Instead it is targeted at all children of that age in the community, their families and the relevant community social networks. The intervention takes an ecological approach in that it is designed to address individual factors in the children (e.g. poor self control), family factors (e.g. harsh parenting) and school factors (e.g. rejection by peers).

The framework is based on community development, ensuring that it is respon-sive and relevant to community issues, and that there are strong efforts to overcome the barriers to participation identified in the local context, with the aim of providing opportunities for immediate and positive change, working alongside other local agencies to support families. It is based in schools because they provide a direct point of connection with the majority of children (see also Chapter 9). The main 'manualised' aspects of the programme are the *Preschool Intervention Programme* (PIP) and the *Family Independence Programme* (FIP). PIP is presented in classrooms and is designed to enhance children's communication and their social competence. FIP incorporates a range of family support activities, some offered in the home and others in groups in community settings, including behaviour-management training, counseling, adult life-skill training, counseling, welfare assistance and playgroups. An evaluation is underway but results have yet to be published.

Case Study: Federal government, Australia, Stronger Families and Communities

There is some tension in Australia between programmes developed by states and plans put forward by the Federal government. Recently, the Federal government in Australia has initiated the *Stronger Families and Communities* strategy as part of a sharper focus on early childhood (ages 0–5 years). This is one of the key programmes designed by the Department of Family and Community Services to help families and communities build strength and capacity so that they can solve local problems, build on their assets and develop opportunities for the future. In the first instance more than 220 million Australian dollars were committed, from 2000/01 to 2003/04 (http://www.facs.gov.au/internet/facsinternet.nsf/aboutfacs/ programs/sfsc-sfcs.htm). Now running from 2004 to 2008, it includes early intervention, prevention and capacity-building initiatives to support and strengthen families and the communities in which they live. There are three broad outcomes: stronger families; stronger communities and economic and social participation; and it is supported by a budget of 365.8 million Australian dollars. Of the four elements – 'Communities for children', 'Early childhood – invest to grow', 'Local answers' and 'Choice and flexibility in child care' – two can be considered geographical community interventions. *Stronger Families and Communities* focuses in addition on specific concerns about children and families such as increases in cases of child abuse and children in foster care, childhood obesity and type 2 diabetes, mental health issues and a broad spectrum of poorer outcomes for the Indigenous children. Thus it could be seen to be community-oriented in a second way, in that communities of interest are catered for in addition to targeted geographical communities.

Communities for children ($110 million) will target up to 35 disadvantaged communities, providing funding for early childhood initiatives, and working with local stakeholders to deliver early childhood development programmes and services. The aim is to provide child-friendly communities with particular attention being paid to those aged 0 to 5 years. The kinds of activities that are planned include home visiting; early learning and literacy; playgroups; early development of social skills and communication skills; parenting programmes and counseling services; child nutrition; peer support for parents of young children; and community events to celebrate the importance of the early years.

Communities for children is designed to operate in a similar way to *Sure Start Local Programmes* in the UK (see next section), although one local organisation will be identified as the lead to drive and manage the local stakeholder committee that will oversee the development of the community action plan. Supporting children's early development and health will be the focus, for children aged 0–5 years. Like *Sure Start* there will be a mix of services including home-visiting, playgroups, parenting programmes and counseling services, community events and services that enhance learning and literacy. The mix of provision will be based on local decision-making. At the time of writing seven community organisations had received funding to work in communities that represent towns (e.g. Launceston, Tasmania; Lismore, New South Wales); several suburbs of a city (e.g. Girrawheen, Koondoola, Balga and Mirrabooka in Perth, Western Australia); or in more rural areas, several towns together (e.g. Coomera, Cedar Creek and surrounds, Queensland).

Local answers ($60 million) is designed to support small-scale initiatives developed by local organisations to give communities the power to develop their own solutions and 'help them help themselves' (FaCS, 2004). The hope is that activities will strengthen disadvantaged communities and give children a better start in life; build community capacity; encourage the development of partnerships; encourage a preventative and early intervention approach; support people through life transitions; develop better integrated and coordinated services; and finally but most importantly, use the evidence and look to the future. The plan will focus in part on economic development by providing services in the community that will assist young parents to further their education or access to training and other services that will help them to make the transition to employment. There will also be activities designed to assist any member of the community to get involved in community life through local volunteering or mentoring of young people, or by helping to get trained so that they can take on community leadership roles in local groups.

It is hoped that small-scale projects can be developed to solve complex problems, based on the notion that only local community members really know what their community needs (FaCS, 2004). The overall aims include building effective parenting skills, partnerships between local services and assisting young parents to further their education. But not all the interventions are directed at early childhood, some are more concerned with parents. For example, *Family as Community* will help Indigenous people living in camps and residences around Alice Springs to build social capital using kinship networks and extended family. An initiative in Enfield, South Australia, identified as one of the most disadvantaged areas with high numbers of single parents within a culturally diverse community, is to be given $200,000 to continue an early childhood and parenting 'café' that will be a central place for services so that families from the area can get help and access to health, education and community resources in one location. Again, an evaluation is planned but has not yet begun to collect data.

Case Study: Ontario, Canada, Better Beginnings, Better Futures

In Ontario a report from the Early Years Reference Group (McCain & Mustard, 1999) called for a community-based and evolutionary approach to enhancing early child development by building on assets in local communities and involving parents in the development of early childhood initiatives in their communities. The overall aim was to optimise development by re-organising existing services into a more coordinated set of integrated early childhood offerings

The *Better Beginnings, Better Futures* Project (*BBBF*) was the main early childhood intervention to come out of this call for new programmes. More clearly than many of the initiatives discussed in this chapter it is a community intervention, based as it is on ecological principles and Bronfenbrenner's model. The model emphasises the importance of taking into account a wide variety of parent, family, neighbourhood, community and broader societal influences on children's development. It is a

25-year longitudinal project, which commenced in 1991, in eight economically disadvantaged communities in Ontario, Canada (see http://bbbf.queensu.ca/index_e.html for more details).

BBBF has three aims: to prevent serious and long-term emotional and behavioural problems; to promote optimal social, emotional, behavioural, physical and cognitive development; and to strengthen disadvantaged communities so that they can respond more effectively to the social and economic needs of children and their families. Community involvement is integral to the idea, with parents participating as equal partners with service-providers in planning, designing and carrying out programmes for children and families in the community through the establishment of partnerships and with existing and new service providers and schools for the joint co-ordination of programmes,

It has been offered either to children aged 0–4 (in five communities) or 4–8 (in three communities) to all those of the eligible age in the area. These locations were chosen in part because of socio-economic disadvantage. For example, among those interviewed before the programmes were in place (to establish a baseline) in the areas where the younger children were to be targeted, 37% of the families were headed by a single parent, and 83% were below Statistics Canada's Low Income Cut Offs (LICOs). A similar proportion (36%) were headed by a single parent in the communities where four- to eight-year-olds would be the focus, and 64% were below the LICOs (Peters et al., 2000). Annual budgets between 1993 and 1998 were $570,000 representing a cost of $1,400 per family for the younger groups, and $1,130 for the older cohorts. The money came from various government departments: the Ministry of Community and Social Service, the Ministry of Health, the Ministry of Education and Training, the Federal Department of Indian and Northern Affairs and Heritage Canada.

The local community areas are relatively small, with the number of children ranging from 250 to 1,125 for 0–4-year-olds and 503 to 530 for 4–8-year-olds. However, while some of the elements of the programme are directed at families with children (e.g. home-visiting, enrichment of child care, parent-training groups), others are for all community members regardless of whether they have children of the target age, or even children at all (e.g. improving neighbourhood safety, increasing levels of voting, community picnics). All the communities were expected to include specific child-related programmes (home visiting and enriched child care in the 0–4 areas; enriched childcare and school-based programmes in the areas chosen to support 4–8-year-olds), but each of the sites was expected also to develop local projects tailored specifically to local community needs. This allowed for a certain degree of uniqueness within the common goals.

Importantly, evaluation was integral from the start. One strand of the evaluation examines how well the different communities implement the programme and the outcomes for children through interviews with staff covering project organisation, the extent of resident participation, the level to which services are integrated and the costs involved. Between 1993 and 1998 it was found (like *Dorchester CARES*; Mulroy, 1997) that meaningful resident involvement required time, trust, support and a balance between project flexibility and clear ground rules (Peters, 2002). It was found that the *BBBF* organisations served as effective catalysts for partnership-building among local service agencies. Through participation in the initiative they became more knowledgeable about the community and more interested in and trusting of each other, leading to more efficient use of scarce resources. The involvement of local residents was achieved by giving them real power on committees that set budgets, wrote job descriptions and planned services, with the appropriate mentoring and support (Peters et al., 2003a). The evaluation team note, however, that it was a formidable challenge to develop local organisation at each site due to the breadth and innovativeness of the programmes as well as the need to establish relationships of trust with residents and build community links. At least two years were devoted to this process with each steering committee having a minimum of 50% local residents as members. However, the *BBBF* projects are now characterised by strong, vested, local leadership with participants reporting 'greater confidence, self-knowledge, assertiveness, awareness of rights, political awareness and public speaking skills' (Peters et al., 2003b, p. 224).

When the programmes were established, the evaluation of the impact on children and families was initiated. Baseline measures on children, families and neigh-bourhoods were collected in 1992–93 before the local programmes were fully operational, on 350 4-year-old children in the younger cohort sites and 200 8-year-old children in the older cohort sites. These children were compared to others of the same age in the same neighbourhood after four years of *Better Beginnings* programming had been provided.

In three of the four *BBBF* locations targeting 0- to 4-year-olds (Kingston, Ottawa and Toronto), there was a decrease in teacher ratings of children's emotional problems from 1993 to 1998 (Peters et al., 2000). In Kingston teachers also rated children showing decreases in behavioural problems and increases in pro-social behaviours when children were assessed at the time they started school, and there was a substantial increase in the children's school readiness over the same time period. In all the younger cohort *Better Beginnings* communities there was improvement on a measure of children's auditory attention and memory, one of the six subtests from a standardised test of general developmental skills. In addition there were some health benefits: parents reported lower rates of smoking, higher rates of breastfeeding and better diet for children and more timely immunisations at 18 months (Peters, 2001).

Results for a five-year period are available for 4-year-olds and their families recruited in 1993 in the three locations offering services to 4–8-year-olds, who were matched socio-demographically (in terms of language and ethnicity) with children in two control communities (Peters et al., 2003b). Findings indicate significant improvements across all three communities for children's emotional and pro-social behaviour as well as general health. However, there were no gains in the children's cognitive functioning despite classroom enrichment programmes in two of the three areas. The authors suggest this lack of impact is probably due to the fact that all children were receiving regular primary school education, so no 'added value' was provided by the BBBF services, although their behaviour was improved, in comparison with areas without the service.

Progress was identified in all three communities in terms of parent health-risk behaviours and overall family social and emotional function. Significant findings were reductions in smoking (notoriously difficult to attain), reductions in stressful life events and improvements in marital satisfaction. Neighbourhood ratings indicated significantly increased satisfaction with the condition of their homes and parents reported significantly improved school contact.

One of the communities had exceptionally good results with significant parent-rated improvements in children's internalising and externalising behaviour as well as both parent- and teacher-rated improvements in three domains of pro-social behaviour. Furthermore, fewer children were referred for special education needs. There were also improvements in the functioning of parents, who reported improved physical and emotional health as well as significant reductions in prescription medication. They described using significantly more consistent parenting and used fewer hostile parenting strategies, reporting a greater sense of parental efficacy and satisfaction. This group also reported significantly improved social support and improved family functioning and they were more satisfied with their neighbourhoods and their children's schools. Apart from these gains at the individual and family levels, there was increased use of community resources by both parents and children such as the toy-lending library, library, sports and other clubs, parent/child drop-in centre and the parent centre (Peters, et al., 2003a).

What makes these improvements interesting is that this community was the most ethnically diverse and the income gap between this already impoverished community and the province showed a relative increase between 1990 and 1995 (Nelson et al., 2004). Unlike one of the other areas, which had community development as its focus and showed the fewest positive gains, this programme had a strong enrichment programme focused on the target children. Additionally there was a strong focus on life-skills development and programmes for parents and children. This supports the contention (McGuire & Earls, 1991) that it is the child's environment that should be the target of interventions designed to improve child outcomes, rather than attempting to achieve those outcomes indirectly through interventions designed to change parenting behaviour.

In all the locations there were improvements for families and the neighbourhood. For example, reduced rates of domestic violence were recorded in the first two years of the programme. Additionally, parents in the areas that targeted younger children (aged 0–4) described feelings of increased safety when out in the neighbourhood at night and, at two of these locations, antisocial and criminal activity (alcohol and drug use, theft, violence) decreased while community cohesion increased. This suggests that the programme has had a positive impact by reducing community disorganisation, which should then lead to greater community cohesion (Peters et al., 2003b).

With respect to costs, they were modest. The average spend per child per annum was $1,475 (Canadian) (Peters et al., 2003b). This compares favourably with other programmes, e.g. the Comprehensive Child Development Project at $21,000 per family per annum (St Pierre et al., 1997). As evaluations of intensive individual-level initiatives such as the Ypsilanti *Perry Preschool Programme* have found (Schweinhart & Weikart, 1997), the costs of not managing child health and behaviour may be far higher, not only in financial terms, but in human capital terms as well. For instance, Reynolds and Ou (2004) cite statistics from various US sources indicating that an amount of $400 billion is lost annually in productivity and tax, as well as to health-compromising behaviour, crime, welfare and remedial education services. By initiating an evaluation at the outset, this community-based initiative has been able to demonstrate that careful planning, encouraging community buy-in, taking time to promote capacity development and following a child-focused model of development, can produce positive, cost-effective child and family outcomes.

Case Study: United Kingdom, Sure Start Local Programmes

In the UK the Labour government launched a strategy to end child poverty by 2020. As part of a multi-pronged effort outlined in the Comprehensive Spending Review (CSR) of July 1998, the Chancellor of the Exchequer introduced the plan for the *Sure Start* programme:

> We plan to bring together quality services for the under-3s and their parents – nursery, childcare and playgroup provision, and pre-natal and other health services. One new feature will be to extend to parents the offer of counselling and help to prepare their children for learning and for school (HM Treasury, July 1998a, p. 5).

The planning was ambitious, designed to create 250 *Local Programmes*, and the government made £452 million available over three years to enable this to happen (HM Treasury, 1998b). The size of the initiative was subsequently doubled so that 524 programmes were eventually created. The need for such an initiative was based on information that disadvantage among young children was increasing in the UK, that this could result in difficulties for these children in later life, and that the earlier intervention was undertaken, the more likelihood there was that poor outcomes could be prevented (HM Treasury, 1998b). The report noted that current services were uncoordinated and patchy, that children under 3 often missed out on services (which tended to concentrate on later age groups), and that the quality of services varied from area to area. There were, nevertheless, said to be examples of good practice based on evidence, and these could inform a new programme aimed at this age group. Among the report's recommendations was a change of approach to the design and delivery of local services: all relevant bodies, both within the local authority and outside it, should jointly plan these. It was said that:

> Sure Start is a cross-Departmental programme. Its aim is "to work with parents-to-be, parents and children to promote the physical, intellectual and social development of babies and young children – particularly those who are disadvantaged – to ensure that they can flourish at home and when they get to school, and thereby break the cycle of disadvantage for the current generation of young children". It is intended to promote joined-up and innovative working at the local level, looking at need from the perspective of young families. In layman's terms they provide better access to family support, advice on nurturing, health services and early learning, through a partnership involving local authorities, health practitioners, parents and voluntary and community organisations (Sure Start Unit, 2002, p. 94).

The *Sure Start Local Programme* (SSLP) areas were to be small, pram-pushing areas and they were to make sense to the local community, reflecting the government's concern with pockets of intense deprivation where the problems of unemployment and crime were said to be acute and hopelessly tangled up with poor health, housing and education (Social Exclusion Unit, 1998). Local partnerships were integral to the plans although these were complex arrangements:

> It has become increasingly common for government initiatives to be delivered through what are confusingly termed "partnerships". Although the words "partners" or "partnership" are used, this does not mean that the initiative will be delivered by a single entity, i.e. legal partnership or incorporated company. In the majority of cases nothing more than a management board/committee has been formed. In other words the partners have not created a single legal entity to deliver the programme, but rather they work together to achieve a single aim. The membership of these partnership programmes generally includes local authorities, police authorities, NHS trusts, doctors, parents, local businessmen, charities, etc. Membership is so wide as the aim of these programmes is to involve the local community in activities which will directly affect them. Although the members may include large local authorities and parents, all parties have an equal say in policy development (Sure Start Unit, 2002, p. 88).

Thus SSLPs were designed to be comprehensive, community-based projects adapted to local needs, making sense of local expertise and enthusiasms, capitalising on shared concerns of community residents (Oliver, Smith & Barker, 1998). They were expected to contribute equally, alongside professionals.

> The Sure Start partnership, although made up of individual members representing a wide range of interests, exists for Sure Start purposes and not to further the aims of any particular member organisation. All members must be clear about their role within the Partnership and feel able to participate as equal partners (Sure Start Unit, 2002, p. 29).

By targeting disadvantaged communities rather than at-risk children and families they were designed to be stigma-free while at the same time addressing the problem of social exclusion. There were government-defined aims and targets (summarised in Box 7.3) but no specified ways to achieve those. It was recommended that while the services provided in each community should be based as much as possible on evidence, the activities in each SSLP should be 'bottom-up', reflecting local needs and capitalising on local strengths.

The whole enterprise has been evaluated from the outset, both nationally and within each local area. The national evaluation is examining whether or not existing services change, by looking at the implementation of SSLPs in England, the cost of providing services and whether children, families and communities benefit. This is being achieved in part by looking at the impact on a large sample of children and parents in 150 of the communities and comparing them with those in areas without *Sure Start*, and by looking at change over time in the communities themselves in the first 260 programmes (NESS Research Team, 2004). Local evaluations are generally more modest in their aims (which are all chosen locally) and many have focused, at least in the first instance, on the process of getting their partnership together (Myers, Barnes & Brodie, 2004).

The national evaluation first examined the process of getting started (Ball & NESS Research Team, 2002). It found that the nature of existing relationships in the Partnership was the most significant factor in setting up a local programme.

Box 7.3   Sure Start Local Programmes in England. Aim and Public Service Agreement (PSA) Targets for 2001/02–2003/04[2]

Aim: To work with parents-to-be, parents and children to promote the physical, intellectual and social development of babies and children – particularly those who are disadvantaged – so that they can flourish at home and when they get to school, and thereby break the cycle of disadvantage for the current generation of young children.

TARGET – IMPROVING SOCIAL AND EMOTIONAL DEVELOPMENT

Reduce the proportion of children aged 0–3 who are re-registered within the space of 12 months on the child protection register by 20 per cent by 2004.

TARGET – IMPROVING HEALTH

Achieve by 2004 a 10 per cent reduction in mothers who smoke in pregnancy.

TARGET – IMPROVING THE ABILITY TO LEARN

Achieve by 2004 for children aged 0–3 a reduction of five percentage points in the number of children with speech and language problems requiring specialist intervention by the age of four.

TARGET – STRENGTHENING FAMILIES

Reduce the number of 0–3 year old children living in households where no one is working.

Sure Start Unit, 2002

The time it took to set up the core and delivery services was generally longer than had been anticipated, because there was always a range of interests on *Sure Start* partnerships, and these had to reach agreement about the details of implementation and make decisions in consultation with parents and the community. Yet it was important to have services operating from the outset, to reassure parents that *Sure Start* had arrived and was going to be an active programme. It was reported

---

[2] These targets have been modified in a number of ways in successive years.

that community consultation could become unbalanced, with discussions about small details taking too much time and insufficient attention to important implementation questions (which might then have to be left until a further meeting). Consultation with sufficient local parents was challenging but more effective when statutory agencies in the area had some history of sharing power with local people. Engagement of parents proved particularly difficult in rural areas, where transport was a key issue.

The successful establishment of partnerships with local agencies depended to a great extent on the skills of the programme managers (Tunstill et al., 2005a) and their ability to develop clear lines of accountability and responsibility. However, there were still issues surrounding the wide range of professionals involved. The evaluation concluded that training to work in multi-agency partnerships was required. Findings from evaluations conducted locally in specific *Sure Start* programmes found that parents on the whole welcomed the opportunity to be members of local partnerships and their presence was seen as vital to the process. However some expressed concern that their own commitment was not always matched by that of the representatives of statutory agencies, and they were sometimes disconcerted by the heavy use of jargon at meetings. They also felt ill-prepared and would have liked more training (Myers, Barnes & Brodie, 2004).

One aspect of implementing an initiative is to decide which services to create or strengthen, and then to spend the money to make this happen. What has become clear is that it is not always easy for these community groups to spend the money allocated to them. In fact it took on average between 24 and 36 months for the full range of services to be offered, to have capital developments (new buildings) in place and to be spending at their peak level, with some SSLPs not fully operational in terms of spending until the fourth year (DfES, 2004).

In addition to the programmes' capacity to plan services and then spend money on them, the implementation module of the national evaluation has examined the balance of services offered by the different programmes. One challenge of targeting services at all eligible children in a community is that the service needs to know who those children are and where they live. The engagement and involvement of the maximum number of eligible children and parents is a key challenge for SSLPs. Although the programmes have been making sustained and diverse attempts to reach their target children and families, most have not been able to document that this rather important target was achieved (Tunstill et al., 2002). Most success has been noted in communities where there is strong support from the health professionals, such as midwives and health visitors, who have access to databases with the relevant information, at least at the point when the children are born, though special effort is required to locate in-movers. This suggests that not all partnerships have reached consensus about SSLPs being a group effort bringing together health, education and child welfare. The health professionals in all the communities will have access to this information as part of the National Health Service database, but clearly not all have shared the names and addresses of eligible children.

Locating children aged 0–3 in the community has in consequence required continuous effort even after programmes have become fully operational.

The national evaluation identified a five-stage continuum of access to children and families, starting with the initial contact (Tunstill et al., 2005b). This embraces as a first step diverse out-reach efforts, including leafleting campaigns; face-to-face outreach work; and community events organised in order to build relationships with the community. At the same time, initial contact of a family with the programme may derive from signposting by a mainstream or local voluntary agency. For example, a mainstream maternity service would make contact with a parent when a woman 'books' her first appointment with a GP and signpost her to the SSLP. A second step on the continuum reflects the work undertaken by *Sure Start* to introduce individual parents to the programme after they have learned about the initiative. The third stage is the point at which a parent decides to take up a service on their own, followed by the fourth point on the continuum, where they spontaneously take up more than one service (SSLPs typically have 30 or more services). Finally, the evaluation team determined that a family could be seen as fully integrated into the community of services when they were confident enough to look beyond the geographically targeted services of the SSLP and explore service provision in the wider area.

While a community-focused service is in theory offered to all children of the target age and their parents, in reality mothers are more likely to become involved than fathers. A themed study examining the involvement of fathers in SSLPs found that fathers had a preference for fun and active sessions over discussion-based ones, and staff indicated that it was easier to involve fathers in outdoor, active, fun-day-type activities than in indoor sessions with children or in sessions related to parenting skills (Lloyd, O'Brien & Lewis, 2003).

Examination of the areas chosen for the programmes confirmed that they were experiencing consistently worse deprivation than elsewhere in England on indicators such as child and adult health, educational achievement, crime, unemployment and benefit dependence (Barnes et al., 2003). However, it has also been revealed that when one applies an intervention in such a large-scale manner, across the country, there are major differences in the pattern and type of deprivation encountered in these communities. As with unhappy families, they are all different! Thus, while some are averagely deprived, or markedly deprived, others are relatively advantaged (Barnes et al., 2005a). Yet other communities are typified by higher concentrations of ethnic minority families. The original policy decision to allow bottom-up local decision-making about how to meet targets and objectives seems sensible, based on this level of variability, but this diversity provides a major challenge for the evaluation of implementation and impact.

Nevertheless, there are some indications that the areas themselves, and the services within them, are changing as a consequence of the presence of the *Sure Start* programmes. Over three years the rates of referral to social services have risen consistently, for all children up to age 16 but particularly for those children under 5 (Barnes et al., 2004; Barnes et al., 2005b). There have also been increases in the proportion of young children identified with special educational needs in the *Sure Start* areas, and in those attending special schools. The eventual aim of the initiative is to help families to be more effective parents, requiring less social service attention. But in the short term it seems likely that the enhanced and more 'joined-up' services have been able to identify more families in need of support and guidance, and more children who would benefit from specialist services to help them attain their potential.

One of the major aims of the initiative was to reduce the number of children living in poverty, and the proportion of children in the target age-range 0–4 living in households dependent on state benefits has dropped in two successive years (Barnes et al., 2004, 2005b). However, it is not clear to what extent the decrease is specific to *Sure Start* areas, since there has also been a drop in England overall. Thus far, few changes can be linked to the length of time programmes have been in operation, or to any other measure of implementation of services.

Although the evaluation of the impact of SSLPs is ongoing, since 2003 there has been a move away from programmes focusing on tightly-defined local geographical community areas, and services are now organised by larger administrative areas defined according to local authority boundaries. The new services are focused around *Children's Centres*, thus taking the concept away from community development although still offering community-based services to children and families (Sure Start Unit, 2003). While some of the aims and targets are similar to those defined for SSLPs, the agenda for the new *Children's Centres* places more emphasis on day care (see Box 7.4). These centres will not be managed by partnerships, reducing some of the community involvement. Instead they will be managed by local authorities. While they are still conceptualised as focusing on areas of disadvantage, the definition of the area to be targeted will be much more loosely adhered to:

> To achieve 'reach' targets local authorities must set a notional catchment area for every children's centre. The Sure Start Unit expects every local authority, within its proposals, to plan to ensure that **at least** 30% of the children to be reached are additional to those served by existing or planned local Sure Start programmes in the area. However, early education and childcare facilities should be available to families beyond the catchment, as it is important to ensure there is a mix of children from all backgrounds. This has been shown to deliver better outcomes for children from disadvantaged areas and will also help ensure day care is sustainable.
>
> Catchment areas will be focused in the main on the 20% most disadvantaged wards, but it will be possible to include pockets of disadvantage. Local authorities should give consideration to current patterns of usage for existing provision when planning. Catchment areas should not be set so rigidly that families lose choice over provision of childcare or early education provider (Sure Start Unit, 2003, p. 8).

This policy shift is interesting in that it suggests that the notion of the small, village-style community may be losing popularity, together with the strong focus on involving all community members in the planning, provision and even evaluation of services. In its place a more pragmatic service is emerging, meeting some community development ideals by bringing services together in convenient, local settings, but designed primarily at the family level, helping parents to move out into the workplace if they should wish, but requiring less participation in the services.

Box 7.4   Children's Centres in England. Aim and public service level targets

AIM

Increase the availability of childcare for all children, and work with parents-to-be, parents and children to promote the physical, intellectual and social development of babies and young children – particularly those who are disadvantaged – so that they can flourish at home and at school, enabling their parents to work and contributing to the ending of child poverty.

PERFORMANCE TARGETS

We will achieve by 2005–06 in fully operational programmes: An increase in the proportion of young children aged 0–5 with normal levels of personal, social and emotional development for their age;

A six-percentage point reduction in the proportion of mothers who continue to smoke during pregnancy;

An increase in the proportion of children having normal levels of communication, language and literacy at the end of the Foundation Stage[3], and an increase in the proportion of young children with satisfactory speech and language development at age two;

A 12 percent reduction in the proportion of young children living in households where no one is working.

SERVICE DELIVERY AGREEMENT TARGETS

All families with new-born babies in SSLP and Children's Centre areas to be visited in the first two months of the baby's life and given information about the services and support available to them.

Information and guidance on breastfeeding, nutrition, hygiene and safety available to all families with young children in SSLP and Children's Centre areas.

Reduce by 10% the number of children aged 0–4 living in SSLP and Children's Centre areas admitted to hospital as an emergency with gastro-enteritis, a lower respiratory infection or a severe injury.

Antenatal advice and support available to all pregnant women and their families living in SSLP and Children's Centre areas.

Sure Start Unit, 2005, pp. 3–4

---

[3] Teacher assessments when children are at the end of the Foundation Stage, from 3–5 years, covering six areas of learning.

IMPLICATIONS FOR COMMUNITY INTERVENTION

The case studies described in this chapter show that the decision to involve communities in the lives of young children and their families has been taken in a number of countries. Many of the initiatives, large and small, are based on ecological ideology and theory, some more explicitly so than others. Bronfenbrenner and others after him have demonstrated that influences beyond the immediate family are important in explaining children's development and family functioning. However, the question remains as to whether the declaration made in *Starting Points* is justified. Should there be an emphasis on strengthening communities in order that they may strengthen family life, which is expected in turn to enhance child development? Possibly it is actually better to devote resources directly to children. It was found in the *Early Head Start* evaluation that children had made cognitive gains, but that this was particularly the case in those areas where the services, provided in centres, were directed specifically at the children. Similarly, the *Better Beginnings Better Futures* programme that identified the greatest gains for children was also one that was providing more services focused directly on children.

In many cases, the implementation of community-focused services, involving local people in decision-making, has not been straightforward. It is challenging to translate participatory and bottom-up ideals and aims into practice, and even more challenging to evaluate the effectiveness of such approaches. Indeed it is not clear that it is feasible to mobilise sufficient collaboration between professionals working in the same neighbourhoods, let alone collaboration between professional groups and local community members. One needs to ask whether it is sensible to insist, as many of these initiatives do, that local families always have some decision-making power about the provision of community-strengthening services, and their evaluation. Many parents find their time sorely stretched just coping with day-to-day life, and those in disadvantaged communities are often unlikely to spend much time involved in community groups (Barnes, 2004).

Clearly one can provide communities with money, and they will report back that partnerships or collaborations have been brought together. Some local parents will become involved and will report that they appreciate the various opportunities offered to them – for additional training, for ways to meet neighbours and for ways to work or play with their children. These groupings between parents and a range of professionals are not created without some difficulty however. Once formed, it is not clear how the community partnerships typical of most of these initiatives translate into better outcomes for parents and children. One thing is apparent, however, and that is that some of these initiatives move from being experimental to widespread, even national, implementation without the benefit of evidence.

Evaluations are in place for many of these programmes, but the reality of evaluation is that, when it is done properly, results take time to emerge and a long-term perspective is essential. Beyond the issues related to any intervention expected to effect change in children's development, or in family functioning, there are many issues relating to the evaluation of communities that are proving taxing to evaluation experts (Hollister & Hill, 1995). What has been shown however in both large and small-scale community development programmes is that there are many teething problems in the early stages if one attempts to implement services that truly address a community's needs. The requirements identified may be quite different from those the programme's instigators consider to be the most important ones, either to promote child development or to prevent parenting problems. Keeping true to community development principles means that a range of community development activities needs to be put in place prior to any programmes designed to support the development of young children or to promote effective parenting. Overall, while community development is an important aim in its own right, the jury is still out on whether it is sensible to direct resources to community development if one wants to enhance child development or to prevent child abuse. It may be better to focus on the children or the parents directly, albeit by providing easily accessible community-based services.

8

CHILDREN'S PARTICIPATION IN COMMUNITY CONSULTATION AND PLANNING

INTRODUCTION

As the quality of children's lives in communities became more of a public policy and research issue through the late twentieth century, concerns to include children and young people in the improvement and revitalisation of communities grew. Governmental organisations and professional groups, from local councillors to environmental planners, became increasingly aware of the need to be child and family sensitive in the complex task of reviving ailing neighbourhoods, cities and service infrastructures (e.g. *Children's rights and habitat*, UNICEF, 1996).

As outlined in Chapter 5 there have also been a number of voices raised to protest about the fear that more recent generations of children have become increasingly restricted in their movements in the local neighbourhood, less like members of the community than young people of the past (Furedi, 1997; Hillman, 1993). While parental perceptions of child abduction and the dominance of motorised traffic on our streets are contributory factors limiting children's quality of life (Hillman, 2001) others have commented on a lack of suitable facilities, or facilities that are provided without consultation with the children themselves (Worpole, 2003).

Ironically, while health experts and psychologists all argue that the opportunity to explore and experience neighbourhoods and communities, without adult supervision, is seen as a necessary experience to foster appropriate child development and to provide youngsters with the tools necessary to cope with the external environment, there has been policy shift in community development towards youth and crime prevention which treats children as either 'victims or villains' with the associated regulation over child freedoms (Waiton, 2001).

Furthermore, current societal obsession with reducing risk and increasing the regulation of children has contributed to fostering mistrust between children, and between children and adults, not to mention contributing to health problems such as asthma and obesity as youngsters are transported by their parents in cars and other vehicles. In sum, the 'safety first' approach has deeply influenced children and young people's perceptions and practices within their neighbourhoods and in some instances reduces the likelihood that they will be involved in community planning.

Nevertheless, on the building sites of many global cities children's drawings and paintings have begun to mingle with scaffolding, as markers of 'child-friendly' urban regeneration. Children and young people are beginning to join adults as users and improvers of the city and neighbourhood environment and an awareness of the importance of working with children, and their families, in their local neighbourhoods and special places is developing. For instance in an important UK Urban Task Force led by the architect, Lord Richard Rogers, in the late 1990s, it was recognised that the quality of life for children is a key barometer of the good enough neighbourhood, city or community.

> In persuading people to re-consider urban living we have to recognise that... the crunch comes with having children. An urban environment, previously perceived as diverse and stimulating, starts to appear unsafe. Schools and health services become more important (Rogers, 1999, p. 35).

Ascertaining children's views on the public services in their communities, whether they be educational, leisure or health, has also become more common (e.g. the *Children's Fund*, DfES, 2005), as Fajerman, Treseder and Connor (2004) declare 'Children are service users too'.

> The needs of children and youth, particularly with regard to their living environment, have to be taken fully into account. Special attention needs to be paid to the participatory processes dealing with the shaping of cities, towns and neighbourhoods: this is in order to secure the living conditions of children and of youth to make use of their insight, creativity and thoughts on the environment (UNICEF: 1996, section 1.13)

Engagement of children and young people in service development represents wider moves to enhance consumer/'user' choice about the extent and quality of public services. It also signifies a shift away from using parents' views as proxies for children's perspectives in line with increasing recognition of children as social actors in their own right (James & Prout, 1990). Central to these developments is the principle of children's *participation* in the society of which they are a part. This entitlement to participate is embedded in legislative and governmental frameworks.

LEGISLATIVE AND GOVERNMENTAL FRAMEWORKS

The movement away from children being perceived as only recipients of welfare or adult care towards ideas that children are 'juristic persons with distinctive rights' or individuals with preferences has a long history (Bainham, 1998, p. 48). The societal process is a gradual democratisation of relationships between the generations which became accelerated across industrialising nations in the post-war period (Archard, 1993). This reconfiguration of formal relationships between adults and children was symbolised by the codification of children's rights in the *UN Convention of the Rights of the Child 1989* http://www.unicef.org/crc/text.htm.

The importance of children's participation has its roots in a series of articles in this legislation, which assumed that children should be active and contributing participants in society and not just receive treatment from those adults around them. Article 12, in particular, has gained great salience in the participation debate. It states that children, depending on their age and maturity, have the right to express an opinion about matters of relevance and to have that opinion taken into account when public decisions are made. The UN Convention has been ratified by most governments across the world and by the British Government in 1991. The Children Act 1989 also placed a duty on public bodies to listen to children and give appropriate weight to their views, as has the Human Rights Act 1998. Accordingly a commitment to involving children and young people has been central to recent policy developments in children's services across the world and to specific guidance for service operational arrangements.

The British Government set up a cross-departmental Children and Young People's Unit (CYPU) in 2001, a precursor to a first children's division, the Child and Family Directorate, within a ministry (Department for Education and Skills) in 2003 and announced:

> The Government wants children and young people to have more opportunities to get involved in the design, provision and evaluation of policies and services that affect them or which they use (CYPU, 2001).

More recently, the guidance has become quite specified.

> We want children, young people and their families to be at the heart of service design and delivery, across both mainstream and more specialist services (DfES, 2003). www.dfes.gov.uk/childrenstrusts/pdfs/guidejan03.pdf

In Britain a further driver for the governmental impetus to engage children and youth perspectives has been an attempt to engage young adults in conventional party political processes as a counter-weight to a perceived 'democratic deficit': 18–24 year olds are much less likely to say they will vote in contrast to 25 year olds and over (18% vs. 43%; Aspden & Birch, 2005). The promotion of 'active citizenship' amongst children and young people, now taught directly though the educational curriculum in many countries also illustrates governmental aspirations to connect children to the public sphere of civic activity.

CHILDREN AS SOCIAL ACTORS

The globalisation of children's rights had its impact on all aspects of children's lives from their relationship with their parents to their participation in school and other social institutions. Towards the end of the twentieth century the representation of children as having a right to 'a life of their own' became commonplace in social analysis and legal discourse (Beck, 1998). Similarly the paradigm of childhood sociology (Jenks, 1996; James & Prout, 1990) emphasising children's position as 'social actors' and as creative and inventive users of the world around them, emerged and transformed how other academic disciplines focusing on children such as psychology and education, approached their province. As Alanen argued at the time:

> Sociologists need not, and should not, content themselves with the notion that children belong primarily to the province of psychology, education and pediatrics (1990, p. 25).

Implicit in childhood sociology was a critique of a developmental psychology paradigm, which had tended to be the main sub-discipline for research on children along with education. These writers have argued that the powerful perspective of developmentalism has rendered children dependent, relegating to them to 'waiting rooms' and to being adults in the making rather than children in the state of being.

Whilst it is the case that developmental psychology had tended to focus on and recognise children only in terms of their developmental needs it was also the case that the academic sub-discipline itself had been in the process of change and self-questioning for many years. Groups of developmentalists both in Europe (e.g. Richards, 1974) and in the US (e.g. Elder, Modell and Parke, 1993) had started to place their study of children in the wider context of cultural and historical change. The new 1990s social studies of childhood nurtured a blossoming of conceptual and empirical explorations of children's competency and agency in a range of diverse settings including neighbourhood contexts (e.g. Corsaro, 1997; Qvortrup, Bardy, Sgritta & Wintersberger, 1994). A focus on generation, particularly relationships between the generations emerged, and analysis of inter-generational age relations as a new social category of inquiry alongside gender and class developed (e.g. Alanen & Mayall, 2001).

WHAT IS CHILDREN'S PARTICIPATION?

Over this period a wide range of definitions concerning the concept of 'children's participation' emerged. Boyden and Ennew (1997) make the distinction between those interpretations which stress the importance of children 'being there' and 'taking part' in the event, decision or project, and those who emphasise the outcome, influence or power which children have in the decision-making process or event itself. Some writers incorporate both dimensions in their definition. For instance in Matthews, Limb and Taylor's (1999) analysis of youth councils, they suggest that 'Participation implies processes of involvement, shared responsibility and active engagement in decisions which affect the quality of life' (1999, p. 136). They recognise, however, that the style or culture of participation can vary considerably; participation can be 'a learning strategy', 'a chance to redefine the structures' or 'the cornerstone of democracy and inclusive citizenship' (1999, p. 143).

While citizenship is now part of the curriculum in the UK, one study in the Isle of Wight in southern England found that few had ever been asked their opinion about any issue relating to their community, although almost three-quarters of those surveyed wanted to give their opinions (Weller, 2003). Accessibility of space was a key issue for the teenagers and in one village youngsters had been active, preserving a bus shelter due for demolition and gaining agreement that the local youth could decorate it themselves and keep it as a meeting place.

The youth in the example above were able to achieve something concrete and were allowed some decision-making. However Hart (1997) highlighted the fact that much 'participation' by children and youth is tokenistic. During the 1990s writers developed and reformed typologies of children's participation, from Roger Hart's (1997) adaptation of Arnstein's eight rungs on the ladder of citizen participation (described in more detail in Chapter 6), to Treseder's (1997) circular rearrangement, reflecting a less hierarchical formation. Hart's model, the most influential in the field, places 'manipulation and deception' at the lowest rung of the children's participation ladder with 'child initiated, shared decision-making with adults' at the highest level. According to Hart's approach, using children's own artefacts, such as photographs, diaries or drawings, for a project in which children are ill informed or indeed deceived, would constitute examples of the lowest rung of participation. Indeed such practices would not now be approved in research ethics committees. Hart places the decorative use of children, for instance in the openings of new community projects or buildings for which they have been un-involved, as on the next rung up, followed by tokenistic children's participation (for instance presence at a neighbourhood advisory committee without clear role clarity, induction or personalised support). Forms of participation still higher up the ladder range from: assigned but informed (adult top-down procedures about which children are informed); consulted and informed (children have some role in creating the procedures and terms of engagement); 'adult-initiated shared decision-making with children' (involving children in all stages of the process, even though the project is adult-initiated); child-initiated and child-directed (activities for instance competitions, games or fund raising events started spontaneously and seen through to completion by children); and finally child-initiated, shared decisions with adults (children's ideas facilitated by relevant and influential adults). (See Box 8.1 for use of this approach with a local *Children's Fund* evaluation.)

Box 8.1   Children's participation in *Children's Fund* projects (5–13 years)

Regional Project leaders were asked which statement was most applicable:

A: Services are initiated and directed by children and young people and decision-making is shared with adults – the adults are involved primarily in a supportive role (9%, 4 of 46).

B. Services are initiated by adults but decision-making is shared with the children and young people (61%, 28 of 46). Adult-initiated, shared decision-making with children *most* common.

C: Children and young people give advice on projects or services that are designed and run by adults. The children and young people are informed about how their input will be used and the outcomes of the decisions made by adults (24%, 11 of 46).

D: Children and young people are assigned a specific role and informed about how and why they are being involved. Assigned but informed *least* common.

E: Children and young people appear to be given a voice, but in practice have little or no choice about what they do or how they participate (7%, 3 of 46).

Source: Lincolnshire Children's Fund, O'Brien et al., 2004.

Hart's dimensions of participation have provided a very helpful platform for practitioners wishing to understand how to promote children's authentic engagement in social and public activities, whilst being criticised for their inherent hierarchical structure and apparent prescriptive quality (Tisdall & Davis, 2004).

A similar hierarchical approach to conceptualising children's participation has been proposed by Shier (2001) who also has incorporated a pragmatic operational emphasis for practitioners. At various points in a snakes and ladders style model, organisations are invited to respond to a checklist of questions in order to assess their level of child participation. His model is organised around five levels of child participation, from level one where 'children are listened to' to level five where 'children share power and responsibility for decision-making' and a linked set of three themes at each level – 'openings', 'opportunities' and 'obligations'. At the inter-face of level and theme lie a series of questions. For example at level four the 'opening' question is 'Are you ready to let children join your decision-making processes?' If the answer is yes then the opportunity available to children is assessed by the question 'Is there a procedure that enables children to join in the decision-making process?' followed by the 'obligation' question, which explores whether 'there is a policy requirement that children must be involved'. Shier's model is built around the UNCRC Article 12.1 where children and young people's views will be given 'due weight', with a suggestion that an organisation is compliant with the Article as it moves from level three to level four in its mode of operation. By level four Shier (2001, p. 113) posits that an organisation has negotiated 'the transition from consultation to active participation'.

Other writers have used the concept of 'organisational cultures' of children's participation in order to enable flexibility in the choice and mode of participatory activity practitioners and children adopt (Kirby et al., 2003). After an audit of several hundred participatory groups and sets of actions in the UK, Kirby et al. suggest that organisations can be characterised as embracing either: 'consultation' focused cultures (users inform service, product or project development); 'participation' focused cultures (context specific and time bound engagement activities) or 'child/youth' focused cultures (where participation is intrinsic and key to the organisational identity and ethos). The writers also trace a range of organisational processes which consultation, participatory and child/youth focused cultures could adopt, showing how involving children and children's perspectives can: unfreeze pre-existing attitudes and behaviours; serve as catalysts for change champions or models of collaborative practice for working with children as partners; enable new shared visions of children's work to emerge and be internalised by organisational actors; and also function to consolidate or institutionalise new ways of working so that they become part of the mainstream service context and no longer marginal. Kirby et al.'s new concepts and handbook of participatory techniques is an important contribution to reframing the field of children's participation in action.

It should also be noted that this general participatory approach is becoming apparent within evaluation methodology, with increasing recognition of children as users, and therefore stakeholders, within children's services and hence necessary contributors to any evaluation of such services (e.g. Clark, McQuail & Moss, 2003; Sinclair, 2004).

CASE STUDIES OF CHILDREN'S PARTICIPATION IN COMMUNITY CONSULTATION AND PLANNING

Case Study. UNESCO Growing Up in Cities project www.unesco.org/ most/growing.htm

Growing Up in Cities uses a participatory action research paradigm to involve young people in low- and mixed-income districts in evaluating their urban environments and collaborating with adults to plan and implement improvements. The project was initiated in the 1970s by Kevin Lynch, an urban designer and advocacy planner, who coordinated eight project locations across Mexico, Argentina, Poland and Australia under the sponsorship of UNESCO. In his early work he recommended choosing areas which had undergone or were currently undergoing, rapid change (Lynch, 1977). He built on urban design work (Lynch 1960) promoting a multi-method, multi-person research design:

- making initial acquaintance with the children, their parents and becoming familiar with the area;
- individual interviews with children, parents and planners about the neighbourhood in the present and in the past;
- spatial discussions, observations and guided tours;
- use of spatial diary;
- group discussions and tours;
- observation of spatial behaviour.

Lynch's view was that an optimal local environment or city should have clarity and vividness for the observer, whether child or adult – an 'imageability'. As he remarked 'Complete chaos without a hint of connection is never pleasurable'

(Lynch, 1960, p. 6); by contrast, he argued, a distinctive image can create a sense of emotional security and familiarity for city dwellers. In his earlier consultation with adults he focused on how the physical and social environment interact and discovered the importance of paths (channels of movements such as streets), edges (boundaries between places such as walls), districts (medium to large sections of cities), nodes (strategic points such as squares or hang-out street corner areas) and finally landmarks (reference points such as a sign or a tree) in creating a sense of connectedness and clarity.

Through his detailed studies of Boston, Jersey City and Los Angeles he portrayed how encouraging sensitivity to environmental imageability amongst both citizens and professionals could be an illuminating experience in itself.

> To some degree, the very process of reshaping a city to improve its imageability may itself sharpen the image, regardless of how unskilful the resulting physical form may be. Thus the amateur painter begins to see the world around him: the novice decorator begins to take pride in her living room and to judge others. Although such a process can become sterile if not accompanied by increasing control and judgement, even awkward "beautification" of a city may in itself be an intensifier of civic energy and cohesion (Lynch, 1960, p. 117).

In 1995 the *Growing Up in Cities* project was revived with the support of the Norwegian Centre for Child Research, Childwatch International of Oslo and the MOST Programme of UNESCO (Management of Social Transformations): this time detailed studies of neighbourhoods in Argentina, Australia, England, India, Norway, Poland, South Africa and the United States were included and some areas were compared over time (see Chawla, 2002; Chawla & Malone, 2003; Driskell, 2002; www.unesco.org/most/growing.htm).

As in the original Lynch investigation, children and youth (mainly 10–15 year olds) were asked to draw the area they lived in and to discuss their drawings. The interview explored their perceptions of this area, what they liked best or least, places they felt 'their own' or places which they avoided. Children's perceptions of neighbourhood changes and future prospects were also examined. Chawla notes how crime, pollution, ethnic tension and traffic were more frequently mentioned in children's accounts of 1990s urban life when contrasted to the 1970s studies. However, commonalities in the features characterising children's positive and negative neighbourhoods, whether they be urban or more rural, was striking. Despite socio-economic variations across communities they found similarities in how children and youth evaluated their cities as positive or negative places to live (see Table 8.1 for a summary).

The positive features or 'indicators of integration' included both the 'physical infrastructure' of place but also the 'social relations' of the neighbourhood setting. The provision of basic needs, such as water and sanitation and security of tenure, were crucial but children also valued having varied places to go to, particularly with friends. As Lynch found, clear imageability, geographically bounded spaces for un-programmed activity or 'hanging out' (for older youth) was a significant positive feature. Having safe green spaces was also valued. By contrast negative features of neighbourhoods or 'indicators of alienation' were places where basic needs could not be met and where environments were insecure or dangerous

Table 8. 1 Indicators of community quality from children's perspectives

Positive indicators	Negative indicators
Social integration: Children feel welcome and valued in their community	**Social exclusion**: Children feel unwelcome and harassed in their community.
Cohesive community identity: The community has clear geographic boundaries and a positive identity that is expressed through activities like art and festivals.	**Stigma**: Residents feel stigmatised for living in a place associated with poverty and discrimination.
Tradition of self-help: Residents are building their community through mutual aid organisations and progressive local improvements.	**Violence and crime**: Due to community violence and crime, children are afraid to move about outdoors.
	Heavy traffic: The streets are taken over by dangerous traffic.
Safety and free movement: Children feel that they can count on adult protection and range safely within their local area.	**Lack of gathering places**: Children lack places where they can safely meet and play with friends.
Peer gathering places: There are safe and accessible places where friends can meet.	**Lack of varied activity settings**: The environment is barren and isolating, with a lack of interesting places to visit and things to do.
Varied activity settings: Children can shop, explore, play sports and follow up other personal interests in the environment.	**Boredom**: Children express high levels of boredom and alienation.
Safe green spaces: Safe, clean green spaces with trees, whether formal or wild, extensive or small, are highly valued when available.	**Trash and litter**: Children read trash and litter in their environment as signs of adult neglect for where they live.
Provision for basic needs: Basic services are provided such as food, water, electricity, medical care and sanitation.	**Lack of provision for basic needs**: When basic services like clean water and sanitation are lacking, children feel these deprivations keenly.
Security of tenure: Family members have legal rights over the properties they inhabit either through ownership or secure rental agreements.	**Insecure tenure**: Children, like their parents, suffer anxiety from fear of eviction, which discourages investment in better living conditions.
	Political powerlessness: Children and their families feel powerless to improve conditions.

Source: Chawla & Malone, 2003, p. 122.

because of traffic, gangs or unfriendliness. Lack of places and spaces to meet other children or to engage in varied activities also created boring and alienating neighbourhoods.

Malone's Australian case study (Chawla & Malone, 2003) illustrates this latest programme of work, which again mainly involved 10 through 15 year olds, in the same neighbourhood covered in the 1990s. Braybrook is a working class estate built in a Melbourne suburb, from cheap building materials ('a concrete jungle') which has had insufficient investment in refurbishment over the years. When Malone commenced her work she was depressed to find that few if any of the recommendations to the local council from the early project had been adopted and furthermore many of the themes of youth dissatisfaction with their neighbourhood continued.

> Empty streets, shuttered shop windows and the deserted treeless parks created an air of anxiety and fear. From behind closed doors and Venetian blinds, residents surveyed the streets. Many of these residents were young people home alone, watching television or babysitting siblings while their parents attended to work or recreation outside the neighbourhood. For most young people, the quintessential experience of growing up in Braybrook, in the 1990s as well as in the 1970s, has been to feel alienated and disconnected from their physical and social surroundings (Chawla & Malone 2003, p. 130).

In working with a group of young people in the neighbourhood Malone facilitated their production of a complaints list which gained a lot of local media attention prompting the local council to fund a *Streetscape* project, aimed at reclaiming the public realm. Alongside the children's complaint list was a wish list including having: secure and safe corridors for moving around without harassment, regulation and surveillance; opportunities to engage in discussions with others about concerns, needs and aspirations; having views listened to and acted on.

Through the *Streetscape* project, a series of detailed child and youth generated designs of new spaces and places were made and presented to the city council, including rose gardens, bike tracks, seats, sculptures, adventure playgrounds. According to Malone, although the youth and children benefited in confidence from the project and engagement in the democratic process, a key objective of the project, it failed to fulfil its other aim, to construct a safe local landscape feature for the children.

As a result of this experience a series of helpful and timely political recommendations were made for future similar work (Chawla & Malone, 2003, pp. 133–134):

- The team's volunteer status may have undermined their credibility and access to key political players. *Response*: Clearly articulate expectations and negotiate a role which can hold policy-makers accountable.
- The project was located in a less powerful and influential section of the council. *Response*: Position the project within a council group which has power, support and cross-sectoral influence.
- Children and youth were seen as a less powerful group in local politics as they lacked voting power. *Response*: Make youth problems be seen as community problems. Embed youth needs in the context of community needs instead of allowing them to be identified as youth-specific, and therefore last on the list or viewed as least significant.
- The project placed too much hope in the one-off impact of the children's presentation. *Response*: Construct timelines, infiltrate management groups and sit on committees which can follow through on young people's recommendations.

Case Study: The Town of Children demonstration project

The *Town of Children* project was created in 1991, in Fano, Italy and was inspired by the Italian psychologist Francesco Tonucci (Baraldi, 2003), whose starting idea was that current everyday life in towns was not safe. According to Tonucci, children are the main victims of this situation, as they can be confined to their houses or educational organisations, and possibly prevented from autonomous actions and movements. He promoted children's participation in decision-making processes and plans about the future of towns as active and conscious instruments for creating urban change. The *Town of Children* project aimed to change town life through children's empowerment in knowing, planning, and discussing their city. The demonstration project in Fano focused on young children aged 6 to 10 and involved professionals, town planners and teachers working with children to discuss environmental and political strategies about town development. Activities included town walks, group observations and model making as well as group discussions.

In Baraldi's (2003) analysis of the different adult styles adopted by professionals he suggests that a 'participated planning' approach, whereby town planners reject a didactic teaching style and instead focus on listening, understanding and discussing the children's perspectives, 'giving voice to personal creativity, without evaluations and without interfering with the children's ideas or direction of the children's activities' (2003, p. 190) promoted greater child engagement and more thoughtful models than formal adult to child teaching. Together with the children, the planner constructed a series of plastic models and drawings representing new child-friendly town spaces, such as squares with fun fountains, designs for school buildings, sculptures and skating parks near the beach where the town was situated.

The project was closely connected to the town council (via the planner) who did indeed use the children's ideas in the construction of a new town statue and a vista point in a park by the seaside. In addition, Baraldi reports anecdotal evidence from parents that after the consultation experience, children paid more attention to social problems and their rights, and read newspapers more regularly. Follow up group discussions and interviews revealed both realism about the feasibility of some of their designs and disappointment at the apparent lack of political will to follow through all the children's ideas, as these comments illustrate (Baraldi, 2003, pp. 199–200):

> Maybe we want too many things in our school, and then where are we going to put all those things?

> We could never make it because it's too difficult.

> I think they won't build it because the builders can't do so many things in two weeks.

> Children's imagination has no limits, so maybe they didn't build it because it wasn't possible.

> Now I understand it was impossible to make.

> I thought they could make it, but now I see things differently and I even laugh because I understand it was impossible.

It was like wonderland, it was really too much.

I think the Town Council worries about important things; but these things are important too.

They actually do the necessary things, but not really all of them, especially [not] things that are important to children.

The practical requirement for community and neighbourhood consultation is to find a space between adult dominated planning processes which can simply ignore children's needs and desires, design them out, or which make ungrounded assumptions about them, and on the other hand a naive idealism which assumes that children can straightforwardly take the roles of adult citizens in a planning process. The need is to take account of the unavoidable complexities arising from different levels of maturity and understanding which largely depend on age and technical training, whilst nevertheless giving enhanced weight to the life-world of children.

Case Study: Improving London

In his book *London: the biography*, Peter Ackroyd (2000, p. 2) argues that London 'is not civilised or graceful...but tortuous, inexact and oppressive...It is a city based on profit and speculation, not need and no mayor or sovereign could withstand its organic will'. For Ackroyd, London has a life deeply embedded in its past. Its inhabitants struggle through and indeed this theme resonates with many empirical studies of the children's accounts, particularly those who live in the poor neighbourhoods of London (e.g Mumford & Power, 2003). It is notable that whilst there has been a long tradition of inquiry into the decline of the quality of life in London, the focus of traditional community studies has tended to be on the adult activities and preoccupations.

Examination of cross-generational perspectives on neighbourhood revitalisation can illuminate whether differences exist between child and adult views. O'Brien et al.'s (1999) study of diverse London neighbourhoods and a comparative new town (see Chapter 5) included an exploration of children's and their parents' aspirations for neighbourhood improvement. Both children and parents were asked to 'name one thing that could be done to make your neighbourhood a better place for children'. This theme was explored in more depth during individual interviews and focus group discussions. What did children think was the one change that would improve the quality of life for children in their neighbourhood and did their parents want the same thing as their children?

There are some commonalities and overlap between children's and parents' most desired neighbourhood improvement but there were differences in the ordering of their wishes (O'Brien, 2003). Four key areas were revealed in the data: more and better play spaces and places (e.g. better parks, play spaces near home, leisure centres for youth), greater security (e.g. cameras, heightened police presence, restriction of dangerous persons), traffic measures (e.g. traffic management/calming, including for example, more zebra crossings, speed bumps) and infrastructural maintenance (e.g. clearing up rubbish, graffiti and dog mess, washing down streets). Children's most desired improvement was for more and better play places and spaces, as one girl puts it:

> Stop building so many houses and ugly buildings, 'cos children want space to play and they can't be expected to stay indoors for the whole of their time – children have to have space (White girl, 11 year old).

Children's emphasis on their improving play and leisure space, found in O'Brien et al.'s study, suggests that contemporary children are expressing a desire to be included in the neighbourhood, to have a public space for themselves. Whilst parents *also* wanted these leisure and play spaces for their children *ensuring security* was uppermost in their minds. As well as traffic concerns (particularly speeding) gang culture and street violence preoccupied parents, especially parents of girls and minority ethnic boys who revealed high levels of parental anxiety about letting their children play out (O'Brien et al. 1999):

> [When you say you worry about him, in which way would you be worried?]

> Possibility of an accident, or being bullied on the way home, because his sister went through that once before, so I worry about that. Anything can happen. And especially at this time that there's darkness around 5 o'clock. I don't like him walking on his own in the dark because of the incidents that happen all the time around this area. It's not safe being in this area you know because of the pickpockets and the things we've witnessed around this area. You can see people fighting or you can see people being shot (Mother of 10 year old boy, African, inner London).

Parental anxiety is amplified in poor, distressed urban environments such as this one. Indeed, in this context the parenting strategy of 'keeping him in/ keeping him close' is a legitimate, protective response. Clearly a balance needs to be struck between an enhanced provision of spaces for children in urban centres such as London and the development of a greater security framework, sensitive to parental anxieties, for children to be able to actually participate in this space.

   This pattern of findings is by no means unique to these areas. In another study the worst feature of four communities was said to be risks to children's health such as dog mess, dangerous litter such as broken glass, needles and polluted water, and fast traffic (Barnes & Baylis, 2004). In all four areas parents put a priority on more activities for their children, while teenagers surveyed in three of the communities agreed that they hoped their communities would provide safe spaces to meet friends (such as parks and shelters) without narrow time restrictions, with good lighting, and that they wanted to be treated with tolerance by other community members (Baylis & Barnes, 2004).

   The importance of asking and involving children as well as parents in research and consultation about neighbourhood improvement is also shown by the unexpected difference between the generations in O'Brien et al.'s (1999) study in their preoccupation with improving the physical infrastructure of the neighbourhood. Interestingly maintenance of the physical dimensions of the neighbourhood infrastructure emerged as much *more* significant to children than to their parents. As one Turkish boy living in inner London put it:

> I'll say just all the street cleaning, the things they throw on the floor, people throw on the floor. I'll say that, clean the streets. Not clean but campaigns for people to learn not to do that, you know. Tell things, make up a group or something, you know, to do it. That's it, say that. That's it.

Many of the photographs of children's unfavoured places included rubbish on streets and corridors of apartment blocks and graffiti drawn on public walls. Children are keen observers of the crumbling infra-structure of their urban environment and because of their size closer than adults to its more offensive features – the broken glass, the uncleared litter and dog dirt. As Colin Ward (1978) and others have remarked the smaller size of children means they are more likely than adults to be closer to ground level. Uneven or 'lumpy' streets and pavements, as children can call them, really matter if you are small in size and riding a bike.

In the inner London focus groups of O'Brien et al.'s (1999) study it was hard to get the children to think about positive aspects to their local living space, and comparisons were often made to other, seemingly better, areas: as one child in inner London said 'the streets are cleaner in other European cities. Bin men are rubbish. Clean the area up. Make the place look better. More parks, more green. Clean up Islington'. The Prime Minister should 'come and see what we're living in'. London children living in less affluent areas ask for more maintenance of streets and buildings and better play spaces. Dissatisfaction with the general level of filth and drab buildings was high for these London children but less of an issue for children living outside London where urban deterioration was not so striking.

It is of note that the arrival of a new Mayor and local government for London (Greater London Authority, GLA) in the late 1990s, created a significant shift towards a new public policy framework for advancing a child-centred urban regeneration programme and was able to take forward many of the issues raised by research. A concerted effort has been made to integrate a strategy to improve the state of London's children with a new spatial plan for the transformation of London's transport, building and neighbourhood developments (The Mayor's Children's Strategy, 2000). Since this first plan there has been further strategic development and the production of two reports on *'The State of London's Children'* (Hood, 2004; www.london.gov.uk) and an updated strategy (Mayor of London, 2004).

Case Study: The Children's Fund Prevention Programme: getting children involved in the development of community based children's services

> The voices of children and young people are at the heart of the Children's Fund, with children and young people being involved in the design, operation and evaluation of the programme.
> http://www.everychildmatters.gov.uk/strategy/childrensfund/

Integrating children's and parent's perspectives on service planning and delivery was a key component to the *Children's Fund Prevention Programme*, a UK government intervention targeted at 5 to 13 year-old children at risk of social exclusion. Launched in 2000 the programme was part of the range of fiscal and social policies introduced by the Labour Government in its efforts to reduce disadvantage associated with child poverty. Initially it was planned to bridge the gap between *Sure Start* (Chapter 7), which focused on the under 5's living in disadvantaged communities, and Connexions, which concentrated on the older child and young adult (National Evaluation of the Children's Fund, 2004). The aim of the programme was to take a preventative approach to working with socially excluded 5 to 13 year-olds in order to reduce truancy, improve educational attainment, reduce youth crime, address health inequalities and encourage more use of services by disabled and minority ethnic children. As well as focusing on prevention the other two guiding principles were partnership and participation. By 2003, 149 multi-agency partnerships were in operation across England, each working within a local authority area and most including representatives from the statutory sector, the voluntary sector, the local community and faith groups.

National guidance to local projects on the importance of encouraging child participation was open-ended, ambitious and linked to governmental monitoring requirements:

> We are not being prescriptive about which methods are used but the participation of children and young people is a requirement (cited in Morris & Spicer, 2003, p. 25).

Local project leaders were encouraged to initiate activities which would be: sensitive to diverse groups of children, taken seriously, be effective and be sustainable beyond the life of the project. There was recognition from government that engaging with children and their families would take time and need resource investment.

Findings from the national evaluation of the *Children's Fund*, through interviews with 149 Children's Fund Programme Managers across England in 2003 showed that a range of participatory activities blossomed and many have been innovative (see Table 8.2 and Box 8.2).

Nationally and locally programme and project managers have shown high levels of commitment to the principles of participation.

> Participation was described as both the most problematic element of the work of the Partnership, as well as its greatest achievement (The National Evaluation of the *Children's Fund*, 2004, p. 27).

Since managers were under high pressure to deliver to several targets on limited time scales (on which continuation funding depended) this context sometimes conflicted with the need for incremental development work to prepare children for participatory activities. The employment of a dedicated participation officer to facilitate work with children and parents helped some local groups considerably.

Table 8.2   Forms of children and young people's participation in the *Children's Fund Prevention Programme*

Strategic development of partnerships	Participation in the strategic-level development of Children's Fund partnerships. Examples include developing, shaping or finalising delivery plans, setting themes and priorities and developing participation strategies through means such as consultation or involvement in children and young people/parents' forums.
Shaping and targeting services	Involvement in the design and targeting of services by defining levels and dimensions of need, identifying issues of access to services, service provision gaps and potential target groups and geographical areas, suggesting ways of locating and engaging target groups through means including consultation participating in children and young people/parents' forums.
Commissioning services	Contribution to commissioning decision-making processes or in some cases the final selection/rejection of proposals and developing service level agreements either through membership of assessment panels or participating in events at which decisions are made.
Recruitment	Involvement in the recruitment of key workers such as Children's Fund staff, local evaluators, participation workers and commissioning consultants through means such as sitting on selection and interview panels.
Management and governance of partnerships and projects	Informing or feeding into the management/governance of Children's Fund partnerships through consultation, sitting on partnership management boards or through children's sub-groups of partnerships. At project/service level involvement through consultation or through project steering groups.
Spending and administering budgets	Active decision-making spending specified budgets and grants within Children's Fund criteria.
Delivery of services and activities	Participating in delivering services and parents' involvement in delivering services and activities for children and young people.
Evaluation and research	Participating in evaluating Children's Fund services or activities at a basic level through feeding back views as users, or more involved levels of engagement such as defining outcomes and measures or being trained to be independent evaluators.
Communication, promotion and awareness	Involvement in producing promotional materials such as newsletters and developing websites.

Source: Spicer & Morris, 2003, p. 26.

Box 8.2   Example of a local *Children's Fund event*

The 'Children's Voices' event involved both children and young people with representatives from Children's Fund Management Team and other agencies. The event
included consultation with children via conversation, a 'graffiti wall' and a drumming
workshop. This event was positively received during feedback and a video was
produced including shots from a 'junior cam' and comments from children. The
video was distributed to all children who took part in the event, all projects and
other interested parties.

Lincolnshire *Children's Fund*, O'Brien et al., 2004.

Workers reported that children and young people were able to articulate their
views on current services and to identify ways in which service provision could
be improved.

Despite significant innovatory and imaginative practice, the national evaluation
findings suggest that there is still lack of clarity amongst programme managers
about how best to work with children, particularly in relation to involving children in formal business and strategic level meetings. One project manager, who
had attempted to engage children in conventional committee meetings reflected:

> Children hated it. It was adult terms and it was adult times and it was adult busi-
> ness, and no matter how much you tried to make it child-friendly there was still the
> business that you had to do that the children found boring (The National Evaluation
> of the *Children's Fund*, 2004, p. 27).

As other studies have shown, there is an increasing need for further training and
knowledge transfer amongst professionals to support new participatory ways of
working as some struggle from a relatively low skills base.

CHALLENGES AND BARRIERS TO CHILDREN'S PARTICIPATION

Although it is now widely accepted that children and young people have a right
to be involved in matters that affect them in the public sphere, a new challenge is
the lack of clarity about how much participation children should be offered and
what precise weight their views should be given in informing decisions. One of
the barriers to understanding the answers to these questions is the lack of clear
attributable evidence for any beneficial impact of children's participation either
on themselves as individuals, on neighbourhood characteristics, or specific children's services. We do not know if children's engagement in the participatory
processes per se is a necessary condition for a more child-friendly neighbourhood
or an improved child-centred service. We do not know the extent to which children's interests need to be represented directly by children themselves for a
particular project, or indirectly by children's advocates or if indeed improvement

could occur through better informed and trained professionals with greater knowledge and awareness about childhood and particular children's requirements. Designing research studies to demonstrate any attributable impact from children's involvement in the complex and fast-changing processes of policy and service development is extremely challenging (Hart et al., 2004; Sinclair, 2004). Those studies that have taken place are typically retrospective, uni-sourced and based on subjective appraisals. A systematic prospective study where data are gathered from different independent sources would be timely. Instead as this chapter has shown we draw on the rich descriptive single case studies abundant in the field, which show the imaginative ways professionals, other adults, children and young people have come together to improve neighbourhoods and services for children.

A further issue which has emerged in the field is the continuing thorny problem of ensuring the authentic representation of the constituency of children, because of course children are a diverse group of individuals. Are the groups of children who 'turn up' to community participation or service improvement activities the dissatisfied, those with time on their hands, or those with more access to facilitating cultural capital resources? For example, formal structures, such as youth councils or parliaments may not be capturing less advantaged children, just attracting the head girls and boys, or the academically and verbally able. Rural children in less spatially accessible neighbourhoods can also be inadvertently left out or disenfranchised from public events organised in central venues. Only a few well-funded research studies are able to assess the representativeness of those groups of children who get involved and participate in specific activities. We know from research on the demographic profile of councillors that civically engaged adults typically tend to be older, male and often with low caring responsibilities (Aspden & Birch, 2005).

Finally it is important to consider which (if any) elements of participatory activity are in fact beneficial to children. Recent international development practitioners have reported concern that the participatory activities may detract 'from the time and energy children could devote to their domestic responsibilities, or from their school work and religious education' (Hart, et al. 2004, p. 32). Some of the case studies reviewed in this chapter suggest that children often prefer not to attend formal committee meetings and in fact become extremely bored during them (as of course do many adults). However, it is precisely these meetings that are typically the influential forum for resource-allocation and strategic decision-making. Arguably the business of childhood is not to spend time at meetings in the company of adults paid to be there, but the problem is that without children's participation how do adults keep 'the child in mind' when making key decisions about the neighbourhood or particular child service? Future research needs to find ways to close the gap between the insights children have about their life-worlds and the organisational and political methods professionals use to respond to children's know-how.

9

SCHOOLS AS COMMUNITIES AND SCHOOLS WITHIN COMMUNITIES

INTRODUCTION

Schools are communities in their own right, but they are also part of their local communities. The unique position of schools within society means that they can be developed to maximise their potential to impact positively on the whole local community, not only the children attending the school, but also their families and other local residents. We argue here that there is enormous potential for schools to become a central resource. This might appear obvious, but traditionally there has been a great deal of reluctance to utilise schools to deliver services to families. The principal role of schools has been to educate children, and the challenge of producing good educational attainment, along with extra-curricular activities such as sport, has left few resources to go beyond that remit. This chapter will review policy developments within the UK (England, in particular), and illustrate a number of different approaches in the UK, the USA and Scandinavia which have attempted in different ways to advance the 'whole school' approach to addressing the needs of children in school, their families and the wider community.

Parents are traditionally seen by schools either as a source of stress for teachers if they do not support the school's directives or, with younger children, as a resource to help teachers in the classroom. However, there is increasing evidence that schools routinely experience aggressive behaviour from parents, even in schools serving young children (Barnes, Belsky, Broomfield & Melhuish, in press). This suggests that it may become increasingly challenging to involve parents in school life. Relationships between schools and parents are normally mediated through institutions such as the Parent Teachers Association and parent governors (responsible to a great extent for fund-raising and general school development), and through 'set piece' events such as parents' evenings where teachers and parents discuss the academic progress (and sometimes behaviour) of children. However, many elementary and primary schools now invite parents in to help with reading and other tasks with younger children. When individual parents become involved in the school it is often when their children are having problems with attendance or behaviour. In such cases in the UK, parents are contacted by Education Welfare Officers[1] or head teachers to get them to do something about the situation.

In recent years there has been a greater recognition that the psychological and emotional well-being of children is crucial to their educational attainment, and that concentrating purely on academic attainment can be counter-productive, especially for children from disadvantaged or disturbed backgrounds. As a result, a number of programmes have been set up to improve the well-being of children in schools. These include school counsellors, peer mentoring, anti-bullying strategies and 'circle time'. Whilst these school-based programmes are helpful in providing a more holistic educational experience for children, families and communities need to be engaged in order to fundamentally change children's attitudes to education and behaviour. The role of parents goes far beyond providing encouragement and helping with homework. The culture of learning created in the home is a crucial factor in determining how children will approach the task of learning and their attitude towards education and training.

A recent review of the research evidence conducted for the UK Department for Education and Skills concluded that parental involvement in their children's education is the single most significant factor in determining the educational attainment of children (Desforges & Abouchaar, 2003). But many parents are not able to give this support, either because their circumstances prevent them from doing so (for example, their work commitments), or because they do not have the skills or the motivation to help their children succeed at or even attend school. In the UK, as in many other developed countries, there has been a two-track 'stick and carrot' policy to address this issue. On the one hand there have been a number of measures which have placed increasing responsibility on parents to ensure that children attend school. The most recent is the *Parenting Order* which can be imposed on parents who persistently refuse to ensure that their children attend school. On the other hand there have been a number of initiatives aimed at supporting parents as a means of preventing children from truanting or being excluded from school and helping them to achieve academically. (See, for example, the *Children's Fund* and *On Track* described in Chapters 8 and 10 respectively.)

In addition to widening the school community to embrace parents, there is developing recognition that schools themselves can do a lot more to become engaged with the local community, in particular to support vulnerable children and families (SEU, 2000). Schools have a unique role in society and within communities. Virtually every child attends a school, and so it is one of the very few genuinely universal public services. Schools are in touch with more parents than any other institution, and they can reach out to parents in a way that no other agency can. In addition schools have a range of health and care professionals working within

---

[1] The Education Welfare Officer's task is to help schools improve pupils' attendance and reduce unnecessary absence and truancy. Education Welfare Officers work closely with schools, children and their parents, and with statutory and voluntary agencies, to promote, encourage and enforce regular school attendance of children.

them, including school nurses, doctors, education welfare officers and educational psychologists. There is clearly potential for closer relationships between parents and schools, not only so that parents can become more engaged in helping their children achieve academically, but equally importantly, so that schools can play a part in supporting vulnerable families within the community.

DEVELOPMENTS IN SCHOOL AND FAMILY POLICY

The links between schools, families and communities have long been recognised by policy makers, and 'community schools' of one sort or another have existed for decades (Ball, 1998). However these links have never been fully developed in policy. Although it is recognised that schools' involvement in the community and engagement with families is an important part of their role, there are counter-vailing (and increasing) pressures on schools to focus very narrowly on delivering the curriculum so that educational targets can be met. Typically schools wishing to provide a wider set of services have to raise the resources from short-term ad hoc funding streams rather than from mainstream educational budgets.

In the UK the impetus towards a wider role for schools was provided by the Joseph Rowntree Foundation, which commissioned two important pieces of work in the late 1990s (Ball, 1998; Dyson & Robson, 1999). These reports advocated strongly for the introduction of extended (or 'full service') schools which could play a much more prominent role in supporting communities and families. Examples of 'full service' or community schools were already being developed in the USA (Dryfoos, 1994).

The UK Government's Social Exclusion Unit's Performance Action Team (PAT) Report 11 on schools, published in 2000 (SEU, 2000), put forward a range of proposals for reforming schools and committed the government to developing full service and extended schools. PAT Report 12 focused on children at risk, and proposed a variety of new approaches to target children at risk of social exclusion.

The Government's subsequent spending review of 2000 resulted in the announce-ment of several new initiatives aimed at supporting school-aged children and their families, and preventing them from becoming socially excluded. Government policy moved decisively towards a more holistic view of the role of schools, and began to take much more seriously the link between education, family support and outcomes for children. The most significant of these new initiatives were the *Children's Fund* and *Connexions*. A further development was the announce-ment by the Government in 2002 of the setting up of the *Parenting Fund* which is aimed at increasing the capacity of the voluntary (NGO) sector to deliver parenting programmes. More recently the Government published the 10-year child care strategy (HM Treasury 2004) which gives a commitment to provide, by 2010, an out-of-school childcare place for all children aged 3–14 between 8am and 6pm each weekday.

However, the most significant policy development in the UK in this area has been the publication of the Green Paper *Every Child Matters* (HM Treasury, 2003)[2]

---

[2] Available online at www.everychildmatters.gov.uk/publications/?asset = document&id = 19783.

and the subsequent *Children Act* (HM Government, 2004) which set out the overall direction of Government policy towards children and families. The main focus is on structural change in the management, configuration and accountability of children's services. The Green Paper provides the framework for improving the outcomes for children by encouraging early intervention, joined-up working between different professionals, better information exchange between agencies and increased accountability workforce reform. In relation to schools the most important development has been the national roll-out of extended schools, which had previously only been piloted in a small number of locations.

In the following section we will describe a number of programmes designed to ensure that schools become more holistic by providing a range of services other than education, and by linking more closely with other agencies and with community members who are not necessarily parents.

Case Study: CoZi: Comer Schools and School of the 21st Century, USA

These two approaches to school transformation both emanate from Yale University and offer complementary approaches to interventions relating to community and schools, but with common features, summarised in Box 9.1. In contrast to the rather laissez-faire approach of the British models described below, these programmes are well structured, with extensive and detailed manuals for the school staff to consult regarding the interventions and their implementation, offering training and certification to those schools who volunteer to implement the programmes. They are attempts to develop holistic approaches to supporting disadvantaged children and families within a school context. Both have been extensively evaluated over the years and have been shown to be effective, not only in improving school attainment, but also in enhancing the overall well-being of children. However the Comer approach is primarily based on the notion of the school-as-community, whereas the School of the 21st Century is based on school-in-community. They have recently been combined to form the *CoZi* initiative.

Box 9.1   Features of *CoZi* initiative schools

The school moves away from an exclusive focus on educational attainment and begins to address six 'developmental pathways':

- Physical
- Cognitive
- Social
- Psychological
- Ethical
- Language

Comer Schools

The *Comer Process*, or the Yale University School Development Program (SDP), was established in 1968 as a collaborative effort between New Haven Public Schools and the Yale Child Study Centre. Since then the programme has been rolled out in several education districts in the USA, and has successfully 'turned round' several failing schools. (For a full description of the process, see Joyner et al., 2004.)

The philosophy underpinning the programme is that schools should be organised to facilitate the natural developmental processes by which children learn and are socialised. The programme mobilises teachers, administrators, parents and others to support students' personal, social and academic growth. It also addresses the way the school is managed and organised, aiming to create a management ethos based on students' needs and on developmental principles. The process is described as an 'operating system', i.e. as a way of managing, organising, coordinating and integrating activities. This was the first holistic school change programme that involved, not simply initiating new interventions in the school, but also addressing the basic ethos, the school management and the involvement of parents and students in decision making.

The *Comer Process* operating system is built on three teams within the school, whose roles are summarised in Box 9.2. All three school teams follow common guiding principles:

- no fault – maintains the focus on problem-solving rather than placing blame;
- consensus decision-making;
- collaboration.

This framework places the students' developmental needs at the centre of the school's agenda and establishes shared responsibility. Concerned adults work together to provide students with the developmental activities that may be lacking outside the school. They also work together to make effective decisions about the programme and curriculum of the school based on student needs.

> The Comer Process provides a structure as well as a process for mobilising adults to support students' learning and overall development. It is a different way of conceptualising and working in schools and replaces traditional school organization and management with an operating system that works for schools and the students they serve (Joyner et al., 2004, p. 18).

The programme has recently been expanded so that in addition to being introduced into individual schools, it now operates also at the school district level. Introducing the process throughout the district enables the philosophy to become more embedded and also creates economies of scale in administration and support.

As we have discussed above, the basic principles and philosophy of this approach are now widely accepted around the world. However the *Schools Development*

Box 9.2   Three teams for the *Comer Process*, and their roles

1. The **School Planning and Management Team**, which develops a comprehensive school plan, sets academic, social and community relations goals and coordinates all school activities, including staff development programmes. Members of the team include administrators, teachers, support staff and parents. The team supervises the key operations for implementing the programme.

- Development of the Comprehensive School Plan. This includes curriculum, teaching and assessment, as well as social and academic climate goals based on a developmental understanding of students
- Provision of Staff Development in the service of achieving the goals of the Comprehensive School Plan
- Assessment and Modification to provide new information and identify new opportunities based on the data of the school's population

2. The **Student and Staff Support Team** promotes desirable social conditions and relationships. Serving on this team are the principal and staff members with expertise in child development and mental health, such as a counsellor, social worker, psychologist, or nurse.

3. The **Parent Team** involves parents in the school by developing activities through which the parents can support the school's social and academic programmes. Composed of parents, this team also selects representatives to serve on the School Planning and Management Team.

Source: Summarised from Joyner, Ben-Avis & Comer, 2004, p. 18.

Program is far more than a general philosophy of education; schools or districts are permitted to call themselves 'fully certified' by the *SDP* only after they have completed the full five-year implementation cycle, and the administrators and major teams have met specific behavioural requirements as well as demonstrated knowledge of the *SDP* approach.

Initially evaluations of the process were conducted internally by *SDP* in-house staff, but more recently the approach has been evaluated more rigorously by external evaluators, most significantly by Millsap and colleagues (2000) who evaluated all the Comer schools in Detroit. This evaluation found that well-implemented *Comer schools* displayed significantly better outcomes for students in educational attainment as well as behaviour and socialisation. However another evaluation (Cook et al., 1999), of *Comer schools* in Prince George's County, Maryland, found that changes in educational attainment could only be found in well-implemented *Comer schools*, and that most of the *Comer schools* were not well implemented. Thus programme fidelity is a crucial component of this approach.

School of the 21st Century (21C)

The *School of the 21st Century (21C)* is a programme that incorporates childcare and family support services into schools. Its overall goal is to promote the optimal growth and development of children, beginning at birth (http://www.yale.edu/bushcenter/21C).

21C was conceptualised by Yale University Professor Edward Zigler and developed for national implementation by Matia Finn-Stevenson, also at Yale. The programme is based on the recognition that changes in patterns of work and family life in recent decades have meant new concerns for parents, especially a pressing need for affordable, quality child care. These same changes have also meant challenges for educators seeking to ensure that children arrive at school ready to learn and that they receive the support they need to succeed academically.

21C was first launched in 1988 in Independence, Missouri. It was one of the first initiatives in the USA to systematically address the links between family and schools. The programme has been implemented in more than 1,300 schools in the USA, and in some school districts and even whole states (e.g. Connecticut, Kentucky and Arkansas).

The fundamental principle behind *21C* is the provision of school-based preschool and after-school care and family support services, all designed to promote the optimal growth and development of children beginning at birth. Its guiding principles are summarised in Box 9.3. Thus the school becomes the basis for a range of services, focused on child care but also including family support, early education, parent training, adult education, youth development and social services.

The *21C* model has been implemented in a number of different contexts, including urban, rural and suburban areas, and in affluent, middle class, and poor communities. The model is flexible – it is not a specific set of services, but rather an approach to developing school-based interventions. This enables individual schools to tailor it to match their own needs and resources. In many communities, *21C* serves as an umbrella for an expanded array of family support services.

Universal access to child care   Unlike the UK and much of Europe, the USA does not provide free access to child care. Many families do not have access to quality child care because they cannot afford high-priced care or because quality, affordable child care is not available in their communities. Thus the first principle is to provide families with this important service.

Strong parental support and involvement   Working parents often find it difficult to spend time with their children's child care providers or to take an active role in the child care or school programme. As we discuss above, however, research shows that parental involvement is essential for the optimal development of children. It is also a crucial factor in the success of any programme aimed at improving educational outcomes. Parents are more likely to take an active role in their child's schooling if they feel encouraged, respected and supported by the school.

> ## Box 9.3   The philosophy, guiding principles and main components of 21C
>
> - Universal access to child care
> - Strong parental support and involvement
> - Focus on the overall development of the child
> - High-quality child care
> - A professional framework for child care providers
> - Non-compulsory programmes
>
> Key services are:
>
> - All-day, year-round child care for preschoolers
> - Before- and after-school and vacation care for school-age children
> - Guidance and support for parents
> - All-day, year-round child care for preschoolers
> - Information and referral services
> - Networks and training for child care providers
> - Health education and services

Focus on the overall development of the child   The 21C model focuses on the overall development of the child by taking a holistic view of child development and working with all aspects of child development including the physical, social, emotional and intellectual, and including attention to the community in which they live.

High-quality child care   Provision of high quality child care is at the core of the 21C programme. Quality is usually determined by staff qualifications and training, high staff-to-child ratios, small groups of children, developmentally-appropriate activities and supportive work environments for employees that prevent high rates of staff turnover.

A professional framework for child care providers   The child care field suffers from a high rate of staff turnover because of low salaries, lack of medical and other benefits, stressful working conditions and low job status with little room for advancement. Quality of care is adversely affected by high staff turnover. Ensuring that employees receive appropriate training and competitive rates of pay is essential to a programme. Providing a supportive and professional environment for employees will also encourage them to stay in the field.

Non-compulsory programmes   Not all families in every community need the same services. Tailoring and administrating programmes for children based on the needs of the community is essential for the success of any educational programme.

Preschool child care The majority of *21C* schools have implemented preschool child care in the school building. However, some programmes, due to space limitations or other considerations, run their preschool programmes at locations outside the school. Preschool child care, whether administered in the school or elsewhere, is not academic in its orientation. By emphasising developmentally-appropriate activities such as play and social interaction, *21C* preschool programmes are designed to lay the groundwork for children's later success in school.

Before- and after-school and vacation care for school-age children One of the most significant services for parents who are employed is the provision of year-round child care for school-age children. This care is non-academic, acting rather 'in loco parentis'. The staff are encouraged to ensure that children feel free to play and make choices about their after-school activities, but also that they do their homework. In *21C* school districts where 5-year-old children are in kindergarten for a full day, before- and after-school care is offered and vacation care for older children. In districts where kindergarten children attend school for only half a day, they participate in child care for the remainder of the day. This can contribute to building the economic and human capital in the wider community by providing parents with the chance to take up opportunities for education and employment.

Guidance and support for parents The *21C* family outreach component is based on Missouri's successful 'Parents as Teachers' programme which educates parents in early child development. *Schools of the 21st Century* are expected to offer regular home visits by trained parent educators, starting before the birth of the child and continuing until the child reaches the age of three. Child development specialists provide parents with age-appropriate information about their child's linguistic, social, cognitive, emotional and motor development. Schools also provide opportunities for group meetings with parents of similar-age children and for health and developmental screening at the school.

Information and referral services *Schools of the 21st Century* are not expected to be the sole provider of child care in their communities; instead they work with community members to expand parents' choices by providing child care slots and information and referral that informs parents of their child care options. In addition they give advice on the criteria for good quality to parents looking for child care. This service also provides information on night-time and weekend child care, health care, financial assistance for eligible parents, and social services and other family support services available in the community.

Networks and training for child care providers *Schools of the 21st Century* maintain a network of family day care providers (akin to registered childminders in the UK) who participate in support groups and training workshops, during which they can share ideas and information. Networks also maintain toy and book-lending libraries, and are used to address issues such as salaries, benefits and running a small business. The relationship between the school and the network is expected to be mutually beneficial: providers have an opportunity to improve the quality of their child care, and the school's information and referral service is better able to inform parents about family day care available in the community. In addition to working with family day care providers, *21C* schools are expected to work with other community child care providers to promote the highest quality preschool care for children.

Health education and services The range of health services offered by fully operational *21C* schools includes: health, nutrition and fitness education, physical health services, care for children with special needs, acute health care, developmental assessments, dental assessments and mental health services. Some *21C* schools integrate current nutrition information into the regular academic programme and also make changes in the school's food service to ensure that it complies with current nutrition guidelines.

Evaluation

The *21C* has been evaluated by the Bush Centre. Finn Stevenson and colleagues (1998) conducted a longitudinal study of two *21C* schools in Montana, and also evaluated various components of the model. The evaluation studied three-year outcomes for a group of 120 children in *21C* schools and 73 control children. It found significant differences for the parents who used the child care facilities, and there were also some differences between the experimental group and the contrast group in academic achievement. However there were no significant differences within schools between those children who attended day care provided by *21C* and those who did not, indicating that there may have been a school effect rather than a programme effect.[3]

The *CoZi* initiative is a new development which combines the *Comer* and the *21C* programmes, providing a whole school change programme together with child care and other community services. This approach too is now being evaluated by the Bush Center.

Case Study: Extended Schools, UK

The *extended school* approach being developed in the UK bears many similarities to both *Comer schools* and the *21C* models. An extended school[4] is one that provides a range of activities and services, often beyond the school day, to help meet the needs of its pupils, their families and the wider community. There are many ways schools can achieve this aim, with no one method or model favoured over any other.

---

[3] According to the *21C* website http://www.yale.edu/bushcenter/21C/research.html, evaluations of the model have demonstrated a much wider range of benefits for children, parents, schools and communities than are reported here. However there are no citations for the research on which these claims are based, and a full internet search by the authors has not revealed any further evaluations of *21C* in the public domain.

[4] Also called *full service schools* and in Scotland *New Community Schools*.

Kinder and colleagues (2003) studied 160 schools and revealed there was great variety amongst schools in terms of the numbers of arenas covered and the degree of investment in them, but they identified six main types of service (summarised in Box 9.4).

While many schools take on board some of the characteristics of an *extended school*, the Government has funded some schools specifically to become extended schools. The *Extended Schools* pathfinder initiative provided additional funding to projects in 25 Local Education Authorities (LEAs) from November 2002 to August 2003. Interim findings from an evaluation of the pathfinders (Dyson, Millward & Todd, 2002; Cummings, Dyson & Todd, 2004) confirmed that there is no single model of 'the extended school' and that there is considerable variation between projects depending on factors including community need, geography and access to other funding streams. The most popular activities with schools are breakfast clubs, after-school and holiday activities for pupils, funding of transport to community activities, adult education, activities bringing art into schools and community use of school facilities. The 'full-service' school in which community services are located on the school site is less common, though many schools are working towards this.

Although there is no single model of the extended school, it is helpful to think in terms of three levels at which projects might work, although the boundaries between these levels are not hard and fast (see Box 9.5). Schools can and do move between them as needs and opportunities change. Nonetheless, those involved in planning extended schools might find them a helpful way to organise their thinking.

Several of the schools evaluated identified the school as a resource for the whole community. Many schools work together in federations or patches to support activities across more than one school and to combine funding streams. Activities are directed towards pupils, families and the community. Adult education is an important part of this but there are many other ways of meeting particular community needs. Examples include a family link worker to

---

Box 9.4   Main types of provision in *extended schools*

- additional schooling provision offering curriculum and leisure opportunities to pupils beyond the traditional school timetable;
- community provision offering learning and leisure opportunities, or general community facilities (e.g. drop-in or advice centres);
- early years provision, such as crèches or preschool facilities;
- family and parent provision involving support relating to their child's learning or to a more general parenting or family role;
- other agency provision (e.g. from Health, Youth or Social Services);
- specialist provision, offering high calibre facilities in areas such as sports, arts, IT or business.

Kinder et al., 2003.

Box 9.5   Levels of *extended school* implementation

Level 1. Developing extended activities. At this level schools are simply concerned to undertake activities for pupils, families and community members that are valuable in their own right. These activities need not be closely related to each other but will meet particular needs or maximise particular opportunities.

Level 2. Developing an extended school. At this level, schools are trying to develop a coherent approach to their relationships with pupils, families and community. They seek to establish a distinctive ethos and to link activities so that they can address in a sustained way underlying issues such as pupils' attainments and motivation, family support for schooling and community attitudes to learning.

Level 3. Developing a local strategy. At this level, the work of the extended school forms part of a wider strategy to address community needs and wishes. The issues at stake – employment opportunities, community cohesion, health, crime and so on – are not simply school concerns. Schools therefore may well work in partnership with other agencies and within the context of policy that is developed at neighbourhood, local authority or even national level. This approach is exemplified by a LEA strategy which provides some funding for schools to co-ordinate extended activities.

---

target support to 'at-risk' families, a breakfast club run by young people and a garden project where pupils who have been underachieving and/or are in danger of exclusion, work with disabled adults to grow plants for sale and to enhance the school environment. Benefits for pupils have included case study evidence of cross-generational awareness, increased confidence, motivation for learning and decreased exclusion.

The evaluation (Cummings, Dyson & Todd, 2004) also found that extended schools impacted on pupils, families and communities in a range of ways generating positive outcomes for all three groups.

- For pupils, there was evidence that activities could have an impact on attainment, behaviour and attendance.
- For families, there was evidence that activities could have an impact on involvement in children's learning.
- For communities, there was evidence that activities could have an impact on community pride and involvement.

In regard to community consultation and involvement the key appeared to be a careful and sustained process of trust-building where partners seek to understand each other's aims, priorities and working methods. This is difficult given the pressures under which all agencies are working, so it is important that the process is given ample time and develops through a series of progressively more ambitious initiatives.

Extended schools are loosely based on programmes initiated in the USA such as those described below. But unlike the USA, the British cultural preference is not to implement specified programmes from the 'top down', but rather to provide funding and general guidance and let schools decide how and what to implement. This approach potentially leads to more 'ownership' of the programme by the school, but it also means that there are inevitably huge variations in implementation – and therefore effectiveness – in different areas.

Case Study: Parent Information Point (PIP), UK

The *Parent Information Point (PIP)* is an example of how a low level and basic intervention can have a real impact on parents. *PIP* was designed by the UK National Family and Parenting Institute (NFPI) and was a response to the Government's pledge in *Every Child Matters* (HM Treasury, 2003) to provide information to all parents at key developmental stages in their children's lives in easily accessible school locations based within the local community. The information is also available to all community members. The intervention itself is relatively straightforward: to offer a universal service consisting of the provision of relevant information about child-development issues and local services (see Box 9.6 for the core features). *PIP* events offer single information sessions to parents on a brief, one-off basis.

The *PIP* events are primarily delivered at school-based meetings to groups of parents with children in one of three key developmental stages – parents with children in a reception (kindergarten) class (aged 4–5 years), pre-teenagers (Year 7, aged 11–12 years) and teenagers (Year 9, aged 13–14 years). *PIP* events have been piloted in three areas: two northern metropolitan boroughs and one inner-city London borough. One of the northern boroughs was situated in an affluent area. The other metropolitan borough was less affluent with a high proportion of parents dependent on benefits. A high proportion of parents from this area were from ethnic minority groups – predominantly Asian (Pakistani and Indian). The inner-city London borough was the least affluent of the three areas, with a high proportion of Bangladeshi parents. The structure of *PIP* included central coordination by NFPI and local coordination by a nominated individual in each pilot area. The pilots were delivered in nine schools, three schools per pilot area – one secondary (high) school and two of its feeder primary (elementary) schools. The

---

Box 9.6   Core features of *Parent Information Point (PIP)* events

- a presentation of ten key child-development points,
- video clips about national and local parenting support services,
- a specially designed '*Who can help parents*?' board game introducing representatives from local support services, and
- an information exchange or 'market place' of stalls setting out for parents what local parenting and family support agencies exist.

pilot was delivered over six months and a rigorous evaluation was built into the design (Bhabra & Ghate, 2004).

There was a considerable degree of diversity in the way *PIP* was delivered in each of the three areas and nine participating schools. None of the areas or schools integrated all four core features of *PIP*. There appeared to be a number of key barriers, as well as key enablers to smooth implementation. A major barrier was the speed with which *PIP* was introduced. This limited the time available for input into a central model from local areas and resulted in limited programme fidelity (consistency of delivery). It was also found to be more challenging for the pilot projects to work with secondary schools due to the schools' other commitments. In areas with high numbers of parents from ethnic minority backgrounds it was difficult to convey information and materials if they were not translated into the languages used in the home. Also 'pupil-post' was found not an ideal way to publicise events. Many parents did not attend *PIP* because they simply had not received the information from their children.

Successful implementation of *PIP* was dependent on a number of factors. Firstly, it was crucial to have a nominated local co-ordinator in each area to organise the events. Good team-working between the local co-ordinator and the schools was very beneficial, especially in primary schools. The support and endorsement of the school staff was a key determinant of successful implementation. It was found that *PIP* was far better attended and was more effective when delivered in schools as opposed to community venues. It was also important to hold *PIP* events at different times throughout the day (morning, afternoon and evenings). A good introduction to the event facilitated parental involvement. Parents were more satisfied when they understood the purpose of *PIP*. The 'market place' was an important component that was enhanced by the presence at the stall of local agency representatives.

PIP users showed a significant increase in self-reported knowledge and awareness of family support services, as well as in their willingness to access them. The session also increased their knowledge of child development and enhanced their parenting confidence. The greatest impact was found amongst groups of parents often deemed 'hard to reach', for example, ethnic minority groups and parents on low incomes. *PIP* also had a significant impact on parents with children in the reception age-group (4–5 years). However it was not particularly successful in reaching fathers in that age-group. It was more successful in reaching them in the pre-teenage and teenage groups. Local agencies benefited from their involvement in *PIP*. They were able to reach a wider variety of parents and also had opportunities to 'network' and share information with other local agencies. Because of the success of the pilot, the National Family and Parenting Institute is now working towards extending *PIP* nationally (Alexander & Goldman, 2005).

Case Study: The Olweus Bullying Prevention Programme

Bullying and school violence have recently become important areas of concern for policy-makers and practitioners concerned about the well-being of children in school. Bullying is one of the major causes of distress for children, causing humiliation, unhappiness and confusion for large numbers of children. Many tend to lose their self-esteem and become anxious and insecure. Often their concentration and learning suffer and they may fear school and refuse to attend. The effects of bullying can persist into adulthood (Olweus, 1993b). In addition, bullies often engage in other forms of violent and anti-social behaviour such as vandalising property, shoplifting, truancy and substance abuse. School bullies also are at increased risk for committing crime in adulthood (Olweus, 1993a).

Rates of bullying and violence in schools are high in many countries around the world (Akiba et al., 2002). For example in the USA, 23% of more than 6,000 middle school students in rural South Carolina reported that they had been bullied several times during the past three months; 20% claimed they had bullied others with the same frequency (Melton et al., 1998). In Australia, Rigby (1997) found that 33.5% of boys and 22.8% of girls aged 8–13 years, and 27.6% of boys and 11.5% of girls aged 13–18 years in South Australia reported having been hit or kicked at some stage in the past year. Grunseit and colleagues (2005) found a number of individual, family and school factors associated with higher levels of violence, including the level of racism in the school, the training of teachers and the approach of the school to violence. A number of different interventions have been developed over the past three decades to combat bullying, some more promising than others (Smith et al., 2004). The common denominator amongst the vast majority of anti-bullying strategies is that they take a 'whole school' approach; they do not target individual bullies or victims for treatment, but rather attempt to create a context within the school in which bullying is discouraged, victims are encouraged to come forward and a 'no blame' or 'restorative' culture is engendered in the school, so that bullies and victims are able to talk to each other rather than settle issues with violence and retaliation.

The first systematic programme to combat bullying in schools was the *Bullying Prevention Programme*, in Bergen, Norway, developed by Dan Olweus after three Norwegian teenagers committed suicide as a consequence of bullying. The original project was implemented between 1983 and 1985. It involved 2,500 students in 42 schools throughout the city. The programme operates at three levels, the school, the classroom and the individual (see Box 9.7). The Olweus programme has been replicated in a number of countries and a range of other programmes have been developed over the past two decades. Some of the programmes have been translated into local or even national anti-bullying strategies (Smith et al., 2004). However, none of the newer programmes has been as systematically researched as the *Bullying Prevention Programme*.

The programme's major goal is to reduce bullying among school pupils by reducing opportunities and rewards for bullying behaviour. School staff are largely responsible for introducing and carrying out the programme, and their efforts are directed toward improving peer relations and making the school a safe and pleasant environment. *Bullying Prevention* increases awareness of and knowledge about the problem, actively involves teachers and parents, develops clear rules against bullying behaviour and provides support and protection for bullying victims.

The use of school, classroom and individual interventions ensures that students are exposed to a consistent, strong message regarding the school's views of and attitudes towards bullying from different sources and in different contexts. In

> **Box 9.7 Levels of operation of the Olweus *Bullying Prevention Programme***
>
> **School**. School personnel disseminate an anonymous student questionnaire to assess the nature and prevalence of bullying, discuss the problem, plan for programme implementation, form a school committee to coordinate programme delivery and develop a system of supervising students during breaks.
>
> **Classroom**. Teachers and/or other school personnel introduce and enforce classroom rules against bullying, hold regular classroom meetings with students, and meet with parents to encourage their participation.
>
> **Individual**. Staff hold interventions with bullies, victims and their parents to ensure that the bullying stops.

addition the whole school approach facilitates involvement and commitment to the programme by school staff.

The original evaluation of the programme (Olweus, 1993a) showed that the frequency of bullying decreased by 50% or more in the two years following the project. These results applied to both boys and girls and to students across all grades studied. In addition, the school climate improved and the rate of anti-social behaviour dropped during the two-year period. In the South Carolina replication site (Melton et al., 1998), the programme slowed the rate of increase in the engagement of youth in anti-social behaviour. In addition, students reported that they bullied other students less after seven months in the programme (a 25% reduction in the rate of bullying).

Further analysis by Olweus (2004) showed that the main factor facilitating successful implementation of the programme was the teachers' attitudes towards it. Teachers who were negative or indifferent to the programme could undermine its effectiveness or even prevent its implementation, even where head teachers or school governors were positive.

In some cases schools have attempted to extend the anti-bullying programme to parents and the wider community. As Pepler and colleagues remark:

> Although bullying is a problem that unfolds most frequently at school, it can occur in other aspects of children's lives. Therefore, the success of transforming the social interactions of children at risk for bullying and victimisation, as well as the social dynamics around bullying, may depend on the extent to which this problem is understood and dealt with outside the school context, in families and community settings (2004, p. 317).

However, they point out that evaluations of such community interventions have shown less impressive results to date than school-based programmes, possibly because the effect is diluted somewhat in the community context. Nevertheless, there are encouraging signs that broader-based strategies to combat bullying may be effective and will reach a wider group of children than school projects alone.

BARRIERS TO ACCESSING SCHOOL INTERVENTIONS

Although the school is known to be a good venue for delivering services such as family support, there has been some concern expressed in the literature that this is not always the case. Research shows that some groups of service-users find it very difficult to access services in schools. This can be because the children are not attending school or because the parents have a history of poor relationships with school. Fathers in particular can prove difficult to engage. There are specific problems depending on whether families are in a rural area or an urban one. It is also more difficult for parents of children at secondary school to link with school-based services.

Hard to Reach: Children not at School

Whilst over 95% of children attend schools, the families of those who do not attend may be those who require the most support. Some of these children (e.g. children educated at home by parents, children with chronic illnesses in hospital, children in jail) are either relatively well-off or are having their educational and welfare needs met in other ways by the institutions in which they are located. However the majority of children not at school are from the most vulnerable and hard-to-reach groups in society. Children excluded from school or truanting are known to be at high risk for a range of difficulties, in particular youth offending (Graham & Bowling, 1995; Kinder et al., 1999). Other groups of children who may not be at school include children of asylum seekers and other children recently brought into the country.[5] Family support programmes based in schools are unlikely to reach out to these groups, especially if families need to physically go into the school to receive the service. Some services deploy outreach workers who can provide a service in the family home, but these are restricted to services which operate on a one-to-one basis.

Hard to Reach: Fathers

One of the key challenges for school-based services is to engage with fathers (Goldman, 2005). School-based services are particularly affected by the challenge of engaging fathers because it is overwhelmingly mothers who come into school to bring and collect children, help in the classrooms, watch school plays and sports days, etc., so fathers tend to see schools as rather alien and perhaps threatening environments. Attempts to involve fathers have not

---

[5] The case of Victoria Climbié, who came to the UK from West Africa with a great aunt and was killed by the aunt and her boyfriend caused a national outcry in the country and has led to a complete overhaul of the child protection system. Victoria was never in school, and this was considered to be one of the major failings of the system.

proved to be particularly successful (Ghate et al., 2000; Henricson et al., 2001). This poses the question of whether the problem is one of engagement (i.e. making services more attractive to fathers, for example, by making fathers feel more welcome in schools or by providing services in the evening), or whether altogether new modes of delivery need to be developed to enable fathers to feel more comfortable accessing the programme.

Services co-located in schools need to be able to reach out to fathers, by employing outreach workers or by providing some services at different venues. There may also be a need to change some of the ways the services work, for example, by opening during evenings and employing male workers.

Confidentiality

Families experiencing problems involving a high level of confidentiality or stigma also have difficulties with access. Although schools provide a generally non-stigmatising environment, and parents routinely go into schools to discuss their children's progress, most parents are not used to going into school to discuss personal problems or family issues. The school can be a welcoming environment for parents who are attending for 'normal' reasons, but can become very threatening if the service offered is more stigmatising and implies poor parenting.

Another issue regarding confidentiality is that parents and/or children may discuss private matters with teachers, and request that they do not disclose to other agencies. Historically teachers have been very reluctant to engage with the child protection system because they are unwilling to breach confidentiality with parents, fearing that this will damage their relationships and may ultimately lead to difficulties for the children (Baginsky, 2000a). Over the past few years there have been a number of attempts to deliver training to teachers about the necessity for referring child protection cases to child protection services (Baginsky, 2000b). Nevertheless there are many problems other than child protection issues which parents may discuss confidentially with teachers, and it is often very difficult for teachers to make a judgement as to whether to refer them on to other services. These issues are much more easily dealt with when there are social workers or other professionals based in the school, and the teachers can then approach them informally to discuss cases without giving names or making an official referral.

Confidentiality is also an issue for children. Like parents, some children may wish to discuss issues confidentially with teachers, whilst other children may not want their teachers to know about issues discussed with school counsellors or other professionals. Children, especially adolescents, are acutely aware of the stigma of being involved in the child protection system or with child and adolescent mental health services (CAMHS), and schools need to handle these issues very carefully. For example, children may resent being called out of class to attend conferences, because they have to explain to their class mates why they were absent.

Poor Relationship with School

Many parents who face difficulties bringing up their children have a history of low academic achievement and conflict or poor relationships with schools, either when they themselves were school students or as parents. These parents are far less likely to see the school as a non-stigmatising environment in which to receive services. School staff need to be helped to understand that some parents are fearful of or resistant to schools. However, reassurance is not always easy to achieve because some parents behave in threatening and even violent ways towards school staff. Violence by parents can create enormous difficulties and conflict for the school, which has to weigh up the welfare of children against the safety of staff.

Because of the potential for alienating some families it is important that they are given a choice of venue, rather than be forced to accept school-based services. However, engagement with the school should be the ultimate aim in all cases – it can never be in children's interests for their parents to be disengaged from their schooling.

Rural/Urban Issues

Schools in rural areas face particular difficulties in providing family support services. This is because the children attending these schools tend to come from a wide geographical area, and it is often difficult for parents to come to school to access services. In addition, rural schools are often smaller than those in urban areas, and so services may be seen as less cost effective than in urban areas. Inner-city schools are physically easier to access but they often serve diverse population groups in areas with multiple problems. School-based services in these areas need to be sensitive to the different groups of families who attend the school, and need to provide culturally sensitive and accessible information to all parents.

Child Age

Parents are more likely to engage with services based in primary schools rather than those in secondary schools. This is because parents (especially mothers) are more likely to be familiar with the school whilst their children are in primary school. Most parents pick their children up from primary school, and virtually all parents attend parents' evenings, school plays, summer fairs or other events at primary (elementary) schools. Parents are also more likely to feel part of the school 'community' and to know other parents because they live close by and because they discuss arrangements for the children to visit one another. Parents of children in secondary (middle or high) schools are far less likely to be familiar with the school community, especially where schools are physically remote from their homes or not easily accessible. Their relation with the school is therefore likely to be more distant. Nevertheless, for many parents the school will continue to be a good location for services. Secondary schools also often have amenities such as sports facilities which can act as a conduit to more specialist services.

Inter-agency Cooperation

One of the key challenges in providing interventions from schools is the question of who should 'own' the initiative. It has been well documented that schools have difficulties relating to professionals from other agencies, especially child protection services (Baginsky, 2000a). There are many reasons for this, including the different professional languages of education, health and social services staff, different understandings of roles (i.e. each agency expecting the other to handle situations), lack of appropriate mechanisms for information sharing, unwillingness of schools to get involved in areas that detract from delivering the curriculum, teachers' fear of alienating parents and lack of training in child protection and child development.

Services 'co-located' in schools can overcome some of these difficulties because the school staff are able to establish personal relationships with the family support staff, and are therefore more likely to establish a degree of trust. However co-location does not resolve all the problems. There still remain problems around, for example, whether social workers or other family support staff should be employed by the school or by another agency. Employment by the school is more likely to allow the support staff to become part of the school staff team, and this will facilitate communication and referrals. However the disadvantage is that families themselves sometimes value a certain distance between the support workers and school staff, mainly because of concerns around confidentiality.

The details of who employs individual members of staff are less important than how the service fits into the ethos of the school. Ideally the services will act as mediators between the school and the other agencies, maintaining the trust and respect of all agencies, and between school and families. They will also work with teachers and others to educate them about child protection and family support issues, and try to encourage schools to become more holistic in their view of children and families. In order to do all these things the practitioners must have the support of the head teacher, senior staff in the school and the pastoral staff, and should have clear protocols around issues such as confidentiality and consent (see below). They also need to be able to work closely with providers in other agencies, and to understand the multi-agency frameworks which govern such matters as referral and information exchange.

Of course, the ideal situation described above does not often prevail, and practitioners may be confronted by a number of conflicts, either within the school, between the school and other agencies and between the school and families. Workers need to be aware of the difficulties and develop strategies to deal with them.

DISCUSSION

This review of policy developments and related service initiatives in the UK, the USA and beyond, suggests that there is enormous potential for schools to deliver a range of services to children and families and to provide a context in which children are able to deal more effectively with issues such as violence and bullying. Schools can play a key role in fostering community connectedness amongst children and families, and are often the fulcrum for community activities, at least for families with children.

Because of their universal provision and their base in the community, schools have been shown to be excellent venues for a range of services aimed at children and families, but they do not reach all families. Over and above the obvious point that some children do not attend school, there are a number of reasons why family members may be reluctant to access school based services. The best way of overcoming this reluctance is to offer families different ways of accessing the service – either through home visits or by holding some sessions in community settings outside the school. When services are in school it is important to make parents and children comfortable by offering privacy and confidentiality (depending on the nature of the service) and by providing adequate facilities for the service.

Like other community interventions, school-based programmes can be difficult to implement. A wide range of stakeholders need to be engaged, and the intervention can easily be undermined by such factors as changes in senior staff in the school, the drying up of funding streams or the overburdening of school staff. A particular issue for schools is that any perception that the broader 'social welfare' or community agenda is undermining educational standards can lead to a refocusing on the school's core task at the expense of the other initiatives.

The most challenging aspect of providing interventions in schools is the relationship between the intervention and the school itself. Without the endorsement of staff, especially the head teacher or principal, programmes will struggle to be established. It is important that teachers be kept 'on side' because many services rely on teachers for referrals and for identifying children at risk. Tension can arise over issues such as confidentiality, children being absent from class to attend sessions and differences of opinion over what actions to take (e.g. to exclude children), and this needs constant dialogue and negotiation.

10

COMMUNITY BASED APPROACHES TO YOUTH SAFETY AND JUVENILE CRIME

THE RELATIONSHIP BETWEEN THE COMMUNITY AND JUVENILE CRIME

There is considerable ambivalence in current public policy and practice regarding the role of adolescents and teenagers in communities. From one perspective (discussed in Chapter 5) there is an increasing recognition that young people have the right to participate more in community life. There is also increasing concern that young people in many Western societies are becoming more sedentary, making less use of their communities for physical activity (Hillman, 2005). This is thought to be contributing to the problems of obesity. So there is a great deal of emphasis in current policy on encouraging teenagers to get out and about more and to be more active in the community. However, once youngsters start to move about in communities without their parents, they are likely to be seen as perpetrators of crime, especially crimes associated with young people such as shoplifting, vandalism and petty theft. They are seen as a potential problem in themselves, just by being there. Teenagers are also more likely to be at risk of becoming victims of crime (Waiton, 2001).

While in the past there was a focus on identifying and supporting individuals who were likely to become delinquent (through association with older family members for instance), considerable attention is now being directed towards prevention and intervention at the community level. This has been facilitated by an increasing understanding of the risk and protective factors related to juvenile crime (Rutter et al., 1998; National Crime Prevention Australia, 1999; Farrington, 2002), and to the increasing sophistication of technology – geographical mapping techniques, for example, allow police forces to map hot spots where perpetrators of specific crimes live (e.g. youth gang attacks), and also where they are likely to commit offences (Mamalian & LaVigne, 1999).

Youth crime is an increasingly important aspect of social policy in all developed countries, and more and more attention is being devoted to initiatives aimed at preventing young people from becoming involved in criminal acts, diverting high risk young people from crime and preventing re-offending. Along-side the policy interest, a large number of research studies have attempted to unpick the relationships and causal pathways between parenting, community and youth crime (Prior & Paris, 2005; Sutton et al., 2004; Utting & France, 2005). These studies tend to show complex relationships, with parenting, peer-group pressure and community disorganisation all playing a role in the development and spatial distribution of youth crime.

Perhaps the most sophisticated recent analysis of these relationships is provided by Weatherburn and Lind (2001). They challenge the prevailing ESIOM (Economic Stress-Induced Offender Motivation) paradigm which asserts that crime levels are high in deprived areas because economic stress creates an inducement for young people to offend. Using evidence from aggregate level studies in the USA they show a strong positive association between economic stress and child neglect (US Department of Health and Human Services, 1988) to support their claim that economic and social stress exert their effects on youth crime by disrupting the parenting process, creating high levels of neglect in those areas. This in turn makes children more susceptible to anti-social influences from peers in the neighbourhood leading to even higher levels of crime. Weatherburn and Lind hypothesise that there is an epidemic or 'tipping' effect. When there is a critical mass of offenders in a community then the level of crime in that community grows exponentially. Their analysis points towards a family-based approach to youth crime prevention, rather than an approach based on increased surveillance and higher levels of policing.

A similar observation about the effects of community on crime – the 'broken window' hypothesis of Wilson and Kelling (1982) described in Chapter 1 – has, paradoxically, led to completely different conclusions about appropriate inter-ventions. Recall that Wilson and Kelling hypothesise that a broken window in a neighbourhood can send a sign to the community that people in the neighbour-hood are not concerned about the community, and that therefore there is a lack of surveillance of behaviour on the street. This invites increasingly disrespectful anti-social behaviour. Law abiding citizens move out or retreat into their homes, leaving the streets to gangs, drunks and prostitutes:

> A piece of property is abandoned, weeds grow up, a window is smashed. Adults stop scolding rowdy children; the children, emboldened, become more rowdy. Families move out, unattached adults move in. Teenagers gather in front of the corner store. The merchant asks them to move; they refuse. Fights occur. Litter accumulates. People start drinking in front of the grocery; in time, an inebriate slumps to the sidewalk and is allowed to sleep it off. Pedestrians are approached by panhandlers (Wilson & Kelling, 1982, p. 30).

Rather than advocating parent-training, day care or even community regeneration as the solution to the problem of neighbourhood degradation, Wilson and Kelling advocate that police should crack down hard on minor misdemeanours to show that they will not be tolerated in the neighbourhood. This will in turn lead to a reduction in major crimes, as potential criminals will be unwilling to take the risk of being apprehended. Police should be given the authority to intervene even in 'extra legal' ways to send a strong message that they are protecting the neighbourhood. This analysis led to the emergence of *broken windows* or *zero tolerance* policing, first tried out in New York City under the then mayor Rudy Giuliani and his police chief William J. Bratton, and soon spread to many other cities in the USA, UK, Australia and elsewhere (Dennis & Bratton, 1998). The concept of *zero tolerance* has become embedded in cultural discourse and this approach has spread to include interventions dealing with weapons and drugs in schools, domestic violence and other social problems. In each case the underlying philosophy focuses on punishment rather than prevention, based on the belief that a strong message that there will be severe consequences for even the most minor misdemeanours will deter all potential offenders.

Despite the popularity of zero tolerance approaches, there has been an extensive debate both about the broken window hypothesis itself and about the effectiveness of zero tolerance policing. The major challenge to the broken window hypothesis has come from the *Project on Human Development in Chicago Neighborhoods* (Sampson et al., 1998) which found that the relationship between community members – *collective efficacy* – was more important in predicting neighbourhood crime levels, than physical signs of disorder such as broken windows or abandoned vehicles. Although zero tolerance policing has many advocates (e.g. Dennis, 1998; Dennis & Mallon, 1998), it also has many detractors (e.g. Harcourt, 2001; Marshall, 1999; Pollard, 1998). The main arguments against the zero tolerance approach are that it reduces police accountability to the community, increases the potential for police brutality, racism and other problems, and that it pulls resources away from detecting and prosecuting serious crime. Another issue is the transferability from its original context – New York City – to communities across the world that have different relationships within the community and between the community and the police. The majority of people who commit the kinds of minor offences targeted by zero tolerance policies are adolescents and young people. Their parents and families are increasingly being seen as significant risk factors in relation to the development of criminal and anti-social behaviour, but also as offering the potential to divert young people away from crime into more socially acceptable conduct.

Whatever the policy consequences, there is emerging evidence that neighbourhood characteristics are strongly related to the anti-social and criminal behaviour of young people, and there is some evidence for the epidemic or social contagion hypothesis discussed in Chapter 2 (Jencks & Mayer, 1990; Crane, 1991; Kupersmidt et al., 1995). Thus work with the leading young offenders in a community is predicted to have 'knock-on' effects in that, if their behaviour is controlled, fewer potential new offenders will be influenced.

This chapter provides examples of a range of different community-based interventions and some that are true community interventions, as defined in Chapter 6, aimed at young people, many of which also involve parents and families. Whilst the majority of interventions either explicitly or implicitly adopt a 'risk/resilience' approach, they come from different theoretical perspectives and have different approaches to targeting and engaging with young people. Although the concept of 'community' is part of the logic model for each of these interventions, few of them explicitly define 'community', and the implicit definitions vary from very small neighbourhoods to much bigger administrative boundaries.

The interventions tend to focus either on children as perpetrators (or potential perpetrators) of crime, and children as victims. The focus on children as victims of crime, bullying and anti-social behaviour is an important recent development in enhancing child safety in the community. There are two main motivations for these developments. Firstly, there has been a general trend in criminal justice policy to include victims' interests and views in the process of the criminal justice system. Until the early 1990s victims had the status of witnesses, and were not offered any services or special consideration for being victims. Children (who until the late 1980s could not give uncorroborated evidence in court in the UK) were not even considered as potential witnesses and therefore there were virtually no resources available to child victims of crime. More recently this has been reversed and it is now recognised that victims of crime require support and consideration in their own right (Home Office, 2003a; Prior & Paris, 2005). Another motivation for aiming services at child victims is that research has shown a significant relationship between being a victim of crime and being a perpetrator (Rutter et al., 1998).

The main area of criminal justice which pioneered the involvement of young victims has been the prosecution of perpetrators of sexual abuse. There are now elaborate arrangements using video-conferencing in court to protect children from having to face perpetrators or hostile questioning from defence counsel (Plotnikoff et al., 1996). More recently there have been several schemes aimed at supporting children who are victims of other crimes such as robbery or assault. Most of these schemes have fallen under the rubric of restorative justice programmes, and in the UK the Youth Justice Board (YJB) has developed a number of restorative justice programmes for young people. Young people commit much of the victimisation that other children experience. Initiatives which seek to reduce the offending behaviour of children and young people may also have a beneficial effect on child victims.

Research into successful schemes to prevent youth offending is increasingly focused on the benefits of community-based work designed to improve personal and social skills and to change behaviour. The provision of affordable and accessible constructive leisure activities is also important. A review of crime prevention programmes by the US Office of Juvenile Justice and Delinquency Prevention (Mihalic et al., 2004) found that the most successful programmes are those that provide high-risk children with home visits, pre-school education and high quality day-care arrangements. Some of the school-focused programmes described in Chapter 9 are also effective in reducing crime and anti-social behaviour. The programmes addressing bullying or behaviour problems that are also described in Chapter 9 are school-based, but there is significant overlap between school-based and neighbourhood-based programmes for young people. In this chapter we describe programmes which are based on geographical neighbourhoods or communities of interest.

Case Study: Youth Works, UK

Youth Works (http://www.youth-works.com) is a programme initiated in the UK in collaboration with commercial organisations by *Groundwork,* an organisation whose main emphasis is community regeneration and environmental improvement (http://www.groundwork.org.uk/). *Youth Works* was set up to engage children-at-risk in community work and to increase their voluntary engagement.

Each *Youth Works* programme is headed by a programme manager who works closely with local agencies. Most of the programmes are in the north of England, and are based within 'problem' housing estates or neighbourhoods in urban areas. Programmes are managed by a local multi-agency steering group. This group normally comprises representatives of local agencies such as the Youth Offending Team, the Police, Groundwork, Education, Social Services and the Probation Service, plus local organisations including drug and health projects, voluntary groups, local businesses, residents' associations and neighbourhood wardens.

Although *Youth Works* programmes take a broad approach to service provision, expecting to engage 150 young people between the ages of 8 and 25 years, they also provide targeted support to up to 50 young people deemed to be particularly 'at risk' of social exclusion.

Youth Works programmes are similar in some respects to the *Youth Inclusion Programmes (YIPs)* described below, but have a wider remit. They also have a greater emphasis on working with the community to reduce anti-social behaviour, which has been found to have a debilitating effect on communities and local traders and causes almost as much anxiety as crime.

Another feature of *Youth Works* is the emphasis on the involvement of local neighbourhood volunteers. Each programme aims to recruit up to 30 residents to assist in delivery. The volunteers can be parents and carers, members of local volunteer groups, long-term unemployed residents, young people on placements, staff and management secondments from local businesses, and local police officers and members of statutory services.

An independent evaluation of 11 *Youth Works* projects by Janice Webb (Webb, 2004) found that it had positive effects on young people themselves, on their anti-social behaviour and on the wider community. Reductions in crime were seen in all 11 communities, and in some areas there were considerable financial savings due to the reduction in youth crime and anti-social behaviour. The evaluation also showed a greater commitment and involvement of young people in their communities as a result of the programme. The evaluation was based on limited data (for example, crime statistics were difficult to obtain for most of the areas), and there were no control groups. So although these findings are positive further research would be necessary to generalise and validate this evaluation.

Case Study: The Violence Intervention Project (VIP) for Children and Families, USA

In 1992, law enforcement officers, community groups, school representatives, and resident council leaders met in the New Orleans police district with the highest level of violence, and together developed a model programme. *VIP* was created in response to the increasing numbers of children exposed to violence as victims or witnesses in the New Orleans metropolitan area (http://www.ncpc.org), with the idea that law enforcement officers are the first people on the scene and can play a crucial role in identifying children who may benefit from intervention (Osofsky, 1997).

VIP involves police, schools and community residents. It focuses particularly on children's networks of caregivers, parents, police, teachers, and health care workers. Police officers are trained by mental health experts on the effects of violence on children and families (Osofsky & Osofsky, 2004). Teachers are given training on working with children who have experienced violence directly or indirectly. Support is given to community groups such as the *'Moms Against Violence'* project, a group of residents whose members' children had died as a result of community violence. This approach involves the whole community in preventing, and intervening against, violence in their community (Scott, 1999).

Case Study: Youth Offending Teams (YOTs)

Since the current UK Government came into power there have been a large number of programmes aimed at curbing youth crime and anti-social behaviour. The Home Office White Paper *No More Excuses* (Home Office, 1997), was the first policy document setting out the new approach to youth justice. *No More Excuses* outlined a new approach to youth crime, stressing personal responsibility and choice, and a new commitment to preventing youth crime as well as convicting offenders. The White Paper set the scene for the establishment of the *Youth Justice Board* (YJB) to lead reforms of the youth justice system under the 1998 Crime and Disorder Act. The YJB provides national management for *Youth Offending Teams (YOTs)*, which deliver co-ordinated youth justice services working to new Youth Justice Plans. Since 2000, all local authorities in the UK have established *YOTs*. These teams are made up of social workers, police officers, education staff, probation officers and health service representatives. There are over 150 *YOTs* in England and Wales with a statutory duty to focus on preventing crime as well as working with convicted young offenders. The majority of *YOTs* cover a local authority area, although some cover more than one local authority, and thus they are serving somewhat large communities in relation to much of the work directed at early childhood and parenting.

YOTs are required to provide a parenting service, and many of them have established successful parenting programmes (Ghate & Ramella, 2002). The majority of these programmes are not preventive, being aimed at families of young people already in the youth justice system. *YOTs* (or other agencies working in conjunction with them) have, however, developed a range of preventive programmes, some with a clear community focus, but all target children at high risk of offending. These preventive programmes were a response to the Audit Commission's report *Misspent Youth* (Audit Commission, 1996), which strongly advocated a refocusing in the youth justice system from reactive to preventive approaches, and particularly preventive programmes targeted at high risk neighbourhoods and individuals. These programmes include:

Youth Inclusion Programmes (YIPs)

YIPs are perhaps the flagship preventive programmes initiated by the YJB. They aim to engage 13- to 16-year-olds who are involved in crime or who are identified as being most at risk of offending, truancy or anti-social behaviour (http://www.youth-justice-board.gov.uk/YouthJusticeBoard/Prevention/YIP).

YIPs aim to reduce youth crime in neighbourhoods. Young people are identified through a number of different agencies who work together in local neighbourhoods (usually a specific housing estate). These include the YOT, police, social services, local education authorities or schools, other local agencies and the community leaders. Key local informants from various agencies complete a 'risk matrix' – based on research evidence on the risk of offending – to identify the 50 young people in the community who are most at risk of offending. These young people are then specifically targeted and encouraged to participate in a range of activities with other young people from the local area.

YIPs are similar to the *Youth Works* projects mentioned above and follow a similar format, but they are much more focused on diverting high-risk young people from crime and anti-social behaviour. The programme operates in 72 of the most deprived/high crime estates in England and Wales.

The programme aims to provide young people with a safe and stimulating environment where they can learn new skills, take part in activities with others and get help with their education and careers guidance. Positive role models – the workers and volunteer mentors – help to change young people's attitudes to education and crime. The programme has specific targets such as the proportion of the 50 most at risk who engage with the programme and the 'dosage' they receive, i.e. the number of sessions. It also has targets for reductions of offending and re-offending by those engaged in the *YIP*, and for reductions of offending in the neighbourhood.

An independent national evaluation of the first three years of the programme (Mackie et al., 2003) found that there were initially a number of difficulties implementing *YIPs*, and that the crime reduction targets had to be lowered somewhat. Nevertheless they were, on the whole, successfully implemented and achieved positive outcomes:

● Arrest rates for the 50 young people considered to be most at risk of crime in each *YIP* had been reduced by 65%.
● Of those who had offended before joining the programme, 73% were arrested for fewer offences after engaging with a *YIP*.
● Of those who had not offended previously but who were at risk, 74% did not go on to be arrested after engaging with a *YIP*.

YIPs are neighbourhood-based programmes, but they are not community-level programmes in the true sense of the word. Rather the community is simply the context within which they conduct their primary objective which is to target 'high risk' individuals.

Youth Inclusion and Support Panels (YISPs)

YISPs aim to prevent anti-social behaviour and offending by 8- to 13-year-olds in a given area who are considered to be at high risk of offending. As in the case of

YIPs, young people at risk are identified by professionals or community workers and referred to a multi-agency panel. The young people are assessed for the degree of risk they pose and the risk assessment is presented to the panel.

Panels are made up of a number of representatives of different agencies (e.g. police, schools, health and social services). The main emphasis of a panel's work is to ensure that children and their families, at the earliest possible opportunity, can access mainstream public services.

Thirteen pilot *YISPs*, funded by the Board and the *Children's Fund*, were set up across England in 2003. Some 92 local authorities including the 13 pilot schemes have chosen to use this funding to establish a *YISP* or multiple *YISPs* in their area. This is set to increase, however. The Government announced plans in its five-year crime strategy (published July 2004) to increase the number of panels by 50% (Home Office, 2004, p. 45).

YISPs cover a wide range of different communities. Some are neighbourhood-based, but others cover much bigger geographical communities and even local authority areas. Nevertheless they are based on similar premises to *YIPs* – in particular the idea that local frontline workers who are well acquainted with young people in the community will be able to identify those children most at risk of offending (or other negative outcomes) and refer them on to preventive programmes. *YISPs* are being evaluated by a team based at Newcastle University (Walker & Coomes, 2003) but no findings have yet been published.

Case Study: The Anti-social Behaviour Order (ASBO)

In addition to these initiatives, a number of new penalties have been developed in the UK for children (or other community members) who offend or commit acts of anti-social behaviour. The most significant of these in relation to community safety are *Anti-social Behaviour Orders* (ASBOs) (details summarised in Box 10.1), designed in part to help neighbourhood residents feel that they could influence what happens in their local area.

Box 10.1   Details of Anti-social Behaviour Orders (ASBOs)

ASBOs were introduced by section 1 of the Crime and Disorder Act 1998. They became available from 1 April 1999, on the application of the police or the local authority, in respect of any person over 10 years of age where:

(a) He or she has acted in an anti-social way, that is to say, in a manner which caused or was likely to cause harassment, alarm and distress to one or more persons not of the same household, and

(b) such an order is necessary to protect persons in that local government area (or neighbouring areas) from further anti-social acts.

ASBOs are not targeted exclusively at young people, nor are they strictly speaking community interventions. We include them here because they have been couched in terms of supporting communities and neighbourhoods, and they represent the 'punitive' end of the preventive continuum, and illustrate the kinds of interventions which stop just short of criminal justice interventions.

The publication of the government White Paper on anti-social behaviour (Home Office, 2003a), the rapid production and progress of the resultant Bill through Parliament, and the launch of the government anti-social behaviour action plan (Home Office, 2003b) demonstrate the significance of anti-social behaviour as a political issue in the UK. Much of the concern about such behaviour relates to young people and an increasingly large proportion of *ASBOs* are issued on children and young people under the age of 18 years.

The effect of the order is to impose prohibitions on the named person considered necessary to prevent a repetition of the anti-social behaviour for a minimum period of two years. There is no upper limit to the order, which can last indefinitely. The scope of the orders is very wide-ranging, and includes prohibitions on entering specific streets or addresses, wearing specific clothes, associating with individuals or even using particular words or phrases.

Initially the take-up of *ASBOs* was very limited and so the Government introduced a number of important legislative changes. These include:

- a significant widening in those who can apply for the orders to include the British Transport Police, Registered Social Landlords, County Councils, Housing Action Trusts in addition to the original bodies;
- enabling the prescriptions in orders to cover any area within, or all of, England and Wales;
- introducing the ability to make interim orders pending consideration of a full application;
- enabling criminal courts on their own motion, or following Crown Prosecution Service/Police representation, to impose an order on conviction for any criminal offence.

By November 2003, the proportion of *ASBOs* served to people under 18 years was 65% (Campbell, 2002a). The number of *ASBOs* taken out in the year up to March 2004 increased by 117% and more than 2,400 had been issued (Thomas, Vuong & Renshaw, 2004). By the end of 2004 a total of 4,649 had been issued, of which 2,057 had applied to children aged 10 to 17. The use of *ASBOs* differed considerably in different parts of the country and a small number of local authority areas accounted for a very high proportion of those served. This suggests that law enforcement officers in some localities have yet to be persuaded that they offer an effective way of reducing crime and disorder.

The introduction of *ASBOs* has proved to be very controversial (Cowan, 2005), and several prominent organisations such as NACRO (National Association for the Care and Rehabilitation of Offenders), NAYJ (National Association of Youth Justice), as well as opposition politicians, have called for them to be discontinued. To date, there has been limited research conducted on the use of *ASBOs*. A Home Office Research Study published in 2002 (Campbell, 2002b) analysed orders made during the first 18 months that they were available. More recently, as a result of concerns in relation to increasing workloads, and the impact on other aspects of YOTs' work, the Home Office commissioned a survey to establish baseline figures for the use of orders across England and Wales (Thomas, Vuong & Renshaw, 2004).

Little research has been conducted on what children and young people themselves feel about these measures.

HOLISTIC APPROACH – SAFETY AND CRIME PREVENTION

Initiatives that incorporate a social support/social capital approach to youth offending and delinquency stress the benefits of encouraging informal systems of support within communities. This is sometimes referred to as 'collective efficacy' (see Chapters 1 and 9). Collective efficacy refers to trust and support between neighbours combined with a willingness to intervene in situations of concern, to the benefit of the whole community (Sampson et al., 1998). The US National Commission on Children in 1991 concluded that enhancing a sense of community and encouraging informal systems of social support for children and families should be a primary goal of social policies at all levels of government. In the UK, as long ago as 1982, the Barclay report into the role of social services (NISW, 1982) emphasised the importance of social networks and communities.

The social approach emphasises the importance of creating better relationships within communities. Aiding better relationships between generations is especially important in reducing fear of crime and creating understanding between older people and young people in communities.

Increasingly, community safety and crime prevention initiatives are adopting a holistic approach. This usually involves partnerships co-ordinating community-based initiatives to address the needs of whole communities rather than just those of individual families or children who are thought to be at risk. The aim is preventive, to stop problems escalating. This work draws on ecological theories discussed in Chapter 1 that place importance on addressing all of the systems influencing children's environments (Garbarino & Kostelny, 1992). Holistic approaches may be comprehensive in terms of involving all relevant agencies, organisations and community groups in the creation of community-wide partnerships. They may also be comprehensive in terms of the scope of the work undertaken, incorporating structural and social aspects to address the underlying causes. Some examples of holistic approaches to crime prevention and community safety are:

Case Study: Communities That Care (CTC)

CTC is a comprehensive community-wide and community-focused initiative designed to deal with a range of problems faced by teenagers, but crime, anti-social behaviour and substance misuse in particular. It establishes partnerships between local people, agencies and organisations and implements local action plans to create safer communities with better outcomes for young people. Its holistic, multi-agency approach was originally developed by David Hawkins and Richard Catalano in the 1980s in the USA (Hawkins & Catalano, 1992). It represents an attempt to combine community empowerment with evidence-based approaches to crime and substance abuse prevention, and its theoretical framework is the 'risk/resilience' model, based on a public health intervention model which has been used to prevent a range of physical illnesses and social difficulties (Roussos & Fawcett, 2000).

CTC involves building a community coalition of key leaders and decision makers who are brought together to form a Community Prevention Board. The Board are provided with training on risk and protective factors for drugs and other problems affecting teenagers. They are also informed about evidence-based prevention programmes. The Board commissions a needs-assessment in the local community, and on the basis of this a range of initiatives and strategies are put into place. Throughout this process the Board is offered Technical Assistance by CTC to enable them to carry out their role, and a range of products and publications have been developed to support this process (see www.communitiesthatcare.org.uk and http://www.channing-bete.com/positiveyouth/pages/CTC/CTC.html).

In the USA, CTC has been established in a large number of communities, and some states have implemented the approach state-wide (Greenberg et al., 2004). Although the model has been much researched, there have been no evaluations of CTC using control groups. The most comprehensive evaluation is that of Greenberg and colleagues (2004) who evaluated 15 CTC sites in Pennsylvania between 1992 and 1998. The evaluation found that there were no significant changes in rates of teenage pregnancy, child abuse or poverty, but that, compared to non-CTC areas (following a 1.8% rise in the first year) delinquency rates declined by 1.5% per year. While encouraging, these reductions do not reach statistical significance. Interestingly, Greenberg et al. found on further analysis that those sites which had implemented CTC more effectively tended to demonstrate higher reductions in youth crime.

Since the late 1990s CTC has been implemented in a number of different countries including the UK, Australia, Ireland and the Netherlands (Utting & France, 2005). In the UK, the Joseph Rowntree Foundation funded three projects, in Barnsley, Swansea and Coventry. Similarly to the process in the USA, in each area key community leaders are identified. These are individuals who can draw together community organisations and resources. The focus is initially on community assessment and capacity building. A local crime prevention board is established and a local crime prevention strategy produced. Data from a number of sources including surveys, demographic data and service analysis are analysed to identify community need. On the basis of the identified need a range of evidence-based interventions are prioritised. This is a long-term process and the strategy is used to identify risk and protective factors in local communities (see Box 10.2).

In Australia CTC has been implemented in three communities in the state of Victoria, and initial research findings indicate that the implementation has been effective (Williams et al., 2005). An outcome evaluation of the programme focusing on reductions in crime and substance abuse by young people is planned but is not yet underway.

> ## Box 10.2 *Communities That Care*, risk and protective factors
>
> Risk factors:
>
> - low income,
> - poor housing,
> - family conflict,
> - parental attitudes condoning problem behaviour,
> - availability of drugs and low school commitment.
>
> Protective factors:
>
> - family attachment,
> - social skills,
> - healthy values,
> - connection to an adult role model,
> - opportunities for social development.

Overall CTC seems to provide a good model for community level interventions aimed at preventing youth crime and substance misuse. The CTC model has been built up over a number of years in a variety of different contexts, and so has been able to mature and develop – unlike many of the programmes discussed in this book, which are often one-off or short-term 'injections' of resources. The CTC approach of building cross-sector partnerships, undertaking neighbourhood needs-assessments and then commissioning a range of evidence-based projects to address local need has formed the basis for a number of other programmes described in this and the preceding two chapters. Many other programmes, however, do not provide the technical support which is a crucial element of CTC, and which is likely to increase sustainability and commitment. Nevertheless it is still not possible to say that CTC 'works' as there have not been any rigorous outcome evaluations of the model, and any judgements about its effectiveness must be tentative.

Case Study: On Track

On Track is an early intervention and prevention programme that was initiated under the Home Office Crime Reduction Programme in the UK. £30 million was originally provided over three years (2000–2003) for the setting up and development of a range of services in local neighbourhoods (see Johnston, 2001 for a fuller description of the programme). *On Track* is based on premises similar to those of CTC, and draws on a similar theoretical and research framework. Specifically, *On Track* is based upon two assumptions:

1. That it is possible to identify children who are at risk of becoming young offenders by identifying individual, family, community, school and peer relationship risk and protective factors (Farrington, 1996; Hawkins et al., 1992).
2. That there is evidence for the effectiveness of particular types of interventions in reducing risks and enhancing protective factors for individual children, families, communities and schools.

The research shows that risk factors are not necessarily causal, but they can be reasonably reliable in predicting outcomes of future youth offending. Prediction is improved if a child can be identified as having multiple risks and low protection (Hawkins et al., 1992). As a result of this evidence, early identification and intervention over the life of a child is seen as a possible solution to tackling youth crime (Farrington, 1996; Prior & Paris, 2005).

Like *CTC*, (and the other community initiatives discussed in this book), *On Track* pilot projects focused on bringing together a range of agencies in the neighbourhood to develop services which would increase the level of early intervention services and would develop a holistic neighbourhood-wide focus on the issue. A particular premise of *On Track* was that children and families at risk would benefit from multiple interventions which would be tailored to meet the individual needs of each child and family within the context of the specific community. *On Track* pilots were also given the task to engage with the most 'hard to reach' children and families within the neighbourhood, and to provide a range of targeted and universal services.

Services were based on five categories of interventions which had been shown by research to be effective:

- home visiting;
- pre-school education;
- parent support and training;
- family therapy;
- family and school partnerships.

In addition there was a sixth category, 'specialist services', which was intended to enable communities to tailor services to their particular needs.

The programme selected 24 deprived and high crime areas that were required to develop community-based projects. These were located within small geographical areas and targeted children aged 4–12 who were 'at risk' of becoming future offenders. At the time *On Track* was set up, the evidence-base for community interventions was well established in the USA but there was limited UK evidence for the effectiveness of early intervention in combating youth crime (Graham, 1998). The programme was therefore aimed at improving the UK evidence-base. Although the sites were provided with definitions of the five categories of interventions, they were given a great deal of flexibility to decide what sort of services they could implement, and the result was a very wide range of interventions. The categories themselves turned out not to be mutually exclusive, and a very high number of activities were classified in the 'specialist' category which became rather a catch-all for activities which did not fit neatly into the five original categories.

Before it was fully implemented, *On Track* was incorporated into the *Children's Fund*, discussed in Chapter 8, and lost its identity as a separate programme, although the 24 communities continued with their own separate structures, and the evaluation continued separately.

On Track was intended as a pilot, and a well-resourced evaluation was commissioned. This addressed implementation issues, impact and cost-effectiveness,[1] and was conducted in two phases. The first phase (which involved a national evaluation team and four local evaluation teams conducting a range of different studies of early implementation) has now reported (Harrington et al., 2004; France et al., 2004a; Parsons et al., 2003). Harrington et al. (2004) discuss the early implementation and process issues, and highlight the practical difficulties faced by projects that were required to create new structures and put new services in place in an unrealistically short timeframe. Five key difficulties for implementation were identified, summarised in Box 10.3.

They also identified how the policy shifts affected and disrupted implementation. A particular challenge for the projects was to change from a needs-based service-delivery model to a risk/resilience-based model, and few of the projects successfully achieved this transition.

France et al. (2004a) focus on the early outcomes. The project data which informed this outcome study was very patchy and rather unreliable, so no firm

---

Box 10.3 Difficulties in the implementation of *On Track*

- Tensions arose over the use of a bidding document for planning service delivery.
- The gap between the presentation of Delivery Plans and Home Office approval of funding was longer than planned, leading to slippage in programme implementation.
- From the beginning project set-up time was included in the model but this was not realistic in the absence of an existing infrastructure.
- Transitional time between the planning stage and action was not included within the model, and this disregarded the need for time to reflect upon the plans and, in many cases, to re-negotiate with partners in order to find the best ways of making partnerships work.
- Project development support was not clearly defined within the model and it remained unclear whose responsibility this was within the Home Office.

(France et al., 2004b, p. 45)

---

[1] For a description of the first phase of the evaluation, see France et al. (2004b). A description of the second phase methodology is available on the website of the Policy Research Bureau www.prb.org.uk.

conclusions can be drawn, but there are some encouraging if rather tentative findings:

> Findings from the evaluation also suggest that On Track could be making a difference. Professionals recorded that between 21 per cent and 36 per cent of children and parents who were identified as having 'risk factors' or problem behaviours improved after On Track intervention. While such results have to be taken with caution because of the subjective nature of recording and the sample size these findings do seem to indicate that On Track can have an effect on different types of risk and problem behaviour (p. 76).

Phase 2 of the evaluation has not yet been reported, but reports are expected to be produced from late 2005 (see www.prb.org.uk and www.dfes.gov.uk/research).

Case Study: Family Group Conferences (FGC)

FGCs are perhaps the best example of youth crime-reduction initiatives based on communities of interest (in this case, extended families and support networks), rather than on geographically defined neighbourhoods or school communities. *FGCs* were originally developed in New Zealand in the early 1980s, being formalised as the primary decision-making mechanism for children and young people in both civil and criminal matters by the Children and Young Persons Act 1989. They were based on the Maori tradition whereby problems with children were resolved by meetings of the extended family or clan, and were developed as a response to the increasing numbers of indigenous children becoming involved in the youth justice and care systems (see Box 10.4 for the main principles underlying *FGCs*). *FGCs* involve a formal meeting between the young person, their immediate and extended family and other significant others in the young person's life. *FGCs* are becoming an increasingly important aspect of the youth justice and child protection systems in most of the developed world.

Box 10.4   Principles of Family Group Conferences (*FGCs*)

FGCs are part of the larger move towards a more 'restorative' approach to youth justice, which is broadly based on the following principles:

- The children most at risk of offending should be identified and helped so that the risk of their offending is greatly reduced.
- These children are likely to be suffering from a range of social, emotional, relationship and behaviour problems, and the help offered should take into account the family and community context of the offending behaviour.
- Families and children themselves need to be involved in decision-making and planning about their cases. The more the family is involved in the decision-making, the more likely they are to be motivated to carry out the plan.

In New Zealand, when *FGCs* are held in the context of the youth justice system, they also involve the victim of the crime (NZ Child, Youth and Family, 2004 http://www. cyf.govt.nz/1254.htm). *FGCs* are coordinated by a trained professional, but no professionals attend the meeting itself. The family then presents the professionals with a plan to address the young person's offending (or the child protection issues), and it is then up to the family and the professionals to negotiate its implementation.

Practitioners from various different agencies should be involved in the assessment and intervention to prevent offending, and partnership between agencies is a necessary factor to ensure success. Although *FGCs* are not neighbourhood-based interventions, they are aimed at the child's or family's community of interest. In that sense they combine the restorative approach with an ecological approach to offending and child protection. The *FGC* is a prime example of an intervention that draws on wider informal social networks rather than on formal services in order to deal with troubled families. Following the implementation of the legislation in New Zealand, there was a significant reduction both in the number of children and young people in state care and in the use of custody for juveniles, reductions which have been attributed to the introduction of the new approach (Maxwell & Morris, 1996). Longitudinal research has demonstrated that *FGCs* can reduce re-offending when they have a high standard of practice (Morris & Maxwell, 1998).

While New Zealand remains the most developed example of how *FGCs* can be used as an integral part of the youth justice system, from the early 1990s a number of projects in the UK pioneered the approach and have become an important part of the child protection system. Over 50% of local authorities use *FGCs* as part of the child protection or 'looked after' process for children under the care of the local authority. 'Working together to Safeguard Children', the Government's guidance on safeguarding children, endorses *FGCs* as an effective model which encourages high levels of participation and engagement from children and their families. *FGCs* have had less of an impact on the youth justice system than on the child protection system, but some *FGCs* have been developed and evaluated in the youth justice system (Lupton, 1998; 2000; Marsh & Crow, 1997). However, of the 46 projects funded by the YJB's Development Fund, only 20 attempted to use *FGCs*, and only five completed six or more conferences during the period of evaluation (Wilcox, 2003). Nonetheless, where *FGCs* have been deployed in a systematic and well-funded manner, there is promising evidence that they are able to reduce offending behaviour among children and young people, to involve significant numbers of victims and to generate high levels of satisfaction from children and their families (Essex County Council, 2002).

Most *FGCs* have to date been focused on interventions within the formal youth justice system rather than being used as a preventive measure, and there is some debate about whether they can be effective preventive interventions. This is partly because of the cost, and partly because many families will be motivated to participate only if there is a real crisis, and may not be prepared to spend several hours (and sometimes days) discussing a relative if there is not a compelling reason to do so.

GENERAL CRIME PREVENTION AND COMMUNITY SAFETY INITIATIVES

The policy focus on youth crime and anti-social behaviour (and children as victims of crime) has been developed in parallel with an increasing focus on community initiatives to combat street crime and promote community safety more generally. Rather than focusing on prevention or diversion, these initiatives aim to reduce crime by improved design of the urban environment and increased surveillance of public spaces. A number of high profile initiatives have been launched to address these issues. Here we provide examples of some of the UK community-based anti-crime initiatives. There are three main foci to these initiatives:

- engaging the whole community more effectively in combating crime;
- changing the physical appearance and layout of communities to improve safety and deter street crime;
- using new technologies such as CCTV.

Whilst the range and extent of initiatives has been rather haphazard and uncoordinated, the overall thrust of policy is to develop community safety strategies within which a range of specific initiatives operate.

- *Neighbourhood Watch* and *Home Watch* (where residents check on the property of others and watch out for suspicious behaviour) can be useful ways to involve local people in crime prevention and to promote surveillance. However their numbers have decreased since the late 1980s and they are less easy to form in high-crime areas. They also suffer a dwindling of involvement by residents over time.
- *The Designing Out Crime Association* (DOCA) aims to provide a forum to promote safer communities and reduce anti-social behaviour by improving the quality of life through the concept, application and practice of designing out crime. www.doca.org.uk/.
- *Operation Gate It* www.gate-it.org.uk/about.html is an initiative by the UK Home Office in partnership with a number of voluntary organisations. It aims to deliver physical environmental improvements to areas which are run-down, badly designed or poorly maintained and have become magnets for anti-social behaviour. The scheme forms part of the Government's TOGETHER campaign to tackle anti-social behaviour.

The *Gate It* scheme is funded by the Home Office's Anti-social Behaviour Unit. The project is to run for two years (from March 2004 to March 2006). It will enable communities across England and Wales to develop schemes that tackle environmental issues such as litter, vandalism and fly-tipping (dumping rubbish, old furniture or commercial waste) in alleyways. It is aimed to help local residents take action to make areas such as alleyways behind houses, bin stores, garages and derelict land near housing estates cleaner, greener and safer and thus to deter anti-social behaviour.

The types of projects being funded include

- improving pathways, open spaces and communal areas to deter joy-riding, fly-tipping and nuisance behaviour;
- securing open spaces by installing gates on alleyways, bollards and fencing;
- installing lighting or CCTV;
- opening up visibility into parks or play areas to make them safer;
- improving areas of neglected or waste land which attract anti-social behaviour.

DISCUSSION

In this chapter we have described a range of community-based interventions aimed at reducing youth crime. These approaches cover a wide range of objectives. Programmes such as *Communities that Care, Youth Works* and *On Track* are primarily focused on **prevention**, whereas *YIPs* and *YISPs* are more focused on **diversion** of those young people at highest risk. *ASBOs* and *FGCs* are aimed at controlling the behaviour of young people who have already offended, although their approaches are at considerable variance with each other. Finally we have described some initiatives which are aimed at reducing the **opportunity** for youth crime. Some interventions focus exclusively on young people themselves, but increasingly families are also becoming part of the intervention strategies. Few of these initiatives take communities as their starting point. Rather they involve community members in the control or rehabilitation of individuals who are known to be at risk of creating problems for the community, in the community. However, they are important to consider since they provide illustrations of the ways that services previously limited to probation or law enforcement have become meshed with a wider array of practitioners and community members.

Some interventions described here have shown promising results, but none of them have (yet) demonstrated long-term effectiveness in crime reduction. It is also not clear to what extent these different approaches complement each other or alternatively undermine each other's effectiveness. However, evaluations of these programmes continue, and knowledge of what is effective is accumulating all the time.

It is possible that the substantial effort devoted to identifying children at risk of offending, and the considerable resources being invested in crime reduction programmes, have contributed to stalling of the rise in youth crime in the UK and the USA in the 1990s. Evaluations of the vast majority of these programmes have demonstrated considerable reductions in offending amongst their client groups and in their neighbourhoods. Overall, however there has been only a modest decline in the actual rate of youth crime in the UK over the past 10 years, and no decline at all between 2001 and 2004 (MORI, 2004). The relationship between the overall rate of offending (or of other social problems related to this age group such as teenage pregnancy, drug misuse, bullying and truanting), and specific programmes, is very difficult to establish. These interventions tend to be short-term projects in a relatively small number of areas, and each one tends to affect a relatively small number of families. Although many of them are nominally pilot projects, implying that they could potentially be implemented on a national basis, it is difficult to see how they could be developed in all, or even most, communities in any particular country or state. Nevertheless, there may well be a collective effect on overall youth-offending rates.

This is perhaps a particular example of the generic problem of the relationship between community initiatives and changes in the behaviour of the population as a whole. As we discuss in Chapter 6, even the most ambitious and successful initiatives are subject to displacement, mis-targeting, variable implementation, etc., all of which undermine their effectiveness. In addition, even the best-funded initiatives can only reach a minority of communities. Finally, it is still not clear to what extent new services or community development projects of any sort are really effective in producing long-term changes in behaviour and social patterns which are caused by structural and cultural factors in society as much as by the lack of service provision. Nevertheless, the recognition that crime, especially youth crime, and anti-social behaviour does have a spatial distribution, and that neighbourhood characteristics do have a bearing on the behaviour of young people, is a significant advance. Although many of the approaches described in this chapter are rather tentative, they could be seen as precursors to a more thought-out and strategic approach to the development of crime-prevention inter-ventions in which community-based programmes would be nested.

11

CONCLUSIONS

From the preceding chapters it is clear that governments, scholars of family life and child development and those involved in helping families are all in agreement that 'place matters' and that, within the places that families occupy – both geographical and virtual – it is desirable for there to be some sense of cohesion, common purpose and support.

Many countries have instigated a range of policy initiatives that are designed to bring local communities together, to encourage people to take shared responsibility for each other and to enhance the places where they live. Not only is there a drive to get people involved in their communities, but in recent years there has been particular attention paid to those members of communities who are often left out of decision making – children. As fertility rates in Western societies decline, children are increasingly being viewed within public policy as a valuable resource for nations, and not only as the concern of their parents. They, and their own special communities – schools, have been at the centre of ideas about bringing together not only local families but also the numerous professional groups who are involved with child and family well-being. Public policy is also addressing the needs and aspirations of parents as parents, rather than viewing them simply as individual citizens. So, for example, child care, maternity and paternity leave and juggling work/home responsibilities have all come within the sphere of politics and policy within the past few years, whereas previously these were considered private matters.

The increasing importance of community and neighbourhood, which characterises both policy making and academic endeavour, can be seen partly as a countervailing impetus to globalisation. It may not be too much of an exaggeration to say that the tensions between globalisation on the one hand and localisation on the other underlie some of the most important social and political developments in the early 21st century. One important recent development in this respect has been the growth of the Internet and the so-called 'digital revolution'. Initially this was heralded as signalling the 'end of geography'. The effects of these processes on children's lives are discussed in Chapter 5. For adults it was predicted that the Internet would provide far more opportunities for tele-working, improved communications, virtual meeting, etc., making face-to-face encounters much less important. This was expected to result in physical location having much less salience than had hitherto been the case. These processes have indeed come about, but there have been some consequences of these developments, which have made neighbourhoods more, rather than less important. The *digital divide*, although primarily relating to age and socio-economic status, has a distinctly geographical aspect to it and the geographical spread of Internet access is not even. In particular rural and remote areas have reduced access to the Internet; and also to mobile telephones in some countries. In addition the huge increase in geo-coding technologies has enabled companies to target individual streets or post codes. As Burrows, Ellison and Woods put it:

> Far from rendering real, physical places unimportant . . . the opposite is the case: digital media, which can appear remote from the immediacies of everyday life, may be having an increasingly tangible impact on how we are sorted – or 'segmented' – in terms of lifestyles, patterns of consumption and, of course, the neighbourhoods in which we live (2005, p. 26).

These technological innovations are therefore bringing together communities of interest, for example enabling virtual communities to form – and increasing the importance of geographical neighbourhoods – providing detailed information about the neighbourhood and people living there. This means that community and neighbourhoods are likely to increase, rather than decrease in their public policy importance over the next decade. This pattern is particularly likely because, as we discuss in Chapter 6, both left and right wing politicians around the world share a focus on community albeit for different reasons. Addition ally, the issues which community interventions are designed to address – social cohesion, crime, educational attainment and so forth – are becoming increasingly important policy concerns. Public policy is also now much more focused on intra familial issues. Parenting, child care, domestic conflict, volunteering, caring responsibilities, custody rights, etc., all of which had previously been considered largely private matters, are now at the centre of public policy debates.

The focus of the majority of this attention has been on deprived areas in major cities, home to many (but certainly not all) of the most vulnerable parents and children. Many of the initiatives described have been designed (in part) to reduce stigma. It relieves families of the pressure of responsibility if interventions are focussed on communities – usually geographical communities though sometimes on communities defined by ethnic group or other characteristics indicating minority status. The principles on which this approach is based are most clearly delineated by Communitarianism:

> Communitarianism springs from the recognition that the human being is by nature a social animal as well as an individual with a desire for autonomy. Communitarians recognize that a healthy society must have a correct balance between individual autonomy and social cohesion. Much recent thinking has focused on an assumed conflict between the rights of the individual and the responsibilities of the government. When you put "community" back into the equation, you find that the apparent conflict between the individual and the government can be resolved by public policies that are consistent with core American values and work to the benefit of all members of our society (Norman Garfinkle, Chairman, Institute for Communitarian Policy Studies, George Washington University, Washington, DC. http://www.gwu.edu/~icps/about.html).

Community interventions are particularly important in relation to children and families because they take into account the contexts in which the children are developing, as well as the characteristics of the children themselves. That is one of the major reasons why the growth of policy interventions in the early years of life has so closely mirrored the growth in community interventions.

In addition to the sharing of responsibility for child and family outcomes there is a sense that efforts are being made to replicate a rural idyll (that famous 'village raising the child') in each urban area throughout the Western world. A strong, close-knit community is cherished as an ideal by city planners, who believe that the built environment can create a sense of community (Katz, 1994). 'New Urbanism' as it is known has been featured on the covers of *Newsweek, The New York Times* and *The Atlantic Monthly* (Fulton, 1996). And yet our analysis has shown that there is also a darker side to communities, which sometimes involves coercive control, social exclusion and isolation. In addition, community interventions are vulnerable to being favoured by governments not only because they are 'bottom up' and empowering, but because they are relatively cheap and may offer an acceptable method of social control.

We have shown some of the complexities in the relationships between children, families and communities. Bronfenbrenner's (1979) ecological theory – in many ways the starting point for the study of families and communities – is usually represented as a series of concentric circles, with the child at the centre and national policy or culture on the perimeter. However it is important to recall that his model also incorporated the complexities of the interactions between children, parents, families and communities (meso-systems); interactions that are likely to change over the course of children's development.

We have discussed the definitional debates surrounding 'community' and the many theoretical approaches that have been taken to understanding just how communities of interest or neighbourhoods might influence families. A major focus of this book has been to explore the related notions of *neighbourhood* and *community* and their implications for understanding more fully the impact of interventions on the lives of families. These are both slippery terms, and there is little consensus either about the definitions or about their true implications for policy and research. Of the two concepts *neighbourhood* is the easier concept to deal with, because the key definitional issue revolves around the geographical size of the physical area and the degree to which people there share a common concept of the area. The term *community* is a far more potent concept, but a lot more difficult to define and operationalise; for example people can belong to several communities at the same time, and communities can be huge or tiny. They can also be geographical areas or communities of interest or membership. There is still a great deal to be learned about the nature of communities and their impact on parenting and families, and ultimately on children's lives. Although it is clear that communities matter, it is not clear whether parents' subjective views of community are more important influences on parenting style than objective 'facts' about the community.

As we have suggested, in this post-industrial era the permanency and predictability of family relationships, including those with children, are more uncertain. Parenting in communities is taking place in an increasing diversity of partnership settings. Children are experiencing less time with their two natural parents and more transitions into and out of household types. Family networks are becoming more complex and less stable for contemporary children although the majority of children still spend significant parts of their childhood in a two-parent family. In some communities a weaker conjugal system is creating some structural marginalisation of fathers in children's lives as more women have children without co-resident male partners or form lone parent households after divorce. With the increased visibility of multi-ethnic and multi-faith groupings across most Western countries, social scientists and public policy-makers will also need to be aware of diverse models of community, parenthood and childhood aspired to by different ethnic and faith groups.

Furthermore, there is evidence of increasing polarisation in children's economic lives linked to their parents' patterns of employment. There is no clear consensus as to whether children's lives are any better or worse in particular types of family; although most commentators agree that economic disadvantage is crucial in undermining children's developmental outcomes. Children's access to space in the public realm raises considerations about principles governing distributive justice and fairness in contemporary urban settings. As Amin has argued:

> A city disposed towards tolerating difference, sharing public spaces and active citizenship is also a source of entrepreneurship and creativity based on the mobilisation of confidence, social interchange and the pooling of resources (1997, p. 15).

In order to create such possibilities for children, a greater degree of trust needs to be engendered at a local level, especially in global cities with their high level of population density, differentiation, anxiety and anonymity. But it is not easy to engender trust. A number of factors such as high levels of population movement, changing work patterns and increased exposure to media reports of abduction, sexual abuse and street crime are making parents and children less trusting of public spaces and of their neighbours. Modern families are faced, therefore, with a yearning for trusted social and geographical spaces on the one hand, but a culture that makes that ideal very hard to achieve.

The recognition that communities are important factors in the lives of children and families has led to enormous interest in developing community or neighbourhood interventions to change the course of child development and to combat family disadvantage. It is clear that some of these interventions have been successful, while there is as yet enthusiasm but no real proof for many of the programmes described. The lack of proof deserves attention. Some of the work that we have described has been carried forward by the logic that where one lives must make a difference to how well one does, and the sheer force of the apparent fairness of enhancing communities, benefiting all residents rather than only a selected few. However there is a dearth of comparative research looking at the relevance of community characteristics for children and parents in different parts of the world; there are few longitudinal studies of key concepts such as social capital; and there is currently only solid effectiveness of a few of the initiatives described, notably some of those designed to enhance early development.

Certainly there have been great strides in enabling professionals to collaborate with each other, and encouraging them to listen carefully to what parents and children have to say when they are planning and implementing services. More sensitivity to user preferences is likely to lead to greater take-up of services. However, this is not necessarily good either for the funders or for the recipients of the service as the Fort Bragg study found when examining a new model of coordinated services for child mental health problems. Take-up of services certainly did increase, but their cost effectiveness was not so good and there were no differences in outcomes for children or families, comparing them to those receiving traditional services (Bickman, 1996). Similarly the *Comprehensive Child Care Development Program* (St Pierre, 1997) was a well resourced, designed and implemented community based intervention that failed to demonstrate positive impacts on families in disadvantaged communities. Many of the initiatives described in this book might have been well advised to study the lessons of these two interventions closely before embarking on services that used the same or similar principles. The book has also discussed some of the considerable challenges to successful implementation that are faced by community interventions. Overall these evaluations show that poorly implemented programmes are more or less guaranteed **not** to have an impact on child and family outcomes, and that effectively implemented evidence based programmes do have a chance, but are not guaranteed to work.

Undoubtedly all the enthusiasm for community development marks an important trend in social policy, and resonates with many urban dwellers' desire for a less alienating social existence. However, it is useful to take a step back and consider just how important (or not) communities and neighbourhoods are in the lives of children and families and the extent to which the relationship between community characteristics and child outcomes can be influenced by public policy or programme interventions.

Many or most of these new programmes may well be important for the communities; people working with families will share information and coordinate their activities, they will talk more to local people, seek opinions and allow people to know more about their neighbours. Some families will benefit from the interventions offered, and will be less resistant to accessing and receiving a range of preventive services. Some parents may become volunteers or even make it to sit on management committees. But we still do not know whether all this activity will make a substantial difference to the lives and well-being of children and parents in those communities.

Much of the work that has been described focuses on large urban environments and particularly on areas of disadvantage. Thus we can say with less certainty that communities matter for affluent children and parents than we can for those experiencing disadvantage or for those defined as disadvantaged – the 'underclass'. One of the reasons why we sound this note of caution is not necessarily because the 'community matters' movement is misguided, but because the evaluation work is in most cases either only just beginning or poorly designed, able to answer only small questions. The bigger ones – such as does community matter, and if so what kind of community is best, and for whom remain unanswered. It is possible that communities, and community interventions are much more salient for some types of families but have relatively little effect on others, but our current state of knowledge is too limited to answer such questions. There have been only limited attempts to distinguish between different theoretical perspectives; for instance is the contagion/epidemic model of understanding community influences more or less powerful than the collective efficacy approach? Much of the work has been pushed forward (as political change often is) on the basis of ideology rather than evidence.

Although the concepts of 'evidence based policy' and 'evidence based practice' are now part of the social fabric, it is very difficult in reality to rely solely on the evidence base. The example of the Fort Bragg intervention is a good case in point. Even though there is little evidence that joined up services produce better outcomes, it makes absolute sense to move in this direction. There is plenty of anecdotal evidence that fragmented services cause distress to needy families, and frustration to the workers who have to operate them. So the idea of joining up simply makes sense – whatever the evidence of their impact on outcomes for children. Similarly it makes sense to believe that services which are set up in partnership with parents and children from the local community are more likely to succeed. So whatever the evidence for effectiveness, participation is likely to be part of the political agenda, despite the thin evidence base for its impact on children.

Another issue relating to the evidence base is how transferable it is from one national context to another. This book has discussed community interventions mainly in the USA, UK and to a lesser extent Australia and New Zealand, and most of the theorising, research and interventions have originated in the USA. However we know that demographically the USA is different from the other Anglo Saxon countries, and that Anglo Saxons, in turn are very different from non-English speaking contexts. So the definitions and conceptualisation around community may well differ considerably in different national contexts, and similar interventions may have different effects in different parts of the world. This applies in particular to indigenous and minority ethnic groups, who are often the target of community interventions but whose position in society differs considerably in different jurisdictions.

It may be that we will have to wait several years before we can really draw this book to a conclusion, but for now we propose that 'considered optimism' is probably the best way to think about much of the work that had been presented. It may be the case that the best strategy for enhancing the health and well-being of children is to focus directly on them as individuals, as well as indirectly through their communities. Thus we finish with this thought:

> There is no finer investment for any community than putting milk into babies (Winston Churchill, radio broadcast, 21 March 1943; published in *Complete Speeches*, vol. 7, 1974).

REFERENCES

6, Perri (1997) *Escaping Poverty*. London: Demos.

Ackroyd, P. (2000) *London: the Biography*. London: Chatto and Windus.

Adams, B.N. & Trost, J. (eds) (2004) *Handbook of World Families*. London: Sage.

Aitken, S.C. (1994) *Putting Children in Their Place*. Washington DC: Association of American Geographers.

Akiba, M., LeTendre, G.K., Baker, D.P. & Goesling, B. (2002) Student victimization: national and school system effects on school violence in 37 nations. *American Educational Research Journal* 39, 829–853.

Alanen, L. (1990) Rethinking socialization, the family and childhood. In P.A. Adler, P. Adler, N. Mandell & C. Spencer (eds) *Sociological Studies of Child Development* Vol. 3 (pp. 13–28). Connecticut: JAI Press.

Alanen, L. & Mayall, B. (eds) (2001) *Conceptualising Child–adult Relations*. London: Falmer Press.

Alcock, P. (2004) Participation or pathology: contradictory tensions in area-based policy. *Social Policy & Society* 3, 87–96.

Alexander, T. & Goldman, R. (2005) *Parent Information Point: Next Steps*. London: National Family and Parenting Institute.

Amin, A. (1997) Placing globalisation. Paper presented at the Royal Geographical Society/Institute of British Geography Annual Conference, Exeter.

Amin, A. (2000) The democratic city. Paper presented at the Royal Geographical Society/Institute of British Geography Annual Conference, London.

Anderson, E. (1990) *Streetwise: Race, Class and Change in an Urban Community*. Chicago: University of Chicago Press.

Anderson, E. (1994) The code of the streets. *Atlantic Monthly* (May), 81–93.

Anenshensel, C.S. & Sucoff, C.A. (1996) The neighbourhood context of adolescent mental Health. *Journal of Health and Social Behavior* 37, 293–310.

Archard, D. (1993) *Children: Rights and Childhood*. London: Routledge.

Armistead, L., Forehand, R., Brody, G. & Maguen, S. (2002) Parenting and child psychosocial adjustment in single parent African American families: is community context important? *Behavior Therapy* 33, 361–375.

Arnstein, S.R. (1969) A ladder of citizen participation. *Journal of the American Planning Association* 35, 216–224.

Aspden, J. & Birch, D. (2005) *New Localism – Citizen Engagement, Neighbourhoods and Public Services: Evidence from Local Government*. London: Office of the Deputy Prime Minister.

Atkinson, T. (1998) Social exclusion, poverty and unemployment. In T. Atkinson & J. Hills (eds) *Exclusion, Employment and Opportunity. CASE Paper 4* (pp. 1–21). London: ESRC Research Centre for the Analysis of Social Exclusion (CASE), London School of Economics and Social Science.

Attwood, C., Singh, G., Prime, D., Creasey, R. (2003) *2001 Home Office Citizenship Survey: People, Families and Communities*. London: Home Office, RDS Publications.

Audit Commission (1996). *Misspent Youth: Young People and Crime*. London: Audit Commission.

Bainham, A. (1998) *Children: The Modern Law* (2nd edn), Bristol: Jordan Publishing Ltd.

Baginsky, M. (2000a) *Child Protection and Education*. London: NSPCC.

Baginsky, M. (2000b) Training teachers in child protection. *Child Abuse Review* 9, 74–81.

Bakardjieva, M. & Feenberg, A. (2002) Community technology and democratic rationalization. *Information Society* 18, 181–192.

Ball, M. (1998) *School Inclusion: the School, the Family and the Community*. York: Joseph Rowntree Foundation.

Ball, M. & the NESS Research Team (2002) *Getting Sure Start Started. National Evaluation of Sure Start*. Nottingham: Department for Education and Skills (DfES) Publications. http:// www.surestart.gov.uk/publications/?Document=100.

Baltimore City Data Collective (BCDC) (2003) *Baltimore's Children. Citywide Statistics of Well-being*. Accessed at http://www.baltimorekidsdata.org/ April 2005.

Baraldi, C. (2003) Planning childhood: children's social participation in the town of adults. In P. Christensen & M. O'Brien (eds) *Children in the City: Home, Neighbourhood and Community* (pp. 184–206). London: RoutledgeFalmer.

Barnes, J. (2004) *Place and parenting: a study of four communities*. Final report of the Families and Neighbourhoods Study (FANS) submitted to the NSPCC. Part 1, quantitative results. London: Institute for the Study of Children, Families & Social Issues, Birkbeck, University of London.

Barnes, J. (2005) Highlights of results: discipline in the home and the neighbourhoods. Paper presented to the Families and Neighbourhoods Study (FANS) conference. Senate House, University of London, April 19.

Barnes, J. & Baylis, G. (2004) *Place and Parenting: a Study of Four Communities*. Final report of the Families and Neighbourhoods Study (FANS) submitted to the NSPCC. Part 2, qualitative results. London: Institute for the Study of Children, Families & Social Issues, Birkbeck, University of London.

Barnes, J., Baylis, G. & Quinn, D. (2004) *Families and Neighbourhoods Study: Children's Perceptions of and Engagement in Three Contrasting Communities*. London: Institute for the Study of Children, Families & Social Issues, Birkbeck, University of London.

Barnes, J., Belsky, J., Broomfield, K.A., Melhuish, E. & the NESS Research Team (2006) Neighbourhood deprivation, school disorder and academic achievement in primary schools in deprived communities in England. *International Journal of Behavioral Development* 30, (in press).

Barnes, J., Broomfield, K., Frost, M., Harper, G., Knowles, J., Leyland, A., McLeod, A. & the NESS Research Team. (2003) *Characteristics of Sure Start local programme areas, Rounds 1 to 4*. Nottingham: Department for Education and Skills (DfES) Publications. http:// www.surestart.gov.uk/publications/?Document=328.

Barnes, J., Broomfield, K., Frost, M., Harper, G., Dave, S., Finn, J., Knowles, J., Desousa, C. & the NESS Research Team. (2004) *Characteristics of Sure Start local programmes 2001/2*. Nottingham: Department for Education and Skills (DfES) Publications. http://www. surestart.gov.uk/publications/?Document=945.

Barnes, J., Broomfield, K., Dave, S., Frost, M., Melhuish, E., Belsky, J. & the NESS research team. (2005a) Disadvantaged but different: variation among deprived communities in relation to child and family well-being. *Journal of Child Psychology and Psychiatry* 46, 952–962.

Barnes, J., Desousa, C., Frost, M., Harper, G. & Laban, D. & the NESS Research Team (2005b) *Changes in the Characteristics of Sure Start Local Programme Areas in Rounds 1 to 4 between 2000/2001 and 2002/2003*. Nottingham: Department for Education and Skills (DfES) Publications. http://www.surestart.gov.uk/publications/?Document=1421.

Barnes, J. & Shay, S. (1996) *Methods of Assessing Community Characteristics Relevant to Child-rearing*. New York: The Foundation for Child Development Neighborhood Research Grants Program.

Barnes McGuire, J. (1997a) The reliability and validity of a questionnaire describing neighborhood characteristics relevant to families and young children living in urban areas. *Journal of Community Psychology* 25, 551–566.

Barnes McGuire, J. (1997b) An ecological approach to child abuse prevention. Theory, practice and evaluation. *Journal of Child Centred Practice* 4, 95–123.

Barry, F. (1991) *Neighborhood Based Approach – What is It?* Background paper for the US. Advisory Board on Child Abuse and Neglect. Ithaca, NY: Cornell University, Family Life Development Center, Department of Human Development and Family Studies.

Barry, F. & Garbarino, J. (1997) Children and the community. In R.T. Ammerman & M. Hersen (eds), *Handbook of Prevention and Treatment with Children and Adolescents* (pp. 59–87). New York: John Wiley.

Bavolek, S. & Comstock, C. (1985) *Nurturing Program for Parents and Children: Program Implementation Manual.* Park City, UT: Family Development Resources.

Baylis, G. & Barnes, J. (2004) *Out and About. Views of 11 Year Olds About Three Contrasting Communities.* Paper presented to 'A place to call home' conference. Social Futures Institute, University of Teesside, Middlesbrough, July.

Baym, N.K. (1993) Interpreting soap operas and creating community: inside a computer-mediated fan culture. *Journal of Folklore Research* 30, 143–177.

Baym, N.K. (1995) The emergence of community in computer mediated communication. In S.G. Jones (ed.), *Cybersociety: Computer Mediated Communication and Community* (pp. 138–163). Thousand Oaks: Sage.

Beck, U. (1998) The Democratization of the Family. In U. Beck (ed.) *Democracy Without Enemies* (pp. 65–83). Cambridge, UK: Polity.

Belsky, J. (1980) Child maltreatment: An ecological integration. *American Psychologist* 35, 320–335.

Belsky, J. (1993) Etiology of child maltreatment: a developmental-ecological analysis. *Psychological Bulletin* 114, 413–434.

Beresford, P. & Croft, S. (1993) *Citizen Involvement: a Practical Guide for Change.* Brighton: Partnership Books.

Bernstein, B. (1960) Language and social class: a research note. *British Journal of Sociology* 11, 271–276.

Bernstein, B. (1974) *Class, codes and control, Volume 1* (2nd edn). London: Routledge and Kegan Paul.

Bertrand, M., Mullainathan, S. & Shafir, E. (2004) A behavioral-economics view of poverty. *The American Economic Review* 94, 419–423.

Berthoud, R., Bryan, M. & Bardasi, E. (2004) *The Dynamics of Deprivation: the Relationship Between Income and Material Deprivation Over Time.* London: Department for Work and Pensions (DWP).

Bhabra, S. & Ghate, D. (2004) *Parent Information Point: Evaluation of the Pilot Phase.* London: National Family and Parenting Institute.

Bianchi, S.M. & Robinson, J. (1997) What did you do today? Children's use of time, family composition, and the acquisition of social capital. *Journal of Marriage and the Family* 59, 332–344.

Bickman L. (1996) A continuum of care. More is not always better. *American Psychologist* 51, 689–701.

Blanchard, A. & Horan, T. (1998). Social capital and virtual communities. *Social Science Computer Review* 16, 293–307.

Blandy, S., Lister, D., Atkinson, R. & Flint, J. (2003) *Gated Communities: a Systematic Review of Research Evidence, Centre for Neighbourhood Research Summary 12.* Bristol: CNR. Available at www.neighbourhoodcentre.org.uk.

Blakeley, E.J, & Snyder, M.G. (1997a) *Putting Up the Gates.* Montclair, NJ: National Housing Institute, Shelterforce Online. http://www.nhi.org/online/issues/93/gates.html.

Blakely, E.J. & Snyder, M.G. (1997b) *Fortress America: Gated Communities in the United States.* Washington, DC: Brookings Institution Press.

Boisjoly, J., Duncan, G.J. & Hofferth, S. (1995) Access to social capital. *Journal of Social Issues* 16, 609–631.

Bonner, K. (1997) *A Great Place to Raise Kids: Interpretation, Science and the Urban-rural Debate.* Quebec: McGill-Queens University Press.

Booth, A. & Crouter, A.C. (eds) (2001) *Does it Take a Village? Community Effects on Children, Adolescents and Families.* Mahwah, New Jersey: Lawrence Erlbaum Associates.

Bourdieu, P. (1986) The forms of capital. In J. Richardson (ed.) *Handbook of Theory and Research in the Sociology of Education* (pp. 241–258). Westport, CT: Greenwood Press.

Bourgois, P. (1996) *In Search of Respect: Selling Crack in El Barrio*. New York: Cambridge University Press.

Boyce, W.F. (2002) Influence of health promotion bureaucracy on community participation: a Canadian case study. *Health Promotion International* 17, 61–68.

Boyden, J. & Ennew, J. (1997) *Children in Focus: a Manual for Participatory Research with Children*. Stockholm: Radda Barnen.

Boyle, M.H. & Lipman, E.L. (1998) *Do Places Matter? A Multilevel Analysis of Geographic Variations in Child Behaviour in Canada. Working Paper W-98–16E*. Hull, QC, Canada: Applied Research Branch, Strategic Policy, Human Resources Development Canada.

Bradley, R.H. & Caldwell, B.M. (1976) The relationship of infants' home environment to mental test performance at fifty-four months: a follow-up study. *Child Development* 47, 1172–1174.

Bradley, R.H. & Corwin, F.C. (2002) Socioeconomic status and child development. *Annual Review of Psychology*, 53, 371–379.

Bradley, R.H. & Whiteside-Mansell, L. (1997) Children in poverty. In R.T. Ammerman & M. Hersen (eds), *Handbook of Prevention and Treatment with Children and Adolescents* (pp. 13–58). New York: John Wiley.

Bradshaw, T.K. (2000) Complex community development projects: collaboration, comprehensive programs, and community coalitions in complex society. *Community Development Journal* 35, 143–145.

Bratton, W. (1998) Crime is down in New York City: blame the police. In N. Dennis (ed.), *Zero Tolerance: Policing a Free Society* (pp. 29–43). London: Institute of Economic Affairs.

Brodsky, A. (1996) Resilient single mothers in risky neighbourhoods: negative psychological sense of community. *Journal of Community Psychology* 24, 347–363.

Bronfenbrenner, U. (1979) *The Ecology of Human Development*. Cambridge, MA: Harvard University Press.

Bronfenbrenner, U. (1988) Foreword. In A. Pence (ed.) *Ecological Research with Children and Families. From concepts to methodology* (pp. ix–xix). New York and London: Teachers College Press.

Bryant, B. (1985) The neighborhood walk. Sources of support in middle childhood. *Monographs of the Society for Research in Child Development* 50 (3, Serial No. 210).

Buchel, F. & Duncan, G.J. (1998) Do parents' social activities promote children's school attainments? Evidence from the German socioeconomic panel. *Journal of Marriage and the Family* 60, 95–108.

Bunge, W.W. (1973) The geography. *Professional Geographer* 25, 331–337.

Burrows, R., Ellison, N. & Woods, B. (2005) *Neighbourhoods on the Net: The Nature and Impact of Internet-based Neighbourhood Information Systems*. York: Joseph Rowntree Foundation.

Bursik, R.J. (1988) Social disorganization and theories of crime and delinquency: problems and prospects. *Criminology* 26, 519–551.

Bursik, R.J. & Webb, J. (1982) Community change and patterns of delinquency. *American Journal of Sociology* 88, 24–42.

Burton, L. & Jarrett, R. (2000) In the mix, yet on the margins: the place of families in urban neighborhood and child development research. *Journal of Marriage and the Family* 62, 1114–1135.

Burton, L., Price-Spratlen, T. & Spencer, M. (1997). On ways of thinking about measuring neighborhoods. Implications for studying context and developmental outcomes for children. In J. Brooks-Gunn, G. Duncan & J.L. Aber (eds) *Neighborhood Poverty. Context and Consequences for Children* (pp. 132–144). New York: Sage.

Burton, P., Goodland, R., Croft, J., Abbott, J., Hastings, A., Macdonald, G. & Slater, T. (2004) *What Works in Community Involvement in Area-based Initiatives? A Systematic Review of the Literature*. Bristol: University of Bristol and University of Glasgow. Home Office Online Report 53/54.

Buysse, V., Sparkman, K. & Wesley, P. (2003) Communities of practice: connecting what we know with what we do. *Exceptional Children* 69, 263–278.

Buysse, V., Wesley, P. & Skinner, D. (1999) Community development approaches for early intervention. *Topics in Early Childhood Special Education* 19, 236–243.

Caldwell, B. & Bradley, R. (1984) *Home Observation for Measurement of the Environment (HOME).* Little Rock, AR: University of Arkansas at Little Rock.

Calhoun, C. (1998) Community without propinquity revisited: communications technology and the transformation of the urban public sphere. *Sociological Inquiry* 68, 373–397.

Campbell, S. (2002a) *Implementing Anti-social Behaviour Orders: Messages for Practitioners.* London: Home Office, Research, Development and Statistics Directorate.

Campbell, S. (2002b). *A Review of Anti-social Behaviour Orders, HORS 236.* London: Home Office, Research, Development and Statistics Directorate.

Cannan, C. & Warren, C. (eds) (1997) *Social Action with Children and Families: a Community Development Approach to Child and Family Welfare.* London: Routledge.

Cantillon, D., Davidson, W.S. & Schweitzer, J.H. (2003) Measuring community social disorganization: sense of community as a mediator in social disorganization theory. *Journal of Criminal Justice* 31, 321–339.

Cappelleri, J.C., Eckenrode, J. & Powers, J. (1993) The epidemiology of child abuse: Findings from the second national incidence and prevalence study of child abuse and neglect. *American Journal of Public Health*, 83 1622–1624.

Carnegie task force on meeting the needs of young children (1994) *Starting Points. Meeting the Needs of Our Youngest Children.* New York: Carnegie Corporation of New York.

Cattell, V. (2001) Poor people, poor places, and poor health: the mediating role of social networks and social capital. *Social Science & Medicine* 52, 1501–1516.

Ceballo, R. & McLoyd, V.C. (2002) Social support and parenting in poor, dangerous neighborhoods. *Child Development* 73, 1310–1321.

Chanan, G. (1992) *Out of the Shadows: Local Community Action and the European Community.* Brussels: Commission of the European Communities.

Chaskin, R.J. (1997) Perspectives on neighborhood and community: a review of the literature. *Social Service Review* 521–547.

Chaskin R. & Garg S. (1997) The issue of governance in neighborhood-based initiatives *Urban Affairs Review* 32, 636–661.

Chawla, L. (2002) *Growing Up in an Urbanizing World.* London: Earthscan Publications.

Chawla, L. & Malone, K. (2003) Neighbourhood quality in children's eyes. In P. Christensen & O'Brien, M. (eds) *Children in the City: Home, Neighbourhood and Community* (pp. 118–141). London: RoutledgeFalmer.

Chen, Z. & Kaplan, H. (2001) Intergenerational transmission of constructive parenting. *Journal of Marriage and the Family* 63, 17–31.

Children's Play Council (CPC) with the Children's Society (2005) *Fit for Play?.* London: National Children's Bureau.

Children and Young People's Unit (CYPU) (2001) *Children's Fund National Guidance.* London: Department for Education and Skills.

Churchman, A. (1990) Resident participation: issues through the prism of Israel's project renewal in N. Carmon (ed.) *Neighbourhood Policy and Programmes* (pp. 164–178). London: Macmillan.

Cicchetti, D. & Lynch, M. (1993) Toward an ecological/transactional model of community violence and child maltreatment. Consequences for children's development. *Psychiatry* 56, 96–118.

Clark, A., McQuail, S. & Moss, P. (2003) *Exploring the Field of Listening to and Consulting with Young Children.* Research Report 445. London: Department for Education and Skills.

Clinton, H.R. (1996) *It Takes a Village: and Other Lessons Children Teach Us.* New York: Simon & Schuster.

Cohen, D., Spear, S., Scribner, R., Kissinger, P., Mason, K. & Wildgen, J. (2000) 'Broken windows' and the risk of gonorrhea. *American Journal of Public Health* 90, 230–236.

Coleman, A. (1985). *Utopia on Trial: Vision and Reality in Planned Housing.* London: Hilary Shipman.

Coleman, J.S. (1988). Social capital in the creation of human capital. *American Journal of Sociology* 94, Supplement S95–S120.

Coleman, J.S. (1990) *Foundations of Social Theory.* Cambridge, MA: Harvard University Press.

Coleman, J.S. (1993) The rational reconstruction of society. 1992 Presidential address. *American Sociological Review* 58, 1–15.

Coltrane, S. (1996) *The Family Man: Fatherhood, Housework and Gender Inequality.* New York: Oxford University Press.

Connell, C., Kubisch, A., Schorr, L. & Weiss, C. (1995) *New Approaches to Evaluating Community Initiatives.* Washington, DC: The Aspen Institute.

Cook. R., Shagle, S. & Degirmencioglu, S. (1997) Capturing social processes for testing mediational models of neighbourhood effects. In J. Brooks-Gunn & J.L. Aber (eds) *Neighborhood Poverty, Vol. II* (pp. 94–119). New York: Sage.

Cook, T.D., Habib, F., Phillips, M., Settersten, R.A., Shagle, S.C. & Degirmencioglu, S.M. (1999) Comer's school development program in Prince George's County, Maryland: a theory-based evaluation. *American Educational Research Journal* 36, 543–597.

Cooper, A., Hetherington, R. & Katz, I. (1997) *A Third Way – a European Perspective of the Child Protection/Family Support Debate.* London: NSPCC.

Cooper, A., Hetherington, R. & Katz, I. (2003) *The Risk Factor – Making the Child Protection System Work for Children.* London: Demos.

Corsaro, W. (1997). *The Sociology of Childhood.* California: Pine Forge Press.

Coulton, C. (1995). Using community-level indicators of children's well-being in comprehensive community initiatives. In J. Connell, A. Kubisch, L. Schorr & C. Weiss (eds) *New Approaches to Evaluating Community Initiatives* (pp. 173–199). Washington, DC: The Aspen Institute.

Coulton, C. (2004) The place of community in social work practice research: conceptual and methodological developments. Aaron Rosen lecture, Society for Social Work Research, New Orleans, January.

Coulton, C., Korbin, J.E., Chan, T. & Su, M. (2001) Mapping residents' perceptions of neighborhood boundaries. A methodological note. *American Journal of Community Psychology* 29, 371–383.

Coulton, C., Korbin, J.E. & Su, M. (1999) Neighborhoods and child maltreatment. A multi-level analysis. *Child Abuse and Neglect* 23, 1019–1040.

Coulton, D., Korbin, J. & Su, M. (1996) Measuring neighborhood context for young children in an urban areas. *American Journal of Community Psychology* 24, 5–32.

Coulton, C., Korbin, J., Su, M. & J. Chow (1995). Community level factors and child maltreatment rates. *Child Development* 66, 1262–1276.

Countryside Agency (1998) *The joint provision of rural services.* London: UK Countryside Agency.

Cowan, R. (2005) ASBO use doubles despite criticism. *The Guardian,* 30 June.

Coward, R. (2005) Lost in London. *The Guardian,* 23 July.

Cox, A.D. (1998) Preventing child abuse. A review of community-based projects: issues arising from reviews and future directions. *Child Abuse Review* 7, 30–43.

Craig, G. (1999) Poverty. *Research Matters. A Digest of Research in Social Services,* 5, April–October, 24–28.

Crane, J. (1991) The epidemic theory of ghettos and neighbourhood effects on dropping out and teenage childbearing. *American Journal of Sociology* 96, 1226–1259.

Crockenberg, S. (1981) Infant irritability, mother responsiveness, and social support influences on the security of infant-mother attachment. *Child Development* 52, 857–865.

CSR, Incorporated. (1996) Cross-site evaluation report: Evaluation of nine comprehensive community-based child abuse and neglect prevention programs. Washington, DC: US. Department of Health & Human Services. National Clearinghouse on Child Abuse and Neglect Information.

Cummings, C., Dyson, A. & Todd, L. (2004) *Evaluation of the Extended Schools Pathfinder Projects.* London: Department for Education and Skills.

Curtis, L.J., Dooley, M.D. & Phipps, S.A. (2004) Child well-being and neighbourhood quality: evidence from the Canadian National Longitudinal Survey of Children and Youth. *Social Science & Medicine* 58, 1917–1927.

Davin, A. (1996) *Growing Up Poor: Home, School and Street in London 1870–1914*. London: Rivers Oram Press.

Deakin, N. (1996) Mister Murray's ark. In R. Lister (ed.) *Charles Murray and the Underclass: the Developing Debate* (pp. 75–80). London: Institute of Economic Affairs, Health and Welfare Unit with the Sunday Times.

Deccio, G., Horner, W. & Wilson, D. (1994) High-risk neighborhoods and high-risk families: replications research related to the human ecology of child maltreatment. *Journal of Social Service Research* 18, 123–137.

Dennis, N. (1998) Editor's introduction. In N. Dennis (ed.) *Zero tolerance: policing a free society* (pp. 1–28). London: Institute of Economic Affairs.

Dennis, N. & Mallon, R. (1998) Confident policing in Hartlepool. In N. Dennis (ed.) *Zero tolerance: policing a free society* (pp. 62–87). London: Institute of Economic Affairs.

Department of Culture, Media and Sport (DCMS) (2001) *Getting Serious About Play: a Review of Children's Play*. London: Her Majesty's Stationery Office.

Department for Education and Skills (DfES) (2003) Guidance for setting up children's trust pathfinders. www.dfes.gov.uk/childrenstrusts/pdfs/guidejan03.pdf.

Department for Education and Skills (DfES) (2004) *Towards Understanding Sure Start local Programmes. Summary of Findings of the National Evaluation*. Nottingham: DfES Publications.

Department for Education and Skills (2005) Children's Fund. http://www.everychildmatters. gov.uk/strategy/childrensfund/accessed 25 August.

Department of the Environment, Transport and the Regions (DETR) (1997). *Regeneration Programmes – the Way Forward: Discussion Paper of 11th November 1997*. London: DETR.

Department of Health (DoH) (2000) *Guidelines for the Framework for the Assessment of Children in Need*. London: The Stationery Office.

Department for Social Security (DSS) (1999) *Opportunity For All: First Annual Report*. London: DSS.

Department of Transport and the Regions (DETR) (2002) *National Travel Survey*. London: HMSO.

Desforges, C. with Abouchaar, A. (2003) *The Impact of Parental Involvement, Parental Support and Family Education on Pupil Achievements and Adjustment: a Literature Review*. Unpublished manuscript. London: Department for Education and Skills.

Driskell, D. (2002) *Creating Better Cities with Children and Youth*. Paris and London: Unesco Publications.

Dryfoos, J. (1994) *Full-service Schools: a Revolution in Health and Social Services for Children, Youth, and Families*. San Francisco: Jossey-Bass.

Dunn, J. & Plomin, R. (1990) *Separate Lives*. New York: Basic Books.

Dunst, C., Trivette, C. & Deal, A.G. (1988) *Enabling and Empowering Families. Principles and Guidelines for Practice*. Cambridge, MA: Brookline Books.

Dunst, C., Vance, S., & Cooper, C. (1986) A social systems perspective of adolescent pregnancy: determinants of parent and parent-child behavior. *Infant Mental Health Journal* 7, 34–48.

Dyson, A. & Robson, E. (1999) *School, Family, Community: Mapping School Inclusion in the UK*. London: National Youth Agency.

Dyson, A., Millward, A. & Todd, L. (2002) *A Study of 'Extended' Schools Demonstration Projects. Research Report 381*. London: Department for Education and Skills.

Earls, F., McGuire, J., & Shay, S. (1994) Evaluating a community intervention to reduce the risk of child abuse. Methodological strategies in conducting neighborhood surveys. *Child Abuse and Neglect* 18, 473–486.

Edwards, R., Franklin, J. & Holland, J. (2003) *Families and social capital: exploring the issues*. London: London South Bank University, Families and Social Capital ESRC Research Group. http://www.lsbu.ac.uk/families/workingpapers/familieswp1.pdf.

Egil Wam, P. (1994) *Targeting Children – Planning Child Orientation in Community Development Programmes*. Asian Dialogue No. 1. Oslo, Norway: Redd Barna.

Elder, G.H., Jr., Modell, J. & Parke, R.D. (eds) (1993) *Children in Time and Place: Developmental and Historical Insights*. New York: Cambridge University Press.

Ellen, I. & Turner, M. (1997) Does neighbourhood matter? Assessing recent evidence. *Housing Policy Debate* 8, 833–866.

Engelbert, A. (1994) Worlds of childhood: differentiated but different. Implications for social policy. In J. Qvortrup, M. Bardy, G. Sgritta & H. Wintersberger (eds) *Childhood Matters: Social Theory, Practice and Policy* (pp. 285–298). Aldershot, UK: Avebury.

Epp, J. (1986). *Achieving Health for All: a Framework for Health Promotion*. Ottawa, Ontario: Health and Welfare Canada.

Ermisch, J., Francesconi, M. & Pevalin, D.J. (2001) *Outcomes for Children of Poverty. Department for Work and Pensions Research Report No. 158*. Leeds: HMSO.

Essex County Council (2002) *Essex Family Group Conference – Young People Who Offend Project. Executive Summary*. Braintree: Essex County Council.

Fajerman, L., Treseder, P. & Connor, J. (2004) *Children are Service Users Too: a Guide to Consulting Children and Young People*. London: Save for Excellence.

Families and Communities Strategy (FaCS) (2004) *Overview. Stronger Families and Communities Strategy. National agenda for early childhood*. Canberra: Australian Government. www.facs.gov.au/sfcs.

Family League of Baltimore City, Inc. (FLBCINC) (2001) *Baltimore's action plan for children and families*. http://www.flbcinc.org/Documents/Research/Overviews%20of%20FLBC%20Research%20and%20Monitoring%20Efforts/baltoevalplan2.pdf.

Farrington, D. (1996). *Understanding and Preventing Youth Crime*. York: Joseph Rowntree Foundation.

Farrington, D. (2002). Developmental criminology and risk-focused prevention, in M. Maguire, R. Morgan and R. Reiner (eds) *The Oxford Handbook of Criminology* (pp. 657–701). Oxford: Oxford University Press.

Federation of Community Work Training Groups (FCWTG) (2001) *Making Changes: a Strategic Framework for Community Development Learning in England*. Sheffield: Federation of Community Work Training Groups.

Feinstein, L., Bynner, J. & Duckworth, K. (2005) *Leisure Contexts in Adolescence and Their Effects on Adult Outcomes*. London: Institute of Education, University of London.

Felton, B. & Shinn, M. (1992) Social integration and social support: moving 'social support' beyond the individual level. *Journal of Community Psychology* 20, 103–115.

Field, F. (1989) *Losing Out: the Emergence of Britain's Underclass*. Oxford: Blackwell.

Finn-Stevenson, M., Desimone, L. & Chung, A. (1998) Linking child care and support services with the school: pilot evaluation of the School of the 21st Century. *Children and Youth Services Review* 20, 177–205.

Fram, M.S. (2003) *Managing to Parent: Social Support, Social Capital, and Parenting Practices Among Welfare-participating Mothers with Young Children*. Discussion paper 1263–03. Washington, DC: Institute for Research on Poverty.

France, A., Hine, J., Armstrong, D. & Camina, M. (2004a) *The On Track Early Intervention and Prevention Programme: from Theory to Action, Home Office Online Report 10/0*. London: Home Office www.homeoffice.gov.uk/rds/pdfs2/rdsolr1004.pdf.

France, A., Hine, J. & Armstrong, D. (2004b) Implementing the On Track crime reduction programme: lessons for the future. In V. Harrington, A. France, A. & S. Trikha (eds) *Process and Early Implementation Issues: Emerging Findings from the On Track Evaluation, Home Office Online Report 06/0* (pp. 44–53). London: Home Office www.homeoffice.gov.uk/rds/pdfs2/rdsolr0604.pdf.

France, A. & Utting, D. (2005) The paradigm of risk and protection-focused prevention and its impact on services for children and families. *Children and Society* 19, 77–90.

Francis, M. & Lorenzo, R. (2002) Seven realms of children's participation. *Journal of Environmental Psychology* 22, 157–169.

Fulton, W. (1996) *The New Urbanism: Hope or Hype for American Communities?* Cambridge, MA: Lincoln Institute of Land Policy.

Furedi, F. (1997) *Culture of Fear: Risk Taking and the Morality of Low Expectation*. London: Cassell.

Furstenberg, F.F. (1993) How families manage risk and opportunity in dangerous neighborhoods. In W.J. Wilson (ed.) *Sociology and the Public Agenda* (pp. 231–258). Newbury Park, CA: Sage Publications.

Furstenberg, F.F. (2001) Managing to make it. Afterthoughts. *Journal of Family Issues* 22, 150–162.

Furstenberg, F.F., Cook, T.D., Eccles, J., Elder, G.H. & Sameroff, A. (1999) *Managing to Make It. Urban Families and Adolescent Success*. Chicago and London: University of Chicago Press.

Furstenberg, F.F. & Hughes, M.E. (1995) Social capital and successful development among at-risk youth. *Journal of Marriage and the Family* 57, 580–592.

Galster, G.C. (1986) What is neighbourhood? An externality-space approach. *International Journal of Urban and Regional Research* 10, 243–261.

Garbarino, J. (1976) A preliminary study of some ecological correlates of child abuse: the impact of socioeconomic stress on mothers. *Child Development* 47, 178–185.

Garbarino, J. (1977) The human ecology of child maltreatment: A conceptual model for research. *Journal of Marriage and the Family* 39, 721–735.

Garbarino, J. (1978) The social maps of children approaching adolescence: studying the ecology of youth development. *Journal of Youth and Adolescence* 38, 7–28.

Garbarino, J. (1985) An ecological approach to child maltreatment. In L.H. Pelton (ed.) *The Social Context of Child Abuse and Neglect* (pp. 228–267). New York: Human Sciences.

Garbarino, J. & Crouter, A. (1978) Defining the community context for parent-child relations: The correlates of child maltreatment. *Child Development* 49, 604–616.

Garbarino, J. & Eckenrode, J. (1997) *Understanding Abusive Families: an Ecological Approach to Theory and Practice*. San Francisco: Jossey Bass.

Garbarino, J. & Kostelny, K. (1992) Child maltreatment as a community problem. *Child Abuse and Neglect* 16, 455–464.

Garbarino, J., Kostelny, K. & Barry, F. (1998) Neighborhood-based programs. In P.K. Trickett & C.J. Schellenbach (eds) *Violence Against Children in the Family and the Community* (pp. 287–314). Washington, DC: American Psychological Association.

Garbarino, J. & Sherman, D. (1980) High-risk neighbourhoods and high-risk families. The human ecology of child maltreatment. *Child Development* 51, 188–198.

García Coll, C.T. & Magnuson, K. (2000) Cultural differences as sources of developmental vulnerabilities and resources. In J.P. Shonkoff & S.J. Meisels (eds) *Handbook of Early Childhood Intervention, Second Edition* (pp. 94–114). New York: Cambridge University Press.

Gauntlet, E., Hugman, R., Kenyon, P. & Logan, P. (2000) *A Meta-analysis of the Impact of Community-based Prevention and Early Intervention Action*. Policy Research Paper No. 11. Canberra: Commonwealth of Australia, Department of Family and Community Services.

Gelles, R.J. (1992) Poverty and violence towards children. *American Behavioral Scientist* 35, 258–274.

Ghate, D. & Hazel, N. (2002) *Parenting in Poor Environments: Stress, Support and Coping*. London: Jessica Kingsley Publishers.

Ghate, D. & Ramella, M. (2002) *Positive Parenting: the National Evaluation of the Youth Justice Board's Parenting Programme*. London: Youth Justice Board for England and Wales.

Ghate, D., Shaw, C., Hazel, N. (2000) *Fathers and Family Centres: Engaging Fathers in Preventative Services*. York: Joseph Rowntree Foundation.

Gibbons, J. (1992) *The Children Act 1989 and Family Support: Principles Into Practice*. London: Her Majesty's Stationery Office.

Gibbons, S. (2002) *Neighbourhood Effects on Educational Achievement: Evidence from the Census and National Child Development Study*. London: Centre for the Economics of Education, London School of Economics.

Gilchrist, A. (2004) *The Well-connected Community. A Networking Approach to Community Development*. London: Community Development Foundation.

Gittell, M., Newman, K., Bockmeyer, J. & Lindsay, R. (1998) Expanding civic opportunity: urban empowerment zones. *Urban Affairs Review* 33, 530–558.

Giorgas, D. (2000) Social capital within ethnic communities. Paper presented to Sociological Sites/Sights, TASA (Australian Sociological Association) Conference, Adelaide: Flinders University, 6–8 December.

Glass, N. (1999) Sure Start: the development of an early intervention programme for young children in the United Kingdom. *Children & Society* 13, 257–264.

Glennerster, H., Lupton, R., Noden, P. & Power, A. (1999) *Poverty, Social Exclusion and Neighbourhood: Studying the Area Bases of Social Exclusion*. London: Centre for the Analysis of Social Exclusion (CASE), London School of Economics.

Glynn, T.J. (1986) Neighbourhood and sense of community. *Journal of Community Psychology* 14, 341–352.

Goldman, R. (2005) *Fathers' Involvement in Their Children's Education: a Review of Research and Practice*. London: National Family and Parenting Institute.

Graham, J. (1998). What works in preventing criminality. In P. Goldbatt & C. Lewis (eds) *Reducing Offending: an Assessment of Research Evidence on Ways of Dealing with Offending Behaviour* (pp. 7–22). London: Home Office.

Graham, J. & Bowling, B. (1995) *Young People and Crime*. London, Home Office.

Grannis, R. (1998) The importance of trivial streets: residential streets and residential segregation. *American Journal of Sociology* 103, 1530–1564.

Grannis, R. (2001) *Street Islands: Social Networks, Street Networks, and Segregation*. Working Paper, Department of Sociology, Cornell University.

Green, J. & Chapman, A. (1992) The British Community Development Project: lessons for today. *Community Development Journal* 27, 242–258.

Greenberg, M., Fineberg, M., Gomez, E. & Osgood, D. (2004) Testing a community prevention model of coalition functioning and sustainability: a comprehensive study of Communities that Care in Pennsylvania. In T. Stockwell, P. Gruenewald, J.W. Toumbourou & W. Loxley (eds) *Preventing Harmful Substance Use: the Evidence Base for Policy and Practice* (pp. 129–142). London: Wiley.

Greer, B.G. (2000) Psychological and social functions of an e-mail mailing list for persons with cerebral palsy. *Cyber Psychology and Behavior* 3, 221–233.

Grundy, E., Murphy, M. & Shelton, N. (1999) Looking beyond the household: intergenerational perspectives on living kin and contacts with kin in Great Britain. *Population Trends* 97, 33–41.

Grunseit, A., Weatherburn, D. & Donnelly, N. (2005) *School Violence and its Antecedents: Interviews with High School Students*. Sydney, NSW: New South Wales Bureau of Crime Statistics and Research.

Gusfield, J.R. (1975) *The Community: a Critical Response*. New York: Harper Colophon.

Guttman, L.M., Friedel, J.N. & Hitt, R. (2003) Keeping adolescents safe from harm: management strategies of African-American families in a high-risk community. *Journal of School Psychology* 41, 167–184.

Halfon, N., Tullis, E., Kuo, A., Uyeda, K., Eisenstadt, N. & Oberklaid, F. (2003) *Report of the International Meeting on Developing Comprehensive Community-based Early Childhood Systems*. Los Angeles, CA: UCLA Center for healthier children, families and communities.

Hampton, K. & Wellman, B. (2003) Neighboring in Netville: how the Internet supports community and social capital in a wired suburb. *City and Community* 2, 277–311.

Hampton, R.L. (1987) Race, class and child maltreatment. *Journal of Comparative Family Studies* 18, 113–126.

Harcourt, B. (2001) *Illusion of Order: the False Promise of Broken Windows Policing*. Cambridge, MA: Harvard University Press.

Harrington, V., France, A. & Trikha, S. (eds) (2004) *Process and Early Implementation Issues: emerging findings from the On Track evaluation*. Home Office Online Report 06/04. London: Home Office www.homeoffice.gov.uk/rds/preventing1.html.

Hart, R. (1979). *Children's Experience of Place*. New York: Irvington Publishers.

Hart, R. (1997) *Children's Participation: The Theory and Practice of Involving Young Citizens in Community Development and Environmental Care*. London: Earthscan; New York: UNICEF.

Hart, R., Newman, J., Ackerman, L. & Feeny, T. (2004) *Children Changing Their World: Understanding and Evaluating Children's Participation in Development*. London: Plan International UK.

Hawkins, J. & Catalano, R. (1992) *Communities That Care: Action for Drug Abuse Prevention*. San Francisco: Jossey Bass.

Hawkins, J., Catalano, R., Morrison, D., O'Donell, J., Abbott, R. & Day, L. (1992) The Seattle social development project: effects of the first four years on protective factors and problem behaviors. In J. McCord & R. Tremblay (eds) *Preventing antisocial behavior: interventions from birth through adolescence* (pp. 139–161). New York: Guildford.

Health Survey for England (2002) cited in Hood, S. (2004) *The State of London's Children Report* (p. 3). London: Greater London Authority.

Heaton, K. & Sayer, J. (1992) *Community development and child welfare*. London: Community Development Foundation.

Hedges, A. & Kelly, J. (1992) *Identification with Local Areas. Summary Report on a Qualitative Study*. London: Department of the Environment (DoE).

Henricson, C., Katz, I., Mesie, J., Sandison, M. & Tunstill, J. (2001) *National Mapping of Family Services in England and Wales – a Consultation Document*. London: National Family and Parenting Institute.

Herbert-Cheshire, L. (2000) Contemporary strategies for rural community development in Australia: a governmentality perspective. *Journal of Rural Studies* 16, 203–215.

Herbert-Cheshire, L. & Higgins, V. (2004) From risky to responsible: expert knowledge and the governing of community-led rural development. *Journal of Rural Studies* 20, 289–302.

Her Majesty's Government (2004) *The Children Act 2004*. London: Her Majesty's Stationery Office. Available at http://www.hmso.gov.uk/acts/acts2004/20040031.htm.

Her Majesty's Treasury (1998a) *Statement by the Chancellor of the Exchequer on the Comprehensive Spending Review – 14 July*. London: HM Treasury. Accessed at http://www.hm-treasury. gov.uk/Spending_Review/spend_csr98/spend_csr98_statement.cfm on 18 July 2005.

Her Majesty's Treasury (1998b) *Comprehensive Spending Review. Chapter 21. Cross departmental Review of Provision for Young children*. London: HM Treasury. Accessed at http://www.archive.official-documents.co.uk/document/cm40/4011/401122.htm on July 18, 2005.

Her Majesty's Treasury (2003) *Every Child Matters*. London: Her Majesty's Stationery Office.

Her Majesty's Treasury (2004) *Choice for Parents, the Best Start for Children. a Ten Year Strategy for Childcare*. London: HM Treasury. http://www.hmtreasury.gov.uk/media/8F5/35/pbr04childcare_480.pdf.

Hernandez, D. (1995) *America's Children: Resources from Family, Government and the Economy*. New York: Russell Sage Foundation.

Hill, N.E. & Herman-Stahl, M.A. (2002) Neighborhood safety and social involvement: associations with parenting behaviors and depressive symptoms among African American and Euro-American mothers. *Journal of Family Psychology* 16, 209–219.

Hillery, G. (1964) Villages, cities, and total institutions. *American Sociological Review* 28, 32–42.

Hillman, M. (1993) One false move. A study of children's independent mobility. In M. Hillman (ed.), *Children, Transport and the Quality of Life* (pp. 7–18). London: Policy Studies Institute.

Hillman, M. (2001) Introduction. In S. Waiton, *Scared of the Kids. Curfews, Crime and the Regulation of Young People* (pp. 9–14). Sheffield: Sheffield Hallam University Press.

Hillman, M. (2006) Children's rights and adult wrongs. *Children's Geographies* (in press).

Hillman, M., Adams, J. & Whitelegg, J. (1990) *One False Move: a Study of Children's Independent Mobility*. London: Policy Studies Institute.

Hobcroft, J. (1998) *Intergenerational and Life Course Transmission of Social Exclusion: Influences of Childhood Poverty, Family Disruption, and Contact with the Police, CASE Paper 15*. London: London School of Economics, Suntory and Toyota International Centres for Economic and Related Disciplines (STICERD).

Hollister, R.G. & Hill, J. (1995) Problems in the evaluation of community-wide initiatives. In J.P. Connell, A. Kubisch, L. Schorr & C. Weiss (eds) *New Approaches to Evaluating Community Initiatives* (pp. 127–172). Washington, DC: The Aspen Institute.

Holloway, S. & Valentine, G. (eds) (2000) *Children's Geographies: Living, Playing and Transforming Everyday Worlds*. London: Routledge.

Home Office (1997) *No More Excuses – A New Approach to Tackling Youth Crime in England and Wales*. London: The Stationery Office.

Home Office (2003a) *Respect and Responsibility – Taking a Stand Against Anti-social Behaviour*. London: The Stationery Office.

Home Office (2003b) *Together – Tackling Anti-social Behaviour*. London: Home Office.

Home Office (2004) *Confident Communities in a Secure Britain: Home Office Strategic Plan 2004–2008*. London: Home Office.

Hood, S. (2004) *The State of London's Children Report*. London: Greater London Authority.

Hudson, P. (1999) Community development and child protection: a case for integration. *Community Development Journal* 34, 346–355.

Hughes, B. (1994) *Lost Childhoods: the Case for Children's Play. Working Paper 3. The Future of Urban Parks and Open Spaces*. Gloucestershire: Comedia.

Hugill, B. (1998) Minded out of their minds. *The Observer*, 29 March.

Humphries, S., Mack, J. & Perks, R. (1988) *A Century of Childhood*. London: Sidgwick & Jackson.

Huttenmoser, M. (1995) Children and their living surroundings for the everyday life and development of children. *Children's Environments* 12, 403–413.

Jack, G. (2000) Ecological influences on parenting and child development. *British Journal of Social Work* 30, 703–720.

Jacobs, J. (1961) *The Death and Life of Great American Cities*. New York: Random House, Vintage Books.

James, A. & James, A.L. (2004) *Constructing Childhood. Theory, Policy and Social Practice*. London: Palgrave.

James, A. & Prout, A. (eds) (1990) *Constructing and Reconstructing Childhood. Contemporary Issues in the Sociological Study of Childhood*. London and Washington, DC: Falmer Press.

Jencks, C. (1996) *Childhood*. London: Routledge.

Jencks, C. & Mayer, S. (1990) The social consequences of growing up in a poor neighborhood. In L.E. Lynn & M.G.H. McGeary (eds) *Inner City Poverty in the United States* (pp. 111–186). Washington, DC: National Academy Press.

Johnston, J. (2001) Evaluating national initiatives: the case of On Track. *Children & Society* 15, 33–36.

Johnston, P. (2005) Whites 'leaving cities as migrants move in'. *Daily Telegraph*, 10 February.

Jones, D., Forehand, R., Brody, G. & Armistead, L. (2003) Parental monitoring in African American single mother-headed families: An ecological approach to the identification of predictors. *Behavior Modification* 27, 435–457.

Joyner, E., Ben-Avie, M. & Comer, J. (2004). *Transforming School Leadership and Management to Support Student Learning and Development*. Thousand Oaks, California; Corwin Press.

Katz, P. (1994) *The New Urbanism: Toward an Architecture of Community*. New York: McGraw Hill.

Karsten, L. (1998) Growing up in Amsterdam: differentiation and segregation in children's daily lives. *Urban Studies* 35, 565–581.

Kaufman, J. & Rosenbaum, J. (1992) The education and employment of low-income black youth in white suburbs. *Educational Evaluation and Policy Analysis* 14, 229–240.

Khan, U. (1998) Putting the community into community safety. In A. Marlow & J. Pitts (eds) *Planning Safer Communities* (pp. 33–41). Dorset: Russell House Publishing.

Kinder, K., Kendall, S., Halsey, K. & Atkinson, M. (1999) *Disaffection Talks*. Slough: NFER.

Kirby, P. (2000) *Involving Young Researchers*. York: York Publishing Services Ltd.

Kirby, P., Lanyon, C., Cronin, K. & Sinclair, R. (2003) *Building a Culture of Participation: Involving Children and Young People in Policy, Service Planning, Development and Evaluation: a Research Report*. London: Department for Education and Skills.

Kjørholt, A.T. (2005) Childhood as a symbolic space. Autonomy, authentic voices and national identity in the area of globalisation. Paper presented at *Childhoods 2005* conference, Oslo.

Korbin, J.E. & Coulton, C. (1997) Understanding the neighborhood context for children and families: combining epidemiological and ethnographic approaches. In J. Brooks-Gunn, L. Aber & G. Duncan (eds) *Neighborhood Poverty: Context and Consequences for Children, Volume II, Policy Implications in Studying Neighborhoods* (pp. 65–79). New York: Russell Sage Foundation.

Kornhauser, R. (1978) *Social Sources of Delinquency*. Chicago: University of Chicago Press.

Kotchick, B.A. & Forehand, R. (2002) Putting parenting in perspective: A discussion of the contextual factors that shape parenting practices. *Journal of Child and Family Studies* 11, 255–269.

Kubisch, A.C., Weiss, C.H., Schoor, L.B. & Connell, J.P. (1995) Introduction. In J.P. Connell, A.C. Kubisch, L.B. Schorr, C.H. Weiss (eds) *New Approaches to Evaluating Community Initiatives. Concepts, Methods and Contexts* (pp. 1–21). Queenstown, MD: Aspen Institute.

Kupersmidt, J., Griesler, P., DeRosier, M., Patterson, C. & Davis, P. (1995) Childhood aggression and peer relations in the context of family and neighbourhood factors. *Child Development* 66, 360–375.

Kytta, M. (1997) Children's independent mobility in urban, small town and rural environments. In R. Camstra (ed.) *Growing Up in a Changing Urban Landscape* (pp. 41–52). Assen, The Netherlands: van Gorcum.

Labonte, R. (1994) Death of program, birth of metaphor: the development of health promotion in Canada. In A. Pederson, M. O'Neill & I. Rootman (eds) *Health Promotion in Canada: Provincial National and International Perspectives* (pp. 72–90). Toronto, Canada: W.B. Saunders.

Lareau, A. (2003) *Unequal Childhoods: Class, Race and Family Life*. Berkeley, CA: University of California Press.

Lee, B.J. & Goerge, R.M. (1999) Poverty, early childbearing and child maltreatment: a multinomial analysis. *Children and Youth Service Review* 21, 755–780.

Lee, P., Murie, A. & Gordon, D. (1995) *Area Measures of Deprivation: A Study of Current Methods and Best Practices in Great Britain*. Birmingham: Centre for Urban and Regional Studies (CURS), University of Birmingham.

Leventhal, T. & Brooks-Gunn, J. (2000) The neighbourhoods they live in: the effects of neighbourhood residence on child and adolescent outcomes. *Psychological Bulletin* 126, 309 337.

Leventhal, T. & Brooks-Gunn, J. (2001) Changing neighborhoods and child well-being: understanding how children may be affected in the coming century. *Advances in Life Course Research* 6, 263–301.

Leventhal, T. & Brooks-Gunn, J. (2003) Moving to opportunity: an experimental study of neighborhood effects on mental health. *American Journal of Public Health* 93, 1576–1582.

Leventhal, T. & Brooks-Gunn, J. (2004) A randomized study of neighborhood effects on low-income children's educational outcomes. *Developmental Psychology* 40, 488–507.

Levitas, R. (1998) *The Inclusive Society? Social Exclusion and New Labour*. Basingstoke, Hampshire: Macmillan Press.

Lewis, O. (1966) *La Vida: A Puerto Rican Family in the Culture of Poverty. San Juan and New York*. New York: Random House.

Lindholm, K.J. & Willey, R. (1986) Ethnic differences in child abuse and sexual abuse. *Hispanic Journal of Behavioral Sciences* 8, 111–125.

Lister, R. (1996) In search of the underclass. In Lister, R. (ed.) *Charles Murray and the Underclass: the Developing Debate*. Choice in Welfare Series Number 33. London: Institute of Economic Affairs.

Livingstone, S., Bober, M. & Helsper, E. (2004) *Active Participation or Just More Information? Young People's Take Up of Opportunities to Act and Interact on the Internet: A Research Report from the UK Children Go Online project*. www.children-go-online.net London: London School of Economics.

Lloyd, N., O'Brien, M. & Lewis, C. (2003) *Fathers in Sure Start Local Programmes*. Nottingham: Department for Education and Skills Publications. http://www.surestart.gov.uk/publications/?Document=117

López Turley, R.N. (2003) When do neighbourhoods matter? The role of race and neighbourhood peers. *Social Science Research* 32, 61–79.

Love, J.M., Kisker, E.E., Ross, C.M., Schochet, P.Z., Brooks-Gunn, J., Paulsell, D., Boller, K., Constantine, J., Vogel, C., Fuligni, A.S. & Brady-Smith, C. (2002) *Making a Difference in the Lives of Infants and Toddlers and Their Families: the Impacts of Early Head Start. Executive Summary*. Washington, DC: US. Department of Health and Human Services, Administration for Children and Families, Head Start Bureau.

Lupton, C. (1998) User empowerment or family self-reliance? The family group conference model. *British Journal of Social Work* 28, 107–128.

Lupton, C. (ed.) (2000) *Moving Forward – on Family Group Conferences in Hampshire*. Portsmouth: University of Portsmouth.

Lupton, R. (2003) '*Neighbourhood Effects': Can We Measure Them and Does It Matter?* CASE Paper 73. London: Research Centre for the Analysis of Social Exclusion (CASE), London School of Economics.

Lynch, K. (1960) *The Image of the City*. Cambridge: M.I.T. Press.

Lynch, K. (ed.) (1977) *Growing Up in Cities: Studies of the Spatial Environment of Adolescence in Cracow, Melbourne, Mexico City, Salta, Toluca, and Warszawa*. London: M.I.T. Press

Maccoby, E., Johnson, J. & Church, R. (1958) Community integration and the social control of juvenile delinquency. *Journal of Social Issues* 14, 38–51.

MacIntyre, D. & Carr, A. (1999) Evaluation of the effectiveness of the Stay Safe primary prevention programme for child sexual abuse. *Child Abuse and Neglect* 23, 1307–1325.

Mackie, A., Burrows, J. & Hubbard, R. (2003) *Evaluation of the Youth Improvement Programme. End of Phase One Report*. London: MHB Consulting/Youth Justice Board.

Mamalian, C. & LaVigne, N. (1999) *The Use of Computerized Crime Mapping by Law Enforcement: Survey Results*. Washington, DC: National Institute of Justice, Research Preview.

Manzi, T. & Smith-Bowers, B. (2005) Gated communities as club goods: segregation or social cohesion? *Housing Studies* 20, 345–359.

Marjoribanks, K. (1979) Ethnicity, family environment and cognitive performance: a regression surface analysis. *Journal of Comparative Family Studies* 10, 5–18.

Marjoribanks, K. (1986) Australian families and adolescents' aspirations: a follow-up analysis. *Journal of Comparative Family Studies* 17, 333–348.

Marjoribanks, K. (1991) Ethnicity, family environment and social status attainment: a follow-up analysis. *Journal of Comparative Family Studies* 22, 15–23.

Marsh, P. & Crow, G. (1997) *Family Group Conferences in Child Welfare*. Oxford: Blackwell.

Marshall, J. (1999) Zero tolerance policing. *Information Bulletin* 9, 1–14.

Massey, D. & Denton, N. (1993) *American Apartheid: Segregation and the Making of the Underclass*. Cambridge, MA: Harvard University Press.

Matthews, H. (1992) *Making Sense of Place: Children's Understanding of Large-scale Environments*. Hemel Hempstead: Harvester Wheatsheaf.

Matthews, H. (1986) Gender, home range and environmental cognition. *Transactions of the Institute of British Geographers* 12, 43–56.

Matthews, H. (2003) The street as liminal space: the barbed spaces of childhood. In P. Christensen & M. O'Brien (eds) *Children in the City: Home, Neighbourhood and Community* (pp. 101–117). London: RoutledgeFalmer.

Matthews, H., Limb, M. & Taylor, M. (1999) Young people's participation and representation in society. *Geoforum* 30, 135–144.

Matthews, H., Taylor, M., Sherwood, K., Tucker, F. and Limb, M. (2000) Growing up in the countryside: Children and rural idyll. *Journal of Rural Studies* 16, 141–153.

Maxwell, G. & Morris, A. (1996) Research on family group conferences with young offenders in New Zealand. In J. Hudson, A. Morris, G. Maxwell & B. Galaway (eds) *Family Group Conferences: Perspectives on Policy and Practice* (pp. 88–110). Annandale, New York: Willow Tree Press.

Maxwell, G. & Morris, A. (1998) *Understanding Re-offending*. Wellington: Institute of Criminology, Victoria University of Wellington.

Mayor of London (2000) *Children and Young People's Strategy*. London: Greater London Authority.

Mayor of London (2004) *Making London Better For All Children and Young People*. London: Greater London Authority. Accessed on 1 August at http://www.london.gov.uk/mayor/strategies/children/docs/main.pdf.

McCain, M.N. & Mustard, J.F. (1999) *Early Years Study: Reversing the Real Brain Drain. Final Report*. Toronto: Ontario Children's Secretariat.

McCubbin, H., Joy, C., Cauble, A., Comeau, J., Patterson, J. & Needle, R. (1980) Family stress and coping: a decade review. *Journal of Marriage and the Family* 42, 855–871.

McCulloch, A. (2003) An examination of social capital and social disorganisation in neighbourhoods in the British household panel study. *Social Science & Medicine* 56, 1425–1438.

McCulloch, A. & Joshi, H. (2001) Neighbourhood and family influences on the cognitive ability of children in the British National Child Development Study. *Social Science & Medicine* 53, 579–591.

McDevitt, S. (1997) Social work in community development: a cross-national comparison. *International Social Work* 40, 341–357.

McGuire, J. & Earls, F. (1991) Prevention of psychiatric disorders in early childhood. *Journal of Child Psychology and Psychiatry* 32, 129–153.

McKendrick, J.H., Fielder, A. & Bradford, M. (1999) Privatisation of collective play spaces in the UK. *Built Environment* 25, 1: 44–57.

McKendrick, J.H. (2000) The geography of children: an annotated bibliography. *Childhood* 7, 359–387.

McKendrick, J.H., Bradford, M. & Fielder, A. (2000) Time for a party!: making sense of the commercialisation of leisure space for children. In S. Holloway & G. Valentine (eds) *Children's geographies: Living, Playing and Transforming Everyday Worlds* (pp. 100–116) London: Routledge.

McMillan, D.W. (1976) *Sense of Community: an Attempt at Definition*. Unpublished manuscript. Nashville, TN: George Peabody College for Teachers.

McMillan, D.W. & Chavis, D.M. (1986) Sense of community: a definition and theory. *Journal of Community Psychology* 14, 6–23.

Melton, G. & Berry, F. (1994) *Protecting Children from Abuse and Neglect: Foundations for a New National Strategy*. New York: Guilford Press.

Melton, G., Limber, S., Cunningham, P., Osgood, D., Chambers, J., Flerx, V., Henggeler, S. & Nation, M. (1998) *Violence Among Rural Youth. Final Report*. Washington, DC: Office of Juvenile Justice and Delinquency Prevention.

Mihalic, S., Fagan, S., Irwin, K., Ballard, D. & Elliott, D. (2004) *Blueprints for Violence Prevention*. Washington DC: Office of Juvenile Justice and Delinquency Prevention.

Millsap, M., Chase, A., Obeidallah, D., Perez-Smith, A., Brigham, N. & Johnston, K. (2000) *Evaluation of Detroit's Comer Schools and Families Initiative*. Cambridge, MA: Abt Associates.

Milner, J. (1994) Assessing physical child abuse risk: The Child Abuse Potential Inventory. *Child Psychology Review* 14, 547–583.

Mitchel, J. & Gelloz, N. (1997) Supporting families and strengthening communities: the role of the 'Specialised prevention' movement in France. *Social Work in Europe* 4, 2–11.

Moore, R. (1986) *Children's Domain: Play and Play Space in Child Development*. London: Croom Helm.

Moran, R. & Dolphin, C. (1986) The defensible space concept: theoretical and operational explication. *Environment and Behavior* 18, 396–416.

MORI (2004) *MORI Youth Survey 2004*. London: Youth Justice Board.

Morris, K. & Spicer, N. (2003) *The National Evaluation of the Children's Fund: Early Messages From Developing Practice*. Birmingham: University of Birmingham, NECF.

Morrow, V. (1999) Conceptualizing social capital in relation to the well-being of children and young people: a critical review. *Sociological Review* 47, 744–765.

Morrow, V. (2001) *Networks and Neighbourhoods: Children's and Young People's Perspectives*. London: Health Development Agency.

Moss, P. & Penn, H. (1996) *Transforming Nursery Education*. London: Penguin.

Moss, P. & Petrie, P. (2002) *From Children's Services to Children's Spaces*. London: RoutledgeFalmer

Mulroy, E.A. (1994) Shared power: how nonprofit organizations collaborate to reduce child abuse and neglect in poverty neighborhoods. Paper presented to the annual meeting of the Association for Research on Nonprofit Organizations and Voluntary Action, Berkeley, CA, 21 October.

Mulroy, E.A. (1997) Building a neighborhood network: interorganizational collaboration to prevent child abuse and neglect. *Social Work* 42, 255–264.

Mumford, K. & Power, A. (2003) *East Enders: Family and Community in East London*. Bristol: Policy Press.

Murray, C. (1989) The emerging British underclass. *Sunday Times Magazine*, November.

Murray, C. (1990) *The Emerging British Underclass*. London: Institute of Economic Affairs, Health and Welfare Unit.

Murray, C., (1994) *Underclass: the Crisis Deepens*. London: Institute of Economic Affairs, Health and Welfare Unit.

Murray, C. (1996) The emerging British underclass. In R. Lister (ed.) *Charles Murray and the Underclass: the Developing Debate* (pp. 23–52). London: Institute of Economic Affairs, Health and Welfare Unit with the *Sunday Times*.

Murtagh, B. (1999a) Listening to communities: locality research and planning. *Urban Studies* 36, 1181–1193.

Murtagh, B. (1999b) Urban segregation and community initiatives in Northern Ireland. *Community Development Journal* 34, 219–226.

Myers, P., Barnes, J. & Brodie, I. (2004) *Partnership Working in Sure Start Local Programmes. Early Findings From Local Programme Evaluations*. London: National Evaluation of Sure Start, Birkbeck, University of London. http://www.ness.bbk.ac.uk/documents/synthesisReports/396.pdf

Nash, J.K. & Bowen, G.L. (1999) Perceived crime and informal social control in the neighbourhood as a context for adolescent behaviour: a risk and resilience perspective. *Social Work Research* 23, 171–186.

Nasman, E. (1994) Individualization and institutionalization of childhood in today's Europe. In J. Qvortrup, M. Bardy, G. Sgritta & H. Wintersberger (eds) *Childhood Matters: Social Theory, Practice and Politics* (pp. 165–188). Aldershot, UK: Avebury.

National Commission on Children (1991) *Beyond Rhetoric: a New American Agenda for Children and Families. Final Report of the National Commission on Children*. Washington, DC: National Commission on Children.

National Crime Prevention Australia (1999) *Pathways to Prevention: Developmental and Early Intervention Approaches to Crime in Australia*. Canberra: National Crime Prevention, Attorney-General's Department. Accessed in May 2005 at http://www.ag.gov.au/www/ncpHome.nsf/0/B78FEDFB9A1D980ACA256B14001A096E?OpenDocument

National Evaluation of the Children's Fund (NECF) (2004) *Children, Young People, Parents and Carers' Participation in Children's Fund Case Study Partnerships*. London: Department for Education and Skills and the University of Birmingham, http://www.ne-cf.org/briefing.asp?section=000100040009&profile=000100080002&id=953.

National Family and Parenting Institute (NFPI) (2004) *Parenting Fund: Guidance 2004*. London: NFPI. www.parentingfund.org.

National Institute of Social Work (NISW) (1982) *Social Workers: Their Role and Tasks (the Barclay Report)*. London: Bedford Square Press.

National Research Council Panel on Research on Child Abuse and Neglect (1993) *Understanding Child Abuse and Neglect*. Washington, DC: National Academy Press.

Nelson, G., Pancer, M., Hayward, K. & Kelly, R. (2004) Partnerships and participation of community residents in health promotion and prevention: experiences of the Highfield community enrichment project (Better Beginnings, Better Futures). *Journal of Health Psychology* 9, 213–227.

Nelson, G., Prilleltensky, I. & Peters, R. DeV. (2003). Prevention and mental health promotion in the community. In W.L. Marshall & P. Firestone (eds) *Abnormal Psychology: Perspectives* (2nd edn) (pp. 462–479). Scarborough, Ontario: Prentice Hall, Allyn & Bacon Canada.

NESS Research Team (2004) The national evaluation of Sure Start local programmes in England. *Child and Adolescent Mental Health* 9, 2–8.

Newman, O. (1972) *Defensible Space: Crime Prevention Through Urban Design*. New York: MacMillan.

Newson, J. & Newson, E. (1968) *Four Years Old in an Urban Community*. Harmondsworth, Middlesex: Penguin.

Newson, J. & Newson, E. (1974) Cultural aspects of childrearing in the English-speaking world. In M.P.M. Richards (ed.) *The Integration of a Child into a Social World* (pp. 53–82). Cambridge: Cambridge University Press.

Novick, M. (1979) *Metro's Suburbs in Transition, Part 1: Evolution and Overview*. Toronto: Social Planning Council of Metropolitan Toronto.

O'Brien, M. (2005) Social Science and Public Policy Perspectives on Fatherhood in Europe. In M.E. Lamb (ed) *The Role of the Father in Child Development* (pp. 121–145). New Jersey: Wiley.

O'Brien, M. (2003) Regenerating children's neighbourhoods: what do children want? In P. Christensen & M. O'Brien (eds) *Children in the city: Home, neighbourhood and community* (pp. 142–163). London: RoutledgeFalmer.

O'Brien, M., Shenitti, I. & Jordan, E. (2004) *The Evaluation of the Children's Fund Projects in Lincolnshire.* Birmingham: National Evaluation of the Children's Fund. http://www.ne-cf.org/localevaluation/evaluator_reports.asp?id=422&section=000100010001&programme=84.

O'Brien, M., Jones, D., Sloan, D. & Rustin, M. (2000) Children's independent spatial mobility in the urban public realm. *Childhood* 7, 257–277.

O'Brien, M., Rustin, M. & Greenfield, J. (1999) *Childhood, Urban Space and Citizenship: Child-sensitive Urban Regeneration.* Final report L12951039. Swindon: Economic and Social Research Council Report.

O'Campo, P., Xue, W., Wang, M. & Caughy, M. (1997) Neighborhood risk factors and low birthweight in Baltimore. A multilevel analysis. *American Journal of Public Health* 87, 1113–1118.

Office of the Deputy Prime Minister (ODPM) (2004) *The Egan Review. Skills for Sustainable Communities.* London: ODPM. Available at www.odpm.gov.uk/eganreview.

Ogbu, J.U. (1981) Origins of human competence: a cultural-ecological perspective. *Child Development* 52, 413–429.

Ogbu, J.U. (1985) A cultural ecology of competence among inner-city blacks. In M.B. Spencer, G.K. Brookins & W.R. Allen (eds) *Beginnings: the Social and Affective Development of Black Children* (pp. 45–66). Hillsdale, NJ: Lawrence Erlbaum Associates, Publishers.

Oliver, C., Smith, M. & Barker, S. (1998) Effectiveness of early interventions. *Treasury Supporting Papers* for the *Cross Departmental Review of Provision for Young Children.* London: HM Treasury.

Olweus, D. (1993a) *Bullying at School: What We Know, What We Can Do.* Oxford: Blackwell.

Olweus, D. (1993b) Victimisation by peers: antecedents and long term outcomes. In K. Rubin & K. & B. Asendorf (eds) *Social Withdrawal, Inhibition and Shyness in Childhood* (pp. 315–342). Hillsdale NJ: Lawrence Erlbaum Associates.

Olweus, D. (2004) Design and implementation issues and a new national initiative in Norway. In P. Smith, D. Pepler & K. Rigby (eds) *Bullying in Schools: How Successful Can Interventions Be?* (pp. 13–36). Cambridge: Cambridge University Press.

O'Neil, R., Parke R.D. & McDowell, D.J. (2001) Objective and subjective features of children's neighborhoods: relations to parental regulatory strategies and children's social competence. *Applied Developmental Psychology* 22, 135–155.

Opie, I. & Opie, P. (1984) *Children's Games in Street and Playground.* Oxford: Oxford University Press.

Orr, L., Feins, J., Jacob, R., Beechcroft, E., Sanbonmatsu, L., Katz, L., Liebman, J. & King, J. (2003) *Moving to Opportunity for Fair Housing Demonstration Program: Interim Impacts Evaluation.* Washington, DC: US Department of Housing and Urban Development.

Osofsky, J.D. (ed.) (1997) *Children in a Violent Society.* London: Guilford Press.

Osofsky, H.J. & Osofsky, J.D. (2004) Children's exposure to community violence. In B. Sklarew, S.W. Twemlow & S.M. Wilkinson (eds) *Analysts in the Trenches: Streets, Schools, War Zones* (pp. 237–256). New York: Analytic Press.

Osofsky, J.D. & Thompson, M.D. (2000) Adaptive and maladaptive parenting: perspectives on risk and protective factors. In J.P. Shonkoff & S.J. Meisels (eds) *Handbook of Early Childhood Intervention* (pp. 54–75). New York: Cambridge University Press.

Panel on Research on Child Abuse and Neglect (1993) *Understanding Child Abuse and Neglect.* Washington DC: National Academy Press.

Parsons, C., Austin, B., Hailes, J. & Stow, W. (2003) *On Track Thematic Report: Community and Schools' Engagement.* London: Home Office.

Pelton, L.H. (1981) *The Social Context of Child Abuse and Neglect.* New York: Human Sciences Press.

Pepler, D., Smith, P. & Rigby, K. (2004) Implications for making interventions work effectively. In P. Smith, D. Pepler & K. Rigby (eds) *Bullying in Schools: How Successful Can Interventions Be?* (pp. 307–324). Cambridge: Cambridge University Press.

Perkins, D. & Taylor, R. (1996) Ecological assessments of community disorder: their relationship to fear of crime and theoretical implications. *American Journal of Community Psychology* 24, 63–107.

Peters, R. DeV. (2001) *Overview of Lessons Learned*. Kingston Ontario: Better Beginnings, Better Futures Research Coordination Unit, Queen's University. http://bbbf.queensu.ca/pdfs/o_stfr.pdf.

Peters, R. DeV. (2002) The Better Beginnings, Better Futures prevention project. Paper presented to the second world conference on the promotion of mental health and prevention of mental and behavioural disorders, London, September.

Peters, R. DeV., Arnold, R., Petrunka, K., Angus, D.E., Brophy, K., Burke, S.O., Cameron, G., Evers, S., Herry, Y., Levesque, D., Pancer, S.M., Roberts-Fiati, G., Towson, S. & Warren, W.K. (2000) *Developing Capacity and Competence in the Better Beginnings, Better Futures Communities: Short-term Findings Report*. Kingston, Ontario: Better Beginnings, Better Futures Research Coordination Unit Technical Report. http://bbbf.queensu.ca/pdfs/r_stfr.pdf.

Peters, R.DeV., Arnold, R., Petrunka, K., Angus, D.E., Bélanger, J.M., Boyce, W., Brophy, K., Burke, S.O., Cameron, G., Craig, W., Evers, S., Herry, Y., Mamatis, D., Nelson, G., Pancer, S.M., Roberts-Fiati, G., Russell, C.C. & Towson, S. (2003a) *Better Beginnings, Better Futures: a Comprehensive, Community-based Project for Early Childhood Development. Highlights of Lessons Learned*. Kingston, Ontario: Better Beginnings, Better Futures Research Coordination Unit technical report.

Peters, R. DeV., Petrunka, K. & Arnold, R. (2003b) The Better Beginnings, Better Futures project: a universal, comprehensive, community-based prevention approach for primary school children and their families. *Journal of Clinical Child and Adolescent Psychology* 32, 215–227.

Phillips, T. (2001) White flight is enforcing segregation. A leading black politician writes an open letter to the home secretary. *The Guardian*, 19 December.

Philo, C. (2000) The corner-stones of my world. *Childhood: A Global Journal of Child Research* 7, 243–256.

Pinderhughes, E.E., Nix, R.L., Foster, E.M., Jones, D. & the Conduct Problems Prevention Research Group (2001) Parenting in context: Impact of neighborhood poverty, residential stability, public services, social networks, and danger on parental behaviors. *Journal of Marriage and Family* 63, 941–953.

Plotnikoff, J., Woolfson, R., Chandler, J. & Lait, D. (1996) *Children in Court*. London: Victim Support.

Pollard, C. (1998) Zero Tolerance: Short term fix, long term liability. In N. Dennis (ed.) *Zero Tolerance: Policing a Free Society* (pp. 44–61). London: Institute of Economic Affairs (IEA).

Portes, A. (1998) Social capital: its origins and applications in modern sociology. *Annual Review of Sociology* 24, 1–24.

Portes, A. & Zhou, M. (1993) The new second generation: segmented assimilation and its variants. *The Annals of the Academy of Political and Social Science* 530 (November), 74–96.

Power, A. & Tunstall, R. (1995) *Swimming Against the Tide: Polarisation or Progress on 20 Unpopular Council Estates, 1980–1995*. York: Joseph Rowntree Foundation.

Preece, J. (1999) Empathic communities: Balancing emotional and factual communication. *Interacting with Computers* 12, 63–77.

Preston, P. (2005) There is no such thing as community. The idea that society comprises homogeneous groups is deluded, *Guardian*, 18 July.

Prior, D. & Paris, A. (2005) *Preventing Children's Involvement: in Crime and Anti-social Behaviour: a Literature Review, a Paper Produced for the National Evaluation of the Children's Fund*. London: Department for Education and Skills (DfES).

Puddifoot, J.E. (1994) Community identity and sense of belonging in a North Eastern English town. *Journal of Social Psychology* 134, 601–608.

Puddifoot, J.E. (1996) Some initial considerations in the measurement of community identity. *Journal of Community Psychology* 24, 327–336.

Punch, S. (2000) Children's strategies for creating playspaces: negotiating independence in rural Bolivia. In S. Holloway & G. Valentine (eds) *Children's Geographies: Living, Playing and Transforming Everyday Worlds* (pp. 48–62). London: Routledge.

Putnam, R.D. (1993) The prosperous community: social capital and public life. *American Prospect* 13, 35–42.

Putnam, R.D. (1995) Bowling alone: America's declining social capital. *Journal of Democracy* 6, 65–78.

Putnam, R.D. (1996) The strange disappearance of civic America. *American Prospect* 24, 34–48.

Putnam, R.D. (2000) *Bowling Alone: the Collapse and Revival of American Community*. New York: Simon & Schuster.

Qvortrup, J., Bardy, M., Sgritta, G. & Wintersberger, H. (eds) (1994) *Childhood Matters: Social Theory, Practice and Politics*. Aldershot: Avebury.

Rankin, B. & Quane, J. (2002) Social contexts and urban adolescent outcomes: the interrelated effects of neighborhoods, families, and peers on African-American youth. *Social Problems* 49, 79–100.

Rasmussen, K. & Smidt, S. (2003) Children in the neighbourhood: the neighbourhood in children. In P. Christensen & O'Brien, M. (eds) *Children in the City: Home, Neighbourhood and Community* (pp. 82–100). London: RoutledgeFalmer.

Raudenbush, S.W. & Sampson, R.J. (1999) 'Ecometrics': toward a science of assessing ecological settings, with application to the systematic social observation of neighborhoods. *Sociological Methodology* 29, 1–41.

Regional Coordination Unit (RCU) (2002) *A Review of Area Based Initiatives*. London: Office of the Deputy Prime Minister.

Reynolds, A.J. & Ou, S. (2004) Alterable predictors of child well-being in the Chicago longitudinal study. *Children and Youth Services Review* 26, 1–14.

Rheingold, H. (1993) *The Virtual Community: Homesteading on the Electronic Frontier*. Reading, MA: Addison-Wesley.

Richards, M.P.M. (ed.) (1974) *The Integration of a Child into a Social World.* Cambridge: Cambridge University Press.

Rigby, K., Smith, P. & Pepler, D. (2004) Working to prevent school bullying: key issues. In P. Smith, D. Pepler & K. Rigby (eds) *Bullying in Schools: How Successful Can Interventions Be?* (pp. 1–12). Cambridge: Cambridge University Press.

Rigby, K. (1997) What children tell us about bullying in schools. *Children Australia* 22, 28–34.

Roberts, I., Norton, R. & Taua, B. (1996) Child pedestrian injury rates: the importance of exposure to risk relating to socioeconomic and ethnic differences. *Journal of Epidemiological Community Health* 50, 162–165.

Robson, B., Bradford, M. & Tye, R. (1995) The development of the 1991 Local Deprivation Index. In G. Room (ed.), *Beyond the Threshold: the Measurement and Analysis of Social Exclusion* (pp. 191–211). Bristol: Policy Press.

Rogers, R. (1999) *Urban Task Force: Towards an Urban Renaissance*. London: Department for the Environment, Trade and the Regions (DETR).

Room, G. (1995) Poverty and social exclusion: the new European agenda for policy and research. In G. Room (ed.) *Beyond the Threshold. The Measurement and Analysis of Social Exclusion* (pp. 1–9). Bristol: The Policy Press.

Room, G. (1998) *Social Exclusion, Solidarity and the Challenge of Globalisation*. Bath: University of Bath, Bath Social Policy Papers.

Rosenbaum, J. (1991) Black pioneers – do their moves to the suburbs increase economic opportunities for mothers and children? *Housing Policy Debate* 2, 1179–1213.

Roseneil, S. & Williams, F. (2004) Public values of parenting and partnering: voluntary organizations and welfare politics in New Labour's Britain. *Social Politics* 11, 181–216.

Ross, N.A., Tremblay, S. & Graham, K. (2004) Neighbourhood influences on health in Montreal, Canada. *Social Science & Medicine* 59, 1485–1494.

Roussos, S. & Fawcett, S. (2000) A review of collaborative partnerships as a strategy for improving community health. *American Review of Public Health* 21, 369–402.

Rutter, M. (1983) Stress, coping, and development: some issues and some questions. In N. Garmezy & M. Rutter (eds) *Stress, Coping, and Development in Children* (pp. 1–42). New York: McGraw-Hill.

Rutter, M., Giller, H. & Hagell, A. (1998) *Antisocial Behaviour by Young People: the Main Messages*. Cambridge: Cambridge University Press.

Sabol, W., Coulton, C. & Polousky, E. (2004) Measuring child maltreatment risk in communities: a life table approach. *Child Abuse & Neglect* 28, 967–983.

Sampson, R.J. (1992) Family management and child development: insights from social disorganization theory. In J. McCord (ed.) *Facts, Frameworks and Forecasts: Advances in Criminological Theory, Vol. 3* (pp. 63–93). New Brunswick, NJ: Transaction Press.

Sampson, R.J. (1997a) Collective regulation of adolescent misbehavior: validation results from eighty Chicago neighborhoods. *Journal of Adolescent Research* 12, 227–244.

Sampson, R.J. (1997b) The embeddedness of child and adolescent development; a community-level perspective on urban violence. In J. McCord (ed.) *Violence and Childhood in the Inner City* (pp. 31–77). Cambridge: Cambridge University Press.

Sampson, R.J. & Groves, W. (1989) Community structure and crime: testing social-disorganization theory. *American Journal of Sociology* 94, 774–802.

Sampson, R.J., Morenoff, J. & Gannon-Rowley, T. (2002) Assessing 'neighborhood effects': social processes and new directions in research. *Annual Review of Sociology* 28, 443–78.

Sampson, R.J. & Raudenbush, S.W. (1999) Systematic social observation of public spaces: a new look at disorder in urban neighborhoods. *American Journal of Sociology* 105, 603–51.

Sampson, R.J. & Raudenbush, S.W. (2004) Seeing disorder: neighborhood stigma and the social construction of 'broken windows'. *Social Psychology Quarterly* 67, 319–342.

Sampson, R.J., Raudenbush, S.W. & Earls, F. (1997) Neighborhoods and violent crime: a multilevel study of collective efficacy. *Science* 277, 918–924.

Sampson, R.J., Raudenbush, S.W. & Earls, F. (1998) Neighborhood collective efficacy: does it help reduce violence? *Protecting Children* 14, 17–19.

Secretary of State for Education and Skills (2005) *Youth Matters. Green Paper*. London: Her Majesty's Stationery Office.

Schorr, L. (1988) *Within Our Reach: Breaking the Cycle of Disadvantage*. New York: Anchor.

Schuler, D. (1996). *New Community Networks: Wired for Change*. New York: ACM Press.

Schweinhart, L.J. & Weikart, D.P. (1997) The High/Scope preschool curriculum comparison study through age 23. *Early Childhood Research Quarterly* 12, 117–143.

Scott, C.L. (1999) Juvenile violence. *Pediatric Clinics of North America* 22, 71–83.

Scott, S., Jackson, S. & Backett-Milburn, K. (1998) Swings and roundabouts: risk anxiety and the everyday worlds of children. *Sociology* 32, 689–705.

Shaver, S. & Tudball, J. (2002) *Literature Review on Factors Contributing to Community Capabilities: Final Report for the Department of Family and Community Services*. Sydney: Social Policy Research Centre.

Shaw, C.R. & McKay, H.D. (1942) *Juvenile Delinquency and Urban Areas*. Chicago: University of Chicago Press.

Shay, S. (1988) *The Influences of a Community Prevention Program on Parenting Beliefs and Parental Competence*. Unpublished report. Ann Arbor, MI: University of Michigan.

Shay, S. (1995) *Building the 21st-century Ark: the CARES Model for Comprehensive Family Support*. Final report to the National Center on Child Abuse and Neglect, Grant No. 90-CA-1417. Washington, DC: US Government Printing Office.

Sheppard, M. & Grohn, M. (2004) *Prevention and Coping in Child and Family Care: Mothers in Adversity Coping with Child Care*. London: Jessica Kingsley.

Shier, H. (2001) Pathways to participation: openings, opportunities and obligations. *Children & Society* 15, 107–117.

Shonkoff, J. & Phillips, D. (eds) (2000) *From Neurons to Neighbourhoods. The Science of Early Childhood Development*. Washington, DC: National Academies Press.

Sidebotham, P. & the ALSPAC Study Team (2000) Patterns of child abuse in early childhood, a cohort study of the 'Children of the Nineties'. *Child Abuse Review* 9, 311–320.

Sidebotham, P., Heron, J., Golding, J. & the ALSPAC Study Team (2002) Child maltreatment in the 'Children of the Nineties': deprivation, class and social networks in a UK sample. *Child Abuse and Neglect* 26, 1243–1259.

Simcha-Fagan, O. & Schwartz, J.E. (1986) Neighborhood and delinquency: An assessment of contextual effects. *Criminology* 24, 667–703.

Sinclair, R. (2004) Participation in practice: making it meaningful, effective and sustainable. *Children and Society* 18, 106–118.

Skelton, T. (2000) Nothing to do, nowhere to go?: teenage girls and 'public' space in the Rhondda Valleys, South Wales. In S. Holloway & G. Valentine (eds) *Children's Geographies: Living, Playing and Transforming Everyday Worlds* (pp. 80–99). London: Routledge.

Smith, D.J. (1992) Defining the underclass. In D.J. Smith (ed.) *Understanding the Underclass* (pp. 3–9). London: Policy Studies Institute.

Smith, F. & Barker, J. (1999) From 'Ninja Turtles' to the 'Spice Girls': children's participation in the development of out of school play environments. *Built Environment* 25, 35–43.

Smith, F. & Barker, J. (2000) Contested spaces: children's experiences of out of school care in England and Wales. *Childhood: A Global Journal of Child Research* 7, 315–333.

Smith, G.R. (1999) *Area-based Initiatives: the Rationale and Options for Area Targeting*. CASE paper 25. London: Centre for the Analysis of Social Exclusion (CASE), London School of Economics.

Smith, P., Pepler, D. & Rigby, K. (eds) *Bullying in Schools: How Successful Can Interventions Be*? Cambridge: Cambridge University Press.

Social Exclusion Unit (1998) *Bringing Britain Together: a National Strategy for Neighbourhood Renewal*. London: SEU. Accessed in June 2005 at http://www.socialexclusion.gov.uk/downloaddoc.asp?id=113.

Social Exclusion Unit (2000) *Schools Plus: Building Learning Communities*. PAT Report 11. London: SEU, http://www.socialexclusion.gov.uk/downloaddoc.asp?id=124.

Social Exclusion Unit (SEU) (2001) *A New Commitment to Neighbourhood Renewal. National Strategy Action Plan*. www.neighbourhood.gov.uk/publicationsdetail.asp.

Social Planning Network of Ontario (SPNO) (2002) *Social Capital Overview*. Toronto, CA: SPNO. Cited by Freiler, C. (2004) *Why Strong Neighbourhoods Matter: Implications for Policy and Practice*. Toronto, CA: Strong Neighbourhoods Task Force.

Somerville, P. (2005) Community governance and democracy. *Policy & Politics* 33, 117–144.

Spilsbury, J. (2002a) *Hazards and Help-seeking in Inner-city Cleveland: The Child's Perception of Neighborhood Danger, Safety, and Support*. Unpublished dissertation. Cleveland OH: Case Western Reserve University.

Spilsbury, J. & Korbin, J. (2004) Negotiating the dance: Social capital from the perspective of neighborhood children and adults. In P. Pufall & R. Unsworth (eds) *Rethinking Childhood* (pp. 191–206). New Brunswick, NJ: Rutgers University Press.

St. Pierre, R.G., Layzer, J.I., Goodson, B.D. & Bernstein, L.S. (1997) *National Impact Evaluation of the Comprehensive Child Development Program: Final Report*. Cambridge, MA: Abt Associates. Accessed May 2005 at http://www.abtassociates.com/reports/D19970050.pdf.

Stack, C. (1974) *All Our Kin: Strategies for Survival in a Black Community*. New York: Harper & Row.

Stone, R. (1996) *Issues in Comprehensive Community Building Activities*. Chicago: Chapin Hall Center for Children at the University of Chicago.

Strong Communities (2005) *What's Different about Strong Communities?* Accessed at http://www.clemson.edu/strongcommunities/resources.html 19 July 2005.

Subramanian, S., Lochner, K. & Kawachi, I. (2003) Neighborhood differences in social capital: a compositional artefact or a contextual construct? *Health & Place* 9, 33–44.

Sure Start Unit (2002) *Sure Start. A Guide to Planning and Running Your Programme*. London: Sure Start Unit.

Sure Start Unit (2003) *Children's Centres – Developing Integrated Services For Young Children and Their Families. Start Up Guidance*. London: Sure Start Unit. Accessed on 18 July 2005 at http://www.surestart.gov.uk/_doc/P0000457.doc.

Sure Start Unit (2005) *Children's Centres Implementation Update No. 5*. London: Sure Start Unit. Accessed on 18 July 2005 at http://www.surestart.gov.uk/publications/index.cfm?document=1017.

Sutton, C., Utting, D. & Farrington, D. (2004) *Support from the Start: Working with Young Children and Their Families to Reduce the Risks of Crime and Anti-social Behaviour*. London: Department for Education and Skills.

Talen, E. (1999) Sense of community and neighbourhood form: an assessment of the social doctrine of New Urbanism. *Urban Studies* 36, 1361–1379.

Taylor, I., Evans, K. & Fraser, P. (1996) *A Tale of Two Cities: a Study of Manchester and Sheffield*. London: Routledge.

Thomas, M., Vuong, K. & Renshaw, J. (2004) *ASBOs and young people*. Association of Youth Offending Team Managers http://www.aym.org.uk/pictures/mainpage_36/id56.doc.

Thompson, R.A. (1995) *Preventing Child Maltreatment Through Social Support: a Critical Analysis*. Thousand Oaks, CA: Sage.

Tisdall, E. & Davis, J. (2004) Making a difference? Bringing children's and young people's views into policy-making. *Children & Society* 18, 131–142.

Tomison, A.M. & Wise, S. (1999) *Community-based Approaches in Preventing Child Maltreatment. Issues Paper No. 11*. Melbourne, Victoria: National Child Protection Clearinghouse, Australian Institute of Family Studies.

Tönnies, F. (1957) *Community and Society*. Translation by C.P. Loomis of *Gemeinschaft und Gesellschaft* (1887) East Lansing, MI: Michigan State University Press.

Treseder, P. (1997) *Empowering Children and Young People*. London: Save the Children.

Tunstill, J., Allnock, D., Meadows, P., McLeod, A. & the NESS Research Team (2002) *Early Experiences of Implementing Sure Start*. Nottingham: Department for Education and Skills publications. http://www.surestart.gov.uk/publications/?Document=97.

Tunstill, J., Allnock, D., Akhurst, S., Garbers, C. & the NESS Research Team (2005a) Sure Start local programmes: implications of case study data for the National Evaluation of Sure Start. *Children & Society* 19, 158–171.

Tunstill, J., Meadows, P., Allnock, D., Akhurst, S., Chrysanthou, J., Garbers, C., Morley, A., Van der Velde, T. & the NESS Research Team (2005b) *Implementing Sure Start Local Programmes: an In-depth Study*. Nottingham: Department for Education and Skills publications. http://www.surestart.gov.uk/publications/?Document=1230.

Twelvetrees, A.C. (1996) *Organising for Neighbourhood Development. A Comparative Study of Community Based Development Organisations*. Aldershot, UK: Ashgate.

United Nations (1989) *Convention of the Rights of the Child 1989*. http://www.unicef.org/crc/text.htm.

United Nations Centre for Human Settlements (UNCHS) (1997) *The Istanbul Declaration and the Habitat Agenda*. Nairobi: UNCHS.

United Nations Children's Fund (UNICEF) (1996) *Children's Rights and Habitat. Housing, Neighbourhood and Settlement*. New York: UNICEF NYHQ.

United States Advisory Board on Child Abuse and Neglect (1993) *Neighbors Helping Neighbors: a New National Strategy for the Protection of Children*. Washington, DC: National Clearinghouse on Child Abuse and Neglect Information.

United States Department of Health and Human Services (1988) *Study Findings: Study of National Incidence and Prevalence of Child Abuse and Neglect*. Washington DC: US Department of Health and Human Services.

United States Department of Health and Human Services (2001) *Building Their Futures: How Early Head Start Programs are Enhancing the Lives of Infants and Toddlers in Low-income Families*. Washington DC: Commissioners Office of Research and Evaluation and the Head Start Bureau.

United States Department of Health and Human Services (2005a) *Early Head Start Almanac*. Accessed July 2005 at http://www.acf.hhs.gov/programs/hsb/programs/ehs/ehsalmanac.htm.

United States Department of Health and Human Services (2005b) *Early Head Start Research and Evaluation Project (EHSRE). 1996–2005. Overview*. Accessed on July 20 at http://www.acf.hhs.gov/programs/opre/ehs/ehs_resrch/index.html.

United Way, Success by 6 (2005) *Background*. http://national.unitedway.org/sb6/aboutsb6/index.cfm.

Urban Task Force (1999) *Towards an Urban Renaissance*. London: Department of the Environment, Transport and the Regions.

Valentine, G., Holloway, S. & Bingham, N. (2000) Transforming Cyberspace: Children's interventions in the new public space. In S. Holloway & G. Valentine (eds) *Children's Geographies: Living, Playing and Transforming Everyday Worlds* (pp. 156–174). London: Routledge.

Valentine, G. & McKendrick, J. (1997) Children's outdoor play: exploring parental concerns about children's safety and the changing nature of childhood. *Geoforum* 28, 219–235.

Vinson, T. (2004) *Community, Adversity and Resilience: the Distribution of Social Disadvantage in Victorian and New South Wales and the Mediating Role of Social Cohesion.* Melbourne: Jesuit Social Services.

Waiton, S. (2001) *Scared of the Kids? Curfews, Crime and the Regulation of Young People.* Sheffield: Sheffield Hallam University.

Walker, A. (1996) Blaming the victims. In R. Lister (ed.) *Charles Murray and the Underclass: the Developing Debate* (pp. 66–74). London: Institute of Economic Affairs, Health and Welfare Unit with the *Sunday Times*.

Walker, D. (2005) View from the top: what exactly is a community? *Guardian Society*, July 27.

Walker, J. & Coombes, M. (2003) *Evaluation of Youth Inclusion and Support Panels: Report of the Scoping Study. Report to the Children and Young People's Unit.* Unpublished report. Newcastle: University of Newcastle.

Ward, C. (1978). *The Child in the City.* London: Architectural Press.

Waters, E., Goldfeld, S. & Hopkins, S. (2001) *The 'Best Start' Indicators.* Melbourne, Victoria: State of Victoria, Department of Human Services. Accessed in May 2005 at http://www.beststart.vic.gov.au/docs/Indicators_Report02v1.2.pdf.

Weatherburn, D. & Lind, B. (2001) *Delinquent Prone Communities.* Cambridge: Cambridge University Press.

Webber, M.M. (1963) Order in diversity: community without propinquity. In L. Wingo, Jr. (ed.) *Cities and Space. The Future Use of Urban Land* (pp. 23–56). Baltimore, MD: Johns Hopkins University Press.

Webber, M.M. (1964) The urban place and the nonplace urban realm. In M.M. Webber, J.W. Dyckman, D.L. Foley, A.Z. Guttenbert, W.L.C. Wheaton & C. Bauer Wurster (eds) *Explorations into Urban Structure* (pp. 63–78). Philadelphia: University of Pennsylvania Press.

Weller, S. (2003) 'Teach us something useful': contested spaces of teenagers' citizenship. *Space and Polity* 7, 153–171.

Wellman, B. (2001) Physical place and cyberplace: the rise of personalized networking. *International Journal of Urban and Regional Research* 25, 227–252.

Wellman, B., Haase, A.Q., Witte, J. & Hampton, K. (2001) Does the Internet increase, decrease, or supplement social capital? Social networks, participation and community commitment. *American Behavioral Scientist* 45, 437–456.

White, M. (1987) *American Neighborhoods and Residential Differences.* New York: Russell Sage Foundation.

Wilcox, A. (2003) Evidence-based youth justice? Some valuable lessons from an evaluation for the Youth Justice Board. *Youth Justice* 3, 19–33.

Wilcox, D. (1994) *The Guide to Effective Participation.* London: Macmillan Press.

Wiles, C. (2004) Social capital and successful neighbourhoods. *Inside Housing*, January 16. www.cih.org/branches/east/socialcapital.htm.

Williams, C.C. (2003) Harnessing social capital: some lessons from rural England. *Local Government Studies* 29, 75–90.

Williams, J., Toumbourou, J., McDonald, M., Jones, S. & Moore, T. (2005) A sea change on the island continent: frameworks for risk assessment, prevention and intervention in child health in Australia. *Children & Society* 19, 91–104.

Williams, T. (1990) *The Cocaine Kids.* Boston, MA: Addison-Wesley.

Willis, D.J. (1995) Psychological impact of child abuse and neglect. *Journal of Clinical Child Psychology* 24, 2–4.

Willmott, P. (1989) *Community Initiatives. Patterns and Prospects.* London: Policy Studies Institute.

Wilson, W.J. (1987) *The Truly Disadvantaged: the Inner City, the Underclass, and Public Policy.* Chicago: The University of Chicago Press.

Wilson, W.J. (1991) Studying inner-city social dislocations: the challenge of public agenda research. *American Sociological Review* 56, 1–14.

Wilson, W.J. & Kelling, G.L. (1982) Police and neighbourhood safety: broken windows. *Atlantic Monthly* 249, 29–38.

Woodhead, P. & Siddall, A. (1995) *Pennywell: A Case Study of Community Development Work in the 1990s*. Newcastle: Save the Children.

Woolcock, M. & Narayan, D. (2000) Social capital: implications for development theory, research and policy. *World Bank Research Observations* 15, 225–249.

Worpole, K. (2003) *No Particular Place to Go? Children, Young People and Public Space*. London: Groundwork. http://www.worpole.dircon.co.uk/Reports/NoParticularPlace. htm.

Wynn, J., Costello, J., Halpern, R. & Richman, H. (1994) *Children, Families, and Communities: a New Approach to Social Services*. Chicago, IL: Chapin Hall Center for Children at the University of Chicago.

Yaqub, S. (2002) Poor Children Grow into Poor Adults: Harmful Mechanism or Over-Deterministic Theory? *Journal of International Development* 14, 1081–1093.

Zeiher, H. (2003) Shaping daily life in urban environments. In P. Christensen & M. O'Brien (eds) *Children in the City: Home, Neighbourhood and Community* (pp. 66–81). London: RoutledgeFalmer.

Zelitzer, V.A. (1985) *Pricing the Priceless Child: the Changing Social Value of Children*. New York: Basic Books.

INDEX

Note: Page references in *italics* refer to tables or boxes.